ENSLAVED

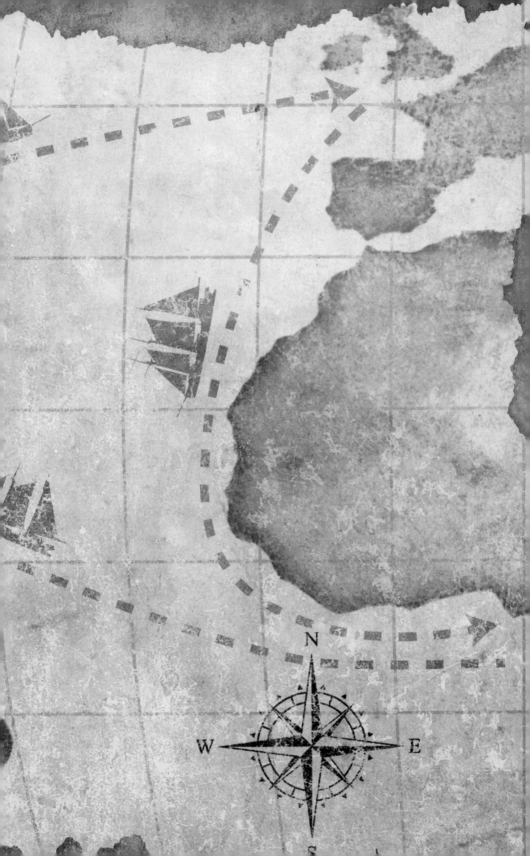

ENSLAVED

THE SUNKEN HISTORY OF THE TRANSATLANTIC SLAVE TRADE

SIMCHA JACOBOVICI
& SEAN KINGSLEY

Preface by Brenda Jones

PEGASUS BOOKS
NEW YORK LONDON

ENSLAVED

Pegasus Books, Ltd.
148 West 37th Street, 13th Floor
New York, NY 10018

First Pegasus Books cloth edition October 2022

Interior design by Maria Fernandez

Library of Congress Cataloging-in-Publication Data is available.

ISBN: 978-1-63936-238-7

10 9 8 7 6 5 4 3 2 1

Printed in the United States of America
Distributed by Simon & Schuster
www.pegasusbooks.com

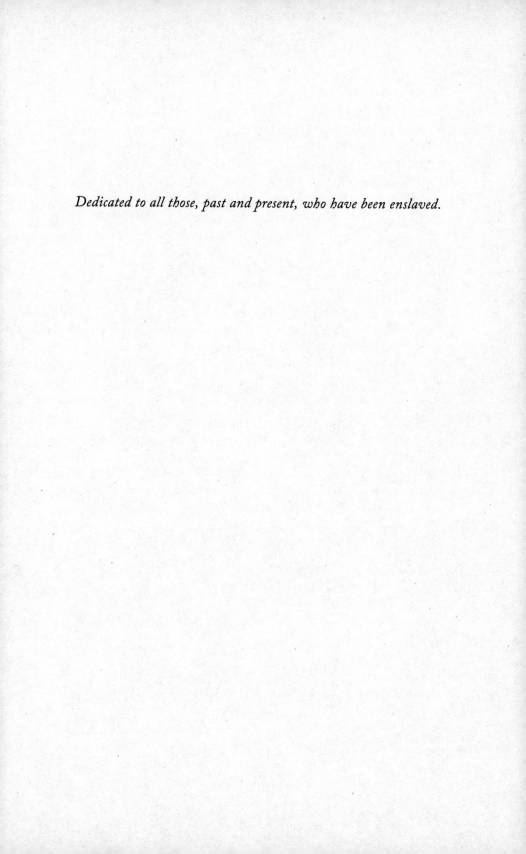

Dedicated to all those, past and present, who have been enslaved.

CONTENTS

PREFACE

by Brenda Jones

The descendants of enslaved peoples represent an inconvenient truth. Conceived in a boiling cauldron of naked ambition and insatiable greed, we are the progeny of a false belief that the vestiges of untold violence, theft, human degradation, and exploitation can somehow escape their unholy origin and launch into a kind of buoyant forgetfulness. This imagined culmination of all the darkness that came before is a wishful, radiant resolution, a voyage into light to a place where every crime is not only forgotten, but somehow erased. The perpetrator is left clean, pure, and fully absolved, regardless of the heaving damage of the original sin.

After all, who could not justify what any creature believes it must commit within the primeval struggle to survive? Existence is paramount above all other values, wouldn't you agree? So, if some threats require the momentary sacrifice of the soul, the choice is swift and overwhelmingly justified. The soul has an infinity of eons to purge any trace of violation and return finally to oneness with the light.

Maybe had you or I felt the gnawing anxiety of that hunger scratching for relief or the humiliated nakedness of a poverty so persistent it birthed a bitter identity . . . maybe if we knew firsthand the generations of longing to be bathed in riches, and maybe if we had barely survived the freezing darkness through ages of deprivation, perhaps we would sympathize with the furious demand of this greed. Perhaps . . . But if we have learned anything over the course of these last six centuries, maybe, just maybe, we now comprehend that what is eternal can never, ever be erased.

We can delay and evade its insurgency, seem to temporarily impede its appearance, but what was meant to be can never be eradicated, even by atomic force. Life can never be completely stamped out. Its remnants will reconstitute if a will beyond our own was its Creator.

Even a valley of dry bones can still be uncovered, unearthed, and scraped together to convey the most salient, present-day truths. Of course, all the gorgeous details are lost—the locks of sumptuous, thick hair, the interesting curl of the lips that runs in the family, those deep-set, penetrating eyes passed down through generations. And the tender details of each individual story are gone too—all the secrets forged in terror, the recollections of amazing grace extended by the Spirit even in the most dire circumstances, the trauma of capture and its impact will never be precisely known or submitted to a lineage of protection passed down by the tribal griot from generation to generation.

Every treasure more than twelve million people were birthed and blessed to convey has been lost. There are spaces in time—lapses—silence across generations of uncertainty. There is so much we will never know, but what we need to know, the essence of the lesson their lives were meant to teach, remains there. It is still available, found in evidence, strewn across the ocean floor waiting to be reconstructed and remembered to share its unvarnished treatise on the human condition.

The descendant's existence conveys the disturbing reminder that there is no "place" to hide as long as the soul remembers even a tinge of its violent origin. Somehow the truth of that inception is always borne out. Our origin can never be erased. You might believe the miseducation, indoctrination, institutionalization, acceptance, wealth, fame, or a subsistent life led in abject obscurity would minimize any trace of memory to its tiniest insignificance. But the truth is the more you have, the more readily you realize that having does not satisfy. The more you have, the more clearly you hear the call of the inner life.

The more you know, the more you realize that forgetting is an illusion. It is remembering that is freeing. References to the Middle Passage resonate throughout African diaspora literature and art. What cannot be recounted by experience is reimagined, repurposed, visited by the mind again and again.

It is remembered in Paule Marshall's *Praisesong for the Widow* and Toni Morrison's Nobel Prize-winning masterpiece *Beloved*. It is the backdrop of Charles Johnson's National Book Award-winning novel *Middle Passage*, the fictional story of a fateful voyage on a slave ship, and also the foundation of V. S. Naipaul's Trinidadian classic by the same name. The great playwright August Wilson begins his tour de force ten-play cycle capturing each decade of the twentieth century with *Gem of the Ocean*, involving a psychic voyage to the bottom of the ocean floor to a great city of bones occupied by the spirits of our ancestors who leapt to their death or were killed and spared the sacrilegious indignities ahead.

In the verse of "Slave Driver," Bob Marley remembers a turmoil he never experienced, and his rage is fresh as though it happened only weeks before. Even a modern-day bard, Jay-Z, speaks of the anomaly in his "Oceans" rap. He muses on the irony of his wealth juxtaposed with the tragic origins of his ancestors. He depicts himself in a tuxedo, riding in a fine car and still remembering what the soul can never release. It has never been forgotten, no, not even by those who know only that it happened and nothing else. Forgetting is an illusion but remembering is well on the path to liberation.

The descendants of enslaved peoples represent all of this inconvenient truth. We are born in innocence, but we learn quickly that we are the living, breathing embodiment of a harvest of crime and centuries of violation others wish they could forget. Our existence is a reminder of an indelible inception, but it also conveys an abiding hope. We mean a mistaken past can indeed lead to a promising future. Yes, we are the living evidence that "truth pressed to earth will rise again," that "you can kill a human being," as activists and revolutionaries say to ward off the terminal potential consequences of protest, "but you cannot kill the idea that person represents."

Secretly, even to the perpetrator caged by his or her knowledge of unforgivable sin, it is a relief to know that, despite the darkest of intentions and the horror of the crime, there is a divine spark that can never be erased. Only so much damage can ever be done. If only they knew our survival is a dynamic part of the offender's dream of salvation. Our existence teaches, the one powerful lesson all war and violence ultimately convey. That truth applied to human existence has the capacity to quench the insatiable hunger and bring an end to shame forever.

The words have been spoken since the beginning of time by poets, sages, and philosophers. Lately a moral leader, Rep. John Lewis, said it best; "We are one people," he would preach, "one family, the human family. And we all live in one house, the American house, the world house. We must learn to live together as brothers and sisters or we will all perish together as fools." He would say, "every human being is a spark of the divine," and once we become deeply aware of the sanctity of all life, we will be destined to build what he called "a Beloved Community, a nation and a world society at peace with itself."

Just imagine what would happen if we finally decided to learn from millennia of mistaken violence; the freedom we are all seeking would not be far behind. Who knew that the conservation law of energy we studied in high school science class had philosophical, historical, and even moral implications? Energy is never destroyed. It is only transmitted, transmuted, and transformed. And this is why to this day, hundreds of years later, this book and the *Enslaved* series that it grew out of can teach. The flesh is gone, but the bones of the lesson are still with us. The more we remember, the more we can heal, and the more we know what happened and how it happened, the more we can transform our future.

—Brenda Jones
Washington, DC

INTRODUCTION

Over four hundred years, twelve million Africans were trafficked to the "New World". The largest forced migration in history. Almost two million died en route.

Portuguese, British, French, Spanish, Dutch, Danish, and American traffickers branded Africans like cattle, cut off their hair, raped women in forts like Elmina in Ghana, and, as the Capuchin priest Dionigi de Carli put it in 1667, herded Africans into ships' holds where they were "press'd together like Herrings in a Barrel . . ."

On the Atlantic waves, male captives were locked in chains. Rebels who refused to eat had their mouths forced open with iron vices or were killed and hanged on masts as warnings to the others. When they were sold onto plantations in the Caribbean and Americas, the names of the trafficked millions were changed to Christian ones. The stripping of a continent's human identity was complete.

At the epicenter of this enforced exodus was the ocean and the ships. Until recently, the technology to find lost and forgotten slave wrecks had been limited. The hatches of sunken history stayed bolted. Now, mixed gas diving, using rebreathers, lets humans descend beyond one hundred meters. Remotely and Autonomously Operated Vehicles (ROVs) extend the limits of exploration beyond four thousand meters in depth.

Taking advantage of these new technologies, over a period of two years from 2017 to 2019, a group of divers from the Florida-based Diving With A Purpose (DWP), an organization affiliated with the National Association of Black Scuba Divers (NABS), dived seven sunken slave ships and two sunken "feedom boats." No one had ever dived so many sunken slave ships. No one had ever dived a sunken freedom boat, confirmed to have spirited runaways from the American South to freedom in Canada.

In this exploration, the divers sought to give voice to the forgotten millions whose memories were drowned by Western greed and profit. They also wanted their discoveries to be springboards inspiring deeper investigations into the transatlantic slave trade.

At the center of the trade was sugar. Prices were kept low by a system of slavery that was meticulously planned at every stage and touched every corner of the globe. The trade *was* driven by sugar, but also by coffee, chocolate, and tea, all highly addictive. The world was hooked. The London bookshop owner William Fox, who opposed the slave trade, warned Britain in 1791 that every spoonful of West Indian sugar taken in tea and coffee was mixed with the blood of Africans. In 1870s England, an aging former African slave called Caesar remembered the evil days of sugar production. He explained how, after wearing his slave chains for decades, "the iron entered into our souls!"

Enslaved is the first book to tell the story of the transatlantic slave trade from the bottom of the sea, but it is far from just a story of victims. Enchained Africans did not accept their fate without a fight. One in ten slaving voyages ended in revolt. Reflecting this reality, ours is also a tale of heroes—resistance, revolution, and the survival of African culture in the face of unimaginable odds.

Diving With A Purpose's efforts were captured in the six-part series *Enslaved: The Lost History of the Transatlantic Slave Trade* that featured Hollywood icon Samuel L. Jackson and has now led to the book you are holding. Writing the book allowed us to dive deeper into the history. It's been an incredible journey. Shipwrecks and marine archaeology are a uniquely tangible way of encountering the past.

For divers Kramer Wimberley, Alannah Vellacott, Kinga Philipps, and Joshua Williams, theirs was also a voyage of self-discovery. They are a very special group of people united by a desire to seek out the truth and to do so fearlessly.

This is their story.

—Simcha Jacobovici & Sean Kingsley,
Tel Aviv & Virginia Water

FOLLOW THE MONEY

It has been said, Will you, for the sake of drinking rum, and sweetening your coffee with sugar, persevere in the most unjust and execrable barbarity?

—Captain John Stedman, *Narrative of a Five Years Expedition Against the Revolted Negroes of Surinam* (1796)

BAD IDEAS

Fort Zeelandia—Paramaribo, Suriname

The transatlantic slave trade would never have happened if it did not generate money. Tons of money. Much of the world we live in today was built on the back of enslaved Africans. Or as the author of *Robinson Crusoe*, Daniel Defoe, put it so crudely in 1713, "No African Trade, no Negroes, no Negroes, no sugar; no Sugar, no Islands, no Islands, no Continent, no Continent, no Trade." Modern historians go even further: no slave trade, no Industrial Revolution, and no Western civilization as we know it.

To find out how such vast machinery—bad ideas, ships, sugar, and coffee factories—made the world smaller, connecting superpowers and capital cities to the most remote parts of Africa, the Caribbean, and Latin America, you need to follow the money.

The bigger the rewards, the greater risks were taken in the worship of profit. Wrecked ships were sometimes the result of this human greed. Even when their trafficked human cargos ended up sunk in some ghastly outpost of empire, Europe still found appallingly innovative ways to win. In Holland and England, you could insure enslaved Africans sunk at sea and still cash in your policy. Sink or sell was a win-win result for heartless traders.

Today, a crack group of intrepid divers, marine archaeologists, dirt archaeologists, historians, and experts in ocean technology, inspired and challenged by the activist and Hollywood legend Samuel L. Jackson and his wife LaTanya Richardson Jackson, are bringing the forgotten back to life. The responsibility falls on the shoulders of a group of Americans: Diving With A Purpose (DWP), which wants answers and action to make sense of centuries of suffering. They plan to dive for truth on a series of slave wrecks and put history on trial. Most of their former exploration has focused on America. Their facemasks, fins, and wetsuits are packed to travel the globe and hunt down the seas' great sunken ships to lay bare these forgotten tragedies.

To come to grips with the demons of the colonial past, Diving With A Purpose's haunting journey will take them to four continents and nine shipwrecks that change the perspective and conversation. Rather than just read what English sea captains wrote and conveniently left out of the pages of history, they want to physically touch and reconstruct the forensic archaeology.

The team seeks justice so the souls of their ancestors can finally rest. This is a personal journey about origins and roots. Above all, this time traveling is giving voice to the silence, breathing new life into people of color still living with unanswered questions. For the first time, the team is telling the history of the transatlantic slave trade from the bottom of the ocean.

DIVING WITH A PURPOSE

Diving With A Purpose (DWP), based in Biscayne National Park, Florida, specializes in education, training, certification, and field experience in maritime archaeology and ocean conservation. DWP's goals are to protect, document, and interpret African slave trade shipwrecks and the maritime history and culture of African Americans worldwide. Its divers learn how to use archaeological remains to tell stories that are not in the history books.

Since 2005, DWP has trained 350 adults and a hundred children. Its divers work on slave ships, World War II plane crash sites, and have joined expeditions with the National Oceanic Atmospheric

Administration (NOAA). DWP is a global partner in the Slave Wrecks Project in collaboration with the Smithsonian's National Museum of African American History and Culture, George Washington University, Iziko Museums of South Africa, and the US National Park Service.

Teams from DWP have partnered in the recovery of the *São José*, a Portuguese slave vessel lost off Cape Town in 1794 on its way from Mozambique to Brazil. Of the 512 African captives onboard, 212 died. DWP was part of the discovery of the *Clotilda* in the Mobile River off Alabama, the last known slave ship to arrive in the United States, fifty-two years after the traffic in enslaved Africans was legally abolished.

Alannah Vellacott, Kramer Wimberley, and Kinga Philipps had crossed the Atlantic to Suriname to listen to a story they did not want to hear. And then to dive a haunted slave wreck they did not want to dive. There was no option. The sinking of the Dutch West India Company trader the *Leusden* in the Maroni River on January 1, 1738, witnessed the single largest human tragedy in the history of the transatlantic slave trade. Diving With A Purpose had flown in their gear to shine a spotlight on one of the most horrific crimes of the transatlantic slave trade, forgotten by the world for three hundred years.

Paramaribo, the capital and leading port city of Suriname, was a Dutch slave colony 350 years ago, colonized with one purpose in mind: to enrich the Netherlands. Built on a perilous reef, its waters choked by rolling sandbars that made navigation hazardous, fertile lands fed by mighty rivers swept far inland. Artificial Dutch canals cut deep into Suriname's rainforests made communications excellent and Paramaribo choice real estate for the grinding cogs of sugar and coffee growing.

The town was a land of order, if not law. Straight streets were lined with orange, tamarind, and lemon trees in what seemed like everlasting bloom. Two- to three-story houses—1,400 by the late eighteenth century—were built of fine timber and brick foundations. At night the Dutch slept in cotton hammocks in rooms stacked with crystal chandeliers, paintings, and china jars.

Life was good. As Captain John Stedman put it in his *Narrative, of a Five Years' Expedition Against the Revolted Negroes of Surinam* in 1796, in Paramaribo, "The town appeared uncommonly neat and pleasing, the shipping extremely beautiful, the adjacent woods adorned with the most luxuriant verdure, the air perfumed with the most utmost fragrance, and the whole scene gilded by the rays of an unclouded sun."

The dive team walked through a forbidding stone archway shrouded in darkness and emerged from the shadows into the courtyard of Fort Zeelandia. Back in the day, the fort was the most striking building in Suriname. Built to store and sell newly landed African captives and goods for export, its prospect looked far more hospitable than the stone prison-castles studded along West Africa's Gold Coast. Four Dutch-style mini manor houses opened onto a large square, its paving made from red tiles set sideways, imitating the streets of Amsterdam. At its center, a tiled floor and stone sundial formed a welcome sanctuary to impress the world about the Netherlands' powerful reach across the waves.

Fort Zeelandia, built by the French in 1640, was this shore's latest incarnation. Lord Francis Willoughby planted an English flag over the Indian village of Torarica in 1651 and, in an act of smug self-glorification, renamed it Willoughbyland. Soon the town bustled with three thousand enslaved Africans and a thousand European settlers. The Dutch repaid the invasion courtesy in 1667 when they swapped control of Nova Zeelandia with the British, at the end of the Second Anglo-Dutch War, in exchange for a swamp they owned elsewhere in the New World that they thought would come to nothing. It was called New Amsterdam, now New York City. As Suriname's new masters put it, by their smart dealing the Dutch "taught the covetous Britons good manners."

The lords from the lowlands ruled over 175 mixed plantations. In the country with no winter, they found paradise. Small deer, stags, and butterflies frolicked across the countryside. In the town, Dutch merchants and plantation masters amused themselves feasting, dancing, riding, playing cards, and visiting their small theater. By the end of the eighteenth century, the colony's five thousand Europeans had seventy-five thousand slaves to attend to their every need.

COLONIAL DUTCH PARAMARIBO

From Captain J. G. Stedman, *Narrative, of a Five Years' Expedition, Against the Revolted Negroes of Surinam, in Guiana . . . from the Year 1772, to 1777 . . . Volume I* (London, 1796).

"The town of Paramaribo has a noble road for shipping, the river before the town being above a mile in breadth, and containing sometimes above one hundred vessels of burthen, moored within a pistol shot of the shore; there are indeed seldom fewer there than fourscore ships loading coffee, sugar, cacao, cotton, and indigo, for Holland, including also the Guinea-men that bring slaves from Africa, and the North American and Leeward Island vessels, which bring flour, beef, pork, spirits, herrings, and mackarel salted, spermaceti-candles, horses, and lumber, for which they receive chiefly melases to be distilled into rum . . ."

"Paramaribo is a very lively place, the streets being generally crouded with planters, sailors, soldiers, Jews, Indians, and Negroes, while the river is covered with canoes, barges, &c. constantly passing and repassing, like the wherries on the Thames, often accompanied with bands of music; the shipping also in the road adorned with their different flags, guns firing, &c.; not to mention the many groupes of boys and girls playing in the water, altogether form a pleasing appearance . . . Their carriages and dress are truly magnificent; silk embroidery, Genoa velvets, diamonds, gold and silver lace, being daily worn, and even the masters of trading ships appear with buttons and buckles of solid gold. They are equally expensive at their tables, where every thing that can be called delicate is produced at any price, and served up in plate and china of the newest fashion, and most exquisite workmanship. But nothing displays the luxury of the inhabitants of Surinam, more than the number of slaves by whom they are attended, often twenty or thirty in one family."

Fort Zeelandia's twenty-one cannons sticking out from two forti-
fied bastions, commanded everything coming in and out of the Atlantic
Ocean, fifteen kilometers away, and the Suriname River. Nothing got by
without the commander tipping his hat. In one sweep from its riverbank,
the eye takes in a panorama of power and profit where slaves arrived and
sugar was sent downstream and on to Europe. The muddy gray waters
saturated with dank forest soils looked less like home in the Florida Keys
and even murkier than the English Channel. Alannah, Kramer, and
Kinga were in for a tough mission.

Today most of old Zeelendia is gone. Paramaribo is sliced up by
concrete bridges spanning the Suriname River. Juggernauts of the sea
slowly haul goods across the water. Most of the city's money comes from
bauxite, the main ore used to make aluminum. Downtown, the gold-
painted wooden beams of the old Dutch Saint Peter and Paul Basilica and
the De Waag, Weighing House, where agricultural goods were sorted
for shipment, still stand.

In Fort Zeelandia's central courtyard, Alannah, Kramer, and
Kinga had arranged to meet Dr. Leo Balai from the University of
Amsterdam. Dr. Balai is a man on a mission who badly needed the
dive team's help.

"I want to tell you a story I think nobody wanted to tell," he began.
"A story I need to tell because it's so important. It's a story about the
biggest mass murder in the history of the transatlantic slave trade. It's
the story of the *Leusden*."

Unlike most slave ships, the *Leusden* was one of the very few Dutch
ships built specially for the slave trade. Its last voyage began in Ghana on
November 19, 1737. The crew enjoyed a smooth trip, taking just forty-
four days to cross the Middle Passage linking West Africa and South
America. Then, on December 30, everything went wrong. It started to
rain; a dense fog fell. Eventually one of the sailors, desperate for relief,
shouted, "Land ahoy!" Crew and captain thought they had reached the
mouth of the Suriname River and the safety of journey's end. They were
about to make a fatal mistake. They had taken a wrong turn, swinging
inland ninety-five kilometers too early into the Maroni River.

THE *LEUSDEN*

- One of last slave ships of Dutch West India Company
- 33.9 meters long, 9.0 meters wide, 3.6 meters deep
- 10 slave voyages, 1719 to 1738
- 6,564 captives embarked, 1,639 died at sea
- Left Elmina in Ghana, November 19, 1737, with 700 African captives, for Suriname
- Wrecked, January 1, 1738, mouth of the Maroni River, Suriname
- The crew bolted closed the hatches; 664 Africans were left to drown
- 23 kilograms of gold for Amsterdam was recovered

THE DUTCH SLAVE TRADE

The earliest Dutch trading voyage to West Africa was made in 1593 by Barent Ericksz. Over the years the Dutch transported nearly 500,000 captives out of West Africa, about 5 percent of Europe's total. During the 175 years of their involvement, their share of the trade approached 10 percent of all traffic, however. For short periods in the 1630s and 1640s, the Dutch were dominant.

Between 1730 and 1791, the West India Company and Dutch free traders combined trafficked 268,792 Africans in 906 ships: on average 1,500 captives a year between 1630 and 1674, 3,000 up to the 1720s, and over 6,000 Africans by the 1760s. The West India Company took the largest number of captives from Keta, Klein Popo, Fida, Jaquin, Offra, Appa, and Patackerie on the Slave Coast, followed by the Gold Coast and the Dutch Loango-Angola Coast (modern Angola and the Republic of the Congo).

Leo Balai stared out over the moody waters beyond the walls of Fort Zeelandia. Somewhere out there to the east the *Leusden* got stuck. "It hit the sandbank," he told the dive team, "and that was the beginning of the end. Here, right here in front of us was where the *Leusden* was supposed to enter the Suriname River to sell the 'cargo'. Imagine, that two hundred to three hundred years ago, this place was all slave plantations. More than six hundred plantations with tens of thousands of slaves to make a profit for people who wanted to get rich. It was here where everything happened, where people were treated like cargo . . ."

From the urban comfort of Paramaribo, it was hard for Alannah, Kramer, and Kinga to imagine the picture Leo Balai was painting. Where he was about to take them would put the fear of God into the friends forever.

HENRY THE NAVIGATOR

It was in Portugal, not Holland, that the trickle of cash made by the slave trade turned into a 350-year torrent of riches. In the popular holiday destination of Lagos on the southwestern spear tip of Portugal, holidaymakers dream of cheap sun closer to home than the Mediterranean. The city has it all: romantic crumbling fortifications, dreamy rocky shores and sandy beaches near the Praia da Rocha, delicious seafood, luxury hotel resorts, and bottomless beer.

How many weekend stag and hen parties know, though, what lurks beneath the flagstones of party central? The Valle da Gafaria cuts through open land just outside Lagos's city walls. A few years ago, archaeologists were rushed in when developers building a new multistorey parking lot were stopped in their tracks. They had disturbed what no developer wants to hit, two ancient cemeteries. One was the city leper colony known from old maps. The other was undocumented, a grisly mass of urban waste thrown away centuries ago.

A stone's throw from the city's ancient harbor, into the six-meter-thick layer of trash sailors had slung the leftover garbage of long-distance sea voyages, from ships' smashed pots to the bones of fish, chicken, pigs, and goats. Littered among the maritime junk were 158 human skeletons, some violently thrown away, still shackled. A woman went to her grave hugging her baby. Rings, necklaces, and sharpened human teeth left no doubt where they once originated in far-off Africa.

At this very spot on August 8, 1444, Lançarote da Ilha, the royal tax collector for Lagos, returned home in six caravel ships crammed with 240 shackled captives taken from the Arguin Bank in Mauritania. Prince

Henry, the son of King John I, ordered the enslaved be paraded in a field near the port for all to cheer Portugal's preeminence. The waterfront was crowded with rubbernecking city folk taking in the exotic spectacle. Prince Henry on horseback pointed out which slaves he wanted as his royal one-fifth *quinto* (royal tax) entitlement for licensing the voyage. The Church was also there, raking in its own rightful one-twentieth of goods promised to the Order of Christ.

In his *Chronicle of the Discovery and Conquest of Guinea*, Gomes Eanes de Zurara described the astonishing birth of the Western slave trade that fateful day:

> Very early in the morning, by reason of the heat, the seamen began to make ready their boats, and to take out those captives, and carry them on shore . . . And these, placed all together in that field, were a marvelous sight; for amongst them were some white enough, fair to look upon, and well proportioned; others were less white like mulattoes; others again were as black as Ethiops, and so ugly, both in features and in body . . . some kept their heads low and their faces bathed in tears, looking one upon another; others stood groaning very dolorously, looking up to the height of heaven . . . others struck their faces with the palms of their hands, throwing themselves at full length upon the ground . . . to increase their sufferings still more, there now arrived those who had charge of the division of the captives, and who began to separate one from another, in order to make an equal partition of the fifths; and then was it needful to part fathers from sons, husbands from wives, brothers from brothers. No respect was shewn either to friends or relations, but each fell where his lot took him . . . the mothers clasped their other children in their arms, and threw themselves flat on the ground with them; receiving blows with little pity for their own flesh, if only they might not be torn from them.

African captives like this ended up dead in Lagos's Valle da Gafaria between 1420 and 1480. DNA analysis has shown how the Africans were taken from the Bantu-speaking groups of West Africa. Born outside the laws of Christendom, these men, women, and children were brutally thrown into the city dump without a prayer, mortally weakened from the horrors of the sea crossing or dying just after landing.

The exiled captives were never baptized, so their corpses were treated no different than animals. Their souls could not be saved. Over the desecrated site of their final resting places, Lagos's Pro Putting Garden modern mini-golf course was built with joyful fountains, bridges, and colorful sculptures of pink, green, and red dancing mother goddesses.

Father of the Slave Trade

The Africans found in the world's oldest slave cemetery were thrown away because they were deemed to have no value. The transatlantic slave trade was born in the shadow of the Valle da Gafaria. From here Portugal seized the lion's share of slave riches for centuries. From Lagos, African slavery and the globe's great sugar rush reached far out to Brazil, sucking in the Dutch, Suriname, and the tragic sinking of the *Leusden*.

All in all, Portuguese slave traders shipped around 5.8 million Africans between the fifteenth and nineteenth centuries, roughly 50 percent of the transatlantic traffic. And the full inhumanity of the machine all began in the city square of Lagos, the lead port for importing Africans between 1444 and 1473.

Dom Henrique, the Prince of Portugal from 1394 to 1460, and more famously known as Henry the Navigator, is credited as the father of the slave trade. For kickstarting Europe's overseas expansion, Henry is seen as a heroic inventor, pioneering scientist, the ideal crusader and promoter of the Catholic faith. Henry became the poster boy for Portugal's Golden Age and the birth of the Age of Exploration. Public polls in Portugal and North America included Henry the Navigator among the twenty-five most important historical figures of the second millennium.

What Dom Henrique did and did not achieve is shrouded in mystery. The truth may never be known after Portugal's archives in Lisbon were destroyed in the great earthquake of 1755. History nevertheless honors Henry as the founder, at windswept Sagres, just west of Lagos, of a scientific citadel with a nautical school bustling with mathematicians, astronomers, cartographers, and instrument makers. The Englishman Samuel Purchas described in 1625 how Henry "caused one Master James, a man skillful in Navigation, and in Cards [charts] and Sea Instruments, to be brought into Portugal, there at his charge, as it were, to erect a school of Marineship, and to instruct his countrymen in that Mysterie."

Sweating over sea maps day and night, legend has it that at Sagres Prince Henry uncovered the hidden secret to long-distance seafaring. The Venetian explorer Cadamosto later wrote that the caravel ships of Portugal could travel anywhere. Africans were struck by eyes painted onto the bows of caravels. They were convinced these gave ships the vision to sail anywhere in the uncharted world.

Caravels with the unmissable square cross logo of the Order of Christ painted onto their sails were the ships of choice for crusading with West Africa. Large rectangular sails inclined at an angle on a mast allowed them to sail close to the wind, make headway under light winds and keep away from pirates. Crucially, because they were small ships of no more than forty to fifty tons, their shallow hulls made them perfect for maneuvering along and exploring the coast of Guinea's shallows and rivers.

In the words of Samuel Purchas, Prince Henry became "The true foundation of the Greatnesse, not of Portugall alone, but of the whole Christian World, in Marine Affairs . . ." The English poet and playwright Dr. Samuel Johnson later called him "the first encourager of remote navigation." Much of the Navigator's red-hot publicity is now thought to be overhyped. Triangular sails date back to the eighth century and the caravel existed in the thirteenth century. And there's no certainty Henry founded a nautical school at Cape Sagres at all. To many, Henry was little more than a pirate, slaver, and corrupt monarch. Whatever the truth, the Infanta Dom Henrique was the first major backer of a Western slave-trading expedition. With power, cash, and vision, he kicked off the deadly game for global colonial supremacy.

Fifty years after the first captives reached Lagos, Portugal was trafficking up to two thousand African captives a year through Oporto and Lisbon. Like in London, some were set to work in domestic service in the big cities. The Flemish traveler Nicolas Cleynaerts, tutor to Henry the Chaste and future king of Portugal, worried in the 1530s that

> Slaves swarm everywhere. All work is done by blacks and captive Moors. Portugal is crammed with such people. I should think that in Lisbon slaves, male and female, outnumber freeborn Portuguese . . . Richer households have slaves of both sexes, and there are individuals who derive substantial profits from the sale of the offspring of their household slaves . . . they raise them much in the same way as one would raise pigeons for sale in the marketplace.

Lisbon boasted twelve slave markets by the mid–sixteenth century. Twenty years later, forty thousand people were enchained in Portugal.

Iberian Sugar

Most of the slaves seized in Portugal's crusading "just war" were set to work in sugar plantations on the island of Madeira. Sugar's stock was rising fast after being brought over from the Middle East with defeated Crusaders. Before becoming the greatest explorer of all time, Christopher Columbus had lived and married on Madeira, where he worked for an Italian firm in the sugar trade. When he sailed to the Caribbean in 1493, he took with him sugarcane cuttings as a symbol of Iberia's wealth.

Madeira became the largest producer of sugar in the Western world, by 1510 turning out 3,701 tons of white and brown granules. Sugar sold as far east as Constantinople and as north as England. Boom time had arrived. The Atlantic sugar rush brought vast bucks. But it was small fry compared to what was to come. When Portuguese hulls took sugarcane and technological expertise into its cash-cow colonies in Brazil, sugar turned into a monster. The world got addicted.

Turning up the heat on the global economy needed a level of manpower that had never been harnessed before. The clock ticked down on the ransacking of Africa.

Tracking down physical traces of Portugal's immense role in the slave trade is hard to do. So far only one Portuguese shipwreck tied to its transatlantic slaving has come to light. Which makes the world's earliest slave cemetery in Lagos all the more telling. But its story is hardly known. Thrill-seeking and playing golf have buried the city's inhumane past.

BOLTING THE HATCHES

Deep down the Maroni River it is difficult to see why Dutch merchants invested fortunes taking Suriname. The dense forest pushes all the way to the riverbanks. The foreboding interior feels full of demons.

In the wildest depths of the Wild Coast, Alannah, Kramer, and Kinga were heading to the town of Albina to meet Leo Balai, his Dutch marine archaeologist, Professor Jerzy Gawronski from the University of Amsterdam, and marine technology expert Steve Moore. From here they would time-travel in search of the *Leusden*, the Dutch trader that sunk with history's greatest loss of trafficked African life.

Palm trees bent above fine sandy beaches along the Maroni River, the border between Suriname and French Guiana. The water was already choppy and murky brown. There was no going back. Diving With A Purpose was all in. Dr. Gawronski is highly respected and experienced. He had worked on land and sea, recently excavating a treasure trove of trade goods under a new metro terminal construction site in Amsterdam. Underwater, Gawronski had been at the heart of projects from Spitsbergen in Norway to Nova Zembla in Russia, the Magalhães Straits in Chile, Sri Lanka, and Curaçao. But he had never found and saved a slave ship in a river.

Balai and Gawronski were in a rush. The *Leusden* had been lost to the world for too long. The ship—the wreck—should be a central pillar in new Dutch consciousness for a country where nobody wanted to confront the dark side of the human past.

DUTCH SHIPPING & WEST AFRICA

Between 1674 and 1740 the West India Company equipped 383 ships for the transport of slaves. Dutch slavers were adapted with a *diep verdeck*, a narrow tween deck between the lower and upper decks. This extra space held slaves and freed up the hold for cargo, food, supplies, and water.

The largest slave trade ships were flutes, pinnaces, and frigates thirty-three to thirty-six meters long, manned by forty-five to sixty sailors, armed with fifteen to twenty guns, and able to transport 600 slaves on average. The largest slave shipment trafficked by a West India Company trader was 952 Africans. Medium-sized frigates, yachts, and galiots, crewed by up to forty-five sailors and with ten cannons maximum, carried 400 slaves. Small barques and hookers had crews of up to thirty men and under ten guns that could carry 200 slaves per voyage. Average voyages sailing the triangular trade from Holland to West Africa, the New World, and home took 516 days.

Once in West Africa, trading voyages up and down the coast searching for trade goods and African human cargo varied from a few weeks to eight-month trips to the Bight of Benin and Biafra. The West India Company preferred fishing vessels like *buizen* (buses), *hoekers* (hookers), and *pinken* for coastal trading, manned by five to fifteen sailors and protected with one or two small cannons, a few muskets, machetes, and swords.

Dutch slave ships were obliged to sail in and out of Africa by way of the fort at Elmina. There captains made sure captives were healthy. Before leaving the Gold Coast a captain had to buy two "Negro Drums" and a wooden stick for the captives to drum as a distraction and entertainment during the crossing.

Abandon Ship

The *Leusden* was one of the last slave ships used by the Dutch West India Company. From the start, between its maiden voyage in 1719 until it sank, it was dedicated to the slave trade. In the fateful year of 1738, it was on its tenth slaving voyage. Through the years the *Leusden* trafficked 6,564 Africans, 1,639 of whom died at sea.

The final crossing was cursed. The captain died shortly after the trader docked at the Dutch fort of Elmina on the Gold Coast. A newly appointed commander, Joachim Outjes, was dispirited to find that stocks of captives were too low to fill the *Leusden* with "cargo" and make a quick turnaround. The eagerness of African kings and middlemen to deal with the Dutch had soured because of the low prices they offered. Whereas the West India Company bartered up to 200 guilders worth of goods for a captive, other Europeans went as high as 280 guilders. Plus, Dutch merchants had been found out for their underhand fobbing Africans off with "poor quality and broken goods."

Rather than wait, the *Leusden* headed 140 kilometers east to the Dutch trading post of Fort Crevecoeur near Accra in Ghana to search out a slave cargo where the Ashanti and Fante had been waging tribal wars. Still the *Leusden* only managed to find 200 Africans. Filling the hold turned out to be hard work. The slaver was forced to sail up and down the coast of Ghana for 192 days before closing the hatches on 700 Africans.

DUTCH TRADE WITH AFRICA

In the fort of Elmina in Ghana, the Dutch held 150–200 sorts of goods to barter with African peoples. Textiles manufactured in Europe, Asia, and Africa were most important at 50 percent of all stores. In the years 1727–1730, the West India Company sent 40,000 sheets of Dutch linen to the Gold Coast. Military stores, firearms, and gunpowder accounted for 12 percent of West India Company trade goods. In the first quarter of the 18th century the Company shipped 68,797 firearms and over 1.5 million pounds of gunpowder. Thirty-three percent was bad stock and dangerous. The Company made a 100 percent profit on firearms.

Around 900,000 pounds of cowrie shells were shipped to Europe from the Maldives Islands by the Dutch and English East India

Companies between 1700 and 1723 (11 percent of imported Dutch goods) to barter with West Africa. Dutch gin and French brandy were welcomed by Africans who also bought beer and wine (4 percent of Dutch imports). Large volumes of iron bars, metal pans, buckets, knives, and locks were imported, as well as luxury beads, trinkets, and mirrors.

As well as trafficking Africans, ivory accounted for 13 percent of West India Company exports to Holland. Between 1676 and 1731, three million pounds of ivory were shipped from Elmina to Europe to manufacture snuff boxes, fans, cutlery, medallions, and furniture inlays. The company exported 14,260 kilograms of gold from Ghana between 1676 and 1731. Out of Africa, Dutch ships also took home "Buenos Aires" hides, cayenne pepper, wax, gum, dyewood, lime juice, cardamom, ostrich feathers, copper, and live civet cats, the secretion from their anal glands used to make perfume.

The crew had every reason to hope their problems were now behind them. The voyage was blissfully smooth from Elmina outward to Suriname. The weather behaved and the captives' health held. Within forty-four days the *Leusden* was off Suriname—its quickest ever crossing.

The crew's luck ran out when, on December 29, 1737, the ship passed Devil's Island, off the coast of French Guiana. In the face of heavy winds, driving rain, and thick fog, the captain ran for the shore. When the weather cleared, the crew spotted a tip of land, which surely had to be Braamspunt at the head of the Suriname River.

A heavy rainstorm clouded over the sight of land once more, and the strong tide pushed the *Leusden* too close to the coast, where it bobbed uncomfortably offshore for hours, waiting for the outgoing tide to float out to the open sea. It never happened. At 4:00 p.m. on January 1, 1738, at a depth of just under six meters, the rudder hit a sandbank. Water flooded the cabin and gunpowder room. The pumps could not work fast enough to stop the *Leusden* from slowly sinking. The crew still had enough time to bolt down the hatches and sit out the night on top of the ship as it turned into a wreck. Seventy-three crew members then abandoned ship and sailed to Paramaribo in the *Leusden*'s launch and sloop. They never looked back.

Left behind in the hold were 664 African men, women, and children. When the slave quarters started flooding with water, the captives pushed higher up the ship to avoid drowning. With the sea at low tide, and the nearshore sandbanks dry and exposed, the Africans could easily have waded to shore and salvation. The Dutch crew had other plans. They made the astonishing decision to nail down the hatches, trapping hundreds of humans to die within sight of shore.

Nobody cared. The crew was more concerned about getting paid a 10 percent salvage award for saving a treasure chest with twenty-three kilograms of gold from the *Leusden*'s hold, recovered "with the greatest peril to their lives," so Captain Outjes reported. The officers and sailors found the time to salvage the ship's treasure chest but not their fellow man.

The tragic loss of the *Leusden* was forgotten. Captain and crew did not lose any sleep over the 664 souls they purposefully allowed to drown. For the Dutch West India Company, it was a minor irritation. In one act of bolting down the hatches, the *Leusden* committed the largest massacre at sea in the history of the transatlantic slave trade.

Mowing the Lawn

Up and down the mouth of the Maroni River, Jerzy Gawronski and Steve Moore have spent years searching for the wreck of the *Leusden* with Leo Balai. They knew it had to be close. This season Diving With A Purpose was adding more eyes and experience to pinpoint the wreck and expose the story to the world.

Gawronski helped the team carry their dive tanks into a small, narrow barge. The team was hunting the ancient Dutch ship not on a high-tech research boat boasting the latest gadgets, but from the same kind of vessel that had sailed these waters for ages. Only now a motor had been bolted onto its stern. Flat-bottomed hulls like these can ride high enough over the shifting sandbanks not to become another casualty.

"The *Leusden* is somewhere out there by the mouth of the Maroni River," Professor Gawronski was convinced. He pointed to where the river met the North Atlantic Ocean. "So, I invite you aboard and let's find it."

The boat chugged past a village of round, thatch-roofed huts lost to time. The branches of the forest trees waved, running all the way down the shore, inviting the divers to plunge in and resurrect the enslaved voices in the shallows.

At Galibi, the nearest village to the mouth of the Maroni River, the team set up camp. Over a worktable they started poring over historic maps that showed how the river's course and sandbanks had changed over time.

Gawronski reconstructed what he and Leo Balai thought was the final route of the confused ship.

"Okay guys," Jerzy began, getting serious. "With these historical maps, together with the crew's testimony, we were able to identify several target areas for the wreck of the *Leusden*. The ship arrived here around the 30th of December, 1737." The marine archaeologist tapped a map showing the coastline ninety-five kilometers east of the Maroni River, where the captain plotted a reading in the ship's log.

"They described that they followed the coast from the east and then early morning on the first of January they saw a river mouth," Jerzy continued. "There were very heavy rains, like a wall of water, very heavy winds. And then in the fog, they saw the corner of land. They hit a sandbank and got stuck, they lost the rudder and there was a massive hole."

In the confusing swirl of atrocious weather, the captain mistook the Maroni for the Suriname River. It was a catastrophic error. The hull opened up like a zipper and rapidly took on water.

"And at that point they knew there was no saving the ship?" Kinga asked.

"In the account," Gawronski clarified, "they called it a 'wreck.' Not a 'ship,' but a 'wreck.' In order to get an idea of what happened, we also have a map from that period. This is a map from 1777 indicating more or less the situation during the wreckage. And you see a number of sandbanks. And on one of these sandbanks, the ship must still be stuck."

The Dutch were excellent seafarers who pioneered early navigational equipment. Onto the 1777 map, their cartographers had inked precise details showing the contours of the sandbanks, their shape and location as they existed 244 years ago.

Kramer had been quiet all the way during the commute from Albina. He had watched the choppy waves and drain-water brown river. This was going to be like diving in pea soup, he realized.

"Jerzy, I'm wondering—with the silt and the currents going through—how that is going to affect the dive?" Kramer asked politely. Alannah screwed up her face and rubbed her chin.

"Well, in these circumstances, the visibility is reduced sometimes to zero because of the presence of all this silt floating in the water. But let's hope for the best," Gawronski replied unconvincingly, the wind already whipping his hair. Kramer was in for a tough shift.

"So, we won't know until we get out there, huh?" Kinga threw in, ever chipper.

"No . . . and it can change day by day," Jerzy added.

The team took once more to the water, this time in a slightly more stable boat.

Kinga summed up the plan to find the *Leusden*. "This river mouth is huge. Over three miles wide, so the first step in pinpointing the ship-wreck is to scan the possible targets on the riverbed with a specialized metal detector. The mission now is to find a trail of metallic debris."

"Could be nails from the ship, ballast, guns, the anchors, of course. The captain used two or three anchors, and also a large amount of shackles to hold down the slaves," Jerzy explained.

Alannah helped deploy overboard into the murky soup a bright yellow Aquascan magnetometer. It looked more like a World War II artillery shell. The boat started towing the bright fish in its wake, meticulously and slowly "mowing the lawn." Hopefully its high sensitivity Fluxgate sensors would pick up the tiniest of metallic objects pinging off the seabed.

The team plowed back and forth over the square mile they had targeted as the last resting place of the *Leusden*. It was tedious but essential groundwork. The mission took days.

Unlike the Florida Keys and English Channel, both maritime highways for centuries, major sea trade off the Maroni River only started with the arrival of the Dutch in the early seventeenth century.

Kramer was optimistic despite the conditions. "There has never been much shipping activity in these waters," he pointed out. "So, if we find any sign of metal, that would strengthen our theory that this is the site of the underwater wreck."

Leo Balai watched the hunt unfold, resolute and strong. "The *Leusden* is so important for the history of the slave trade. We have to find it," he told the crew, keeping them motivated.

After five days surveying the waters, the team failed to pick up any signals on the Aquascan. It was a painful wake-up call for how hard it can be to track down wrecks that do not want to be found.

But then, as so often happens in archaeology, on the last day, everything changed in an instant.

From inside the boat's cabin, it was Steve Moore's job to guide the survey track lines and watch the profile of metallic bumps and lumps register on his laptop's software. As the boat reached the end of another grid line, he spotted something familiar.

"I think we got something . . ." Steve announced. "Yeah, yeah definitely. We are seeing some sort of target or something metallic down there. We need to pull it in and have a look." On the computer the graph showed a double low dip, registering a big metallic hit on the seabed.

The dive team was relieved. They finally had their purpose, their lead. The boat shut down its engines and swayed from side to side on the choppy water. It was time to get eyes on the prize and verify the target. It now looked like, almost three hundred years after the disastrous sinking of the *Leusden*, the crew could be floating right over the wreck.

TWISTED TONGUES

To make sense of what the Dutch were up to in Suriname means turning the spotlight on Brazil, the country where the slave trade began in earnest in 1440. Along the hilltops of Recife on the country's central east coast, the achingly beautiful scenery has not changed for five hundred years. Field after field of lush green sugarcane rolls as far as the eye can see. It was in this paradise that the torture of African slave labor first took hold in the New World. From these soils, enslavement encircled the Caribbean and on to Suriname.

Sugar factories have been part of Brazil's landscape since 1542. Today Black workmen, direct descendants of trafficked Africans, still cut the cane, now dressed in their favorite football team shirts. White supervisors on horseback keep a beady eye on their investment. Until now the best "machine" for cutting sugarcane is people. In Brazil sugar production reached new levels of efficiency and profit.

Just as Brazil is the biggest exporter of sugar in the world today, so it was ground zero for sugar destined for Europe's markets five centuries ago. For fifty years Holland and Portugal fought a relentless war to control global commerce. At stake, in what has been called the first true world war, was new overseas empires and earning the bragging rights to be the supreme superpower of the Western world.

Portugal sent the first sugar technician to Brazil in 1516 to oversee a sugar mill start-up. Within a decade you could buy Brazilian sugar in Lisbon and Antwerp. The experiment took root. More skilled experts were contracted from Portugal, Italy, Galicia in Spain, the Canary Islands, Belgium, and Madeira to turn Brazil into the West's newest cash cow. Plantings shipped from Madeira were grafted into the soil between São Vicente in the south and Pernambuco in the north, flat lands with fertile ground conveniently near the shore for export and covering four thousand square miles, three quarters the size of Connecticut.

Production skyrocketed beyond the limits of the small island of Madeira, the former capital of sugar cultivation. From 1570 to 1585 the number of sugar factories in Brazil rose from 60 to 128 with Pernambuco and Bahia controlling three quarters of the country's output. Where a sugar mill on Madeira could turn out 15 metric tons of sugar a year, Brazilian mills bagged 130 tons.

At first, the Portuguese enslaved natives seized in what the Church called a "just war." The Indigenous people, though, were found to be poor workers, no doubt often deliberately. In any event, Indigenous people had no immunity to European diseases. Between 1492 and 1700, smallpox, chicken pox, and typhoid killed an estimated fifty-five million natives, or 90 percent of Indigenous people in the Americas. Some twenty-first-century climate scientists have suggested that the mass deaths and the resulting abandonment of agricultural land led to a "terrestrial carbon uptake," when the land was reclaimed by nature. Put simply, so many people died that this may have led to the Little Ice Age between the fourteenth and nineteenth centuries. The Europeans now had a problem. They needed cheap labor and they had to fill the hole left by the millions of dead. Enter the Africans.

Africans were the polar opposite of the Indigenous people of the Americas. They had been tried and tested in Portugal's sugar plantations on Madeira. Cane cutting took man and woman teamwork. The man cut and his companion bound the canes into faggots. Harsh quotas of around 4,200 canes had to be met every day or else. Conditions were ruthless. Failure to hit quotas was punished by slaves being scorched with hot wax, branded on the face or chest, or having their ears or noses chopped off. Sexual brutality was also common in Portuguese Brazil. The lucky ate food made from manioc flour, salt meat, fish, rice, and bananas, topped off with whale meat. The unfortunate swallowed whatever they could get their hands on. Even rats caught in sugarcane fields were boiled in cooking pots.

PLAGUE IN BRAZIL

Plague appeared on the Brazilian coast as a serious problem in 1559. Disease, probably smallpox, killed over six hundred enslaved Indigenous people in Espirito Santo the next year. Overall, an estimated thirty thousand perished. Father do Valle described children dying on their mothers' breasts for lack of milk, people so weak that they could not dig graves for the dead or collect water for the living. On some sugar plantations, ninety to one hundred slaves perished. In 1563, measles struck the weakened population. Another thirty thousand died. It was no accident that the importation of Africans began in the 1570s.

Many plantation masters cared little about their slaves' well-being, dismissing them as no better than "mute orangutans." But not everyone liked what they saw. Priests like the Italian Padre António Vieira detested the horrific conditions the Africans had to put up with, describing in 1633:

> And truly who sees in the blackness of night those tremendous furnaces perpetually burning; the flames leaping . . . the Ethiopians or cyclopses, bathed in sweat, as black as they are strong, feeding the hard and heavy fuel to the fire, and the tools they use to mix and stir them; the cauldrons, or boiling lakes, continually stirred and restirred, now vomiting froth, exhaling clouds of steam, more of heat than of smoke . . . the noise of the wheels and chains, the peoples the color of the very night working intensely and moaning together without a moment of peace or rest; who sees all the confused and tumultuous machinery and apparatus of that Babylon can not doubt though they may have seen Vesuvius or Mount Etna that this is the same as Hell.

By the time Brazil's pure-as-snow end product was packed, it was welcomed in Europe as the most prized commodity on earth. Already by 1625 almost fourteen thousand tons of sugar headed to the West a year, its prices marked up 60 percent higher than in Brazil. Even during the country's eighteenth-century gold rush, the value of Brazilian sugar exports exceeded all other commodities. From Brazil the sugar industry was copied across Barbados and the Caribbean. Sweetening coffee and tea became an inescapable craze of daily Western life. African slaves continued to be shackled and shipped to Brazil until 1855.

New Holland

For all the profit that the slave trade generated, there was an unimaginable loss. A loss counted in murdered Africans and wrecked ships. After jealously watching Portugal rake in colossal profits in Europe's great cities, Amsterdam decided to get in on the act. In 1623, the Dutch sent out war fleets to Brazil. All were repelled until, seven years later, sixty-seven ships and seven thousand soldiers took Olinda and Recife. Amsterdam now planted a flag in the sweet soils of New Holland.

Portugal had trafficked one hundred thousand Africans to its Brazil plantations in the first quarter of the seventeenth century. Now the Dutch duplicated its success. One hundred and sixty-six sugar mills were turning in Dutch Brazil by 1639. All Holland needed to power up its foothold in the Americas was an enchained army. The answer to Johan Maurits, the prince of Nassau-Siegen and governor of Dutch Brazil, was to try and capture Luanda, Portugal's slave market in Angola. A fleet of twenty-one ships set out. Without African slaves, Brazil's economy would be doomed.

In May 1641, Luanda and the great Portuguese slave port on the island of São Tomé were in Dutch hands. The Dutch West India Company was at the peak of its powers. It planned to ship to Brazil fifteen thousand slaves a year, aged fifteen to thirty-six. The Dutch West India Company reckoned the slave trade to Brazil should rake in six million guilders a year. Sugar and slaves were the richest prize on earth.

Even though the lowlanders were all too swiftly thrown out of Brazil in 1654, they kept a chokehold over slave trafficking by dominating former Portuguese lands in West Africa, including the jewel in Lisbon's crown, the mighty fort of Elmina in modern Ghana. Portuguese Brazilian slavers planning to trade on the Guinea Coast were forced to pay a 10 percent toll on the value of their cargo to Dutch authorities.

Down the decades, the Dutch would traffic around five hundred thousand slaves to the Americas, making it the fifth largest trader in slaves after Portugal, Britain, France, and Spain. It was after the loss of Brazil that Dutch merchants turned to nearby Suriname to grow their sugar and coffee ambitions.

New Blacks City

From a small business in the town of Lagos in Portugal, the slave trade became a worldwide moneyspinner, creating cities like Rio de Janeiro. It may surprise people, but only 4 percent of all enslaved Africans were sent to North America. The Caribbean received 36 percent. Fourteen percent went to Spanish America. But, between 1560 and 1852, 46 percent of the total—4.8 million Africans—arrived in Brazil.

In these years Rio de Janeiro was distastefully known as the "Black City." A graphic memory of the capital's shamed past came to light when Rio was being developed for the 2016 Olympics. Fast and furious construction work in the port area of Valongo, the Long Valley, uncovered the old city wharf where captive Africans first landed in the Americas. Archaeologists discovered a historic site covered with the memories Africans brought with them: tobacco pipes, beads, rings, magical cowrie shells from the Gulf of Guinea, good luck charms, anthropomorphic stones, and crystals. The dock formed part of a large slave quarters, including the quarantine station where captives infected with contagious diseases were locked up, and the Cemetery of Pretos Novos ("New Blacks"), where the victims of abusive sea voyages and the diseases they caught during crossings were discarded as worthless.

The cemetery itself came to light by chance when a young couple bought a new house and began home improvements. Digging in the foundations turned up human bones. And then more and more bones. Their home had been built on the cemetery of the New Blacks where Africans fresh off the boat were buried. Most had died on landing after forty-five to sixty days crossing the Middle Passage. To begin with, the bodies were laid to rest in orderly graves. Space quickly ran out as the dead reached unmanageable numbers. The cemetery deteriorated into an unmarked mass grave. Then, Rio's residents started using it as a general garbage dump.

When the smell got too bad, the locals burned down the garbage heap, and then the process started all over again, filling it up with discarded Africans and trash. Over thirty thousand Africans ended their lives in a random hellhole in the ground. Just like in Lagos, the enslaved of no economic value were cast off in the easiest and cheapest way possible.

Valongo's history fascinated the archaeologists. They immediately knew that the wharf was the setting for one of the greatest crimes in humanity. In the shadow of this place of unspeakable suffering, the dig's lead archaeologist, Tania Andrade Lima, wrote how

> We took Valongo out of the ground with our heart in our hands, with great respect and deep emotion. Considered one of the most notable places of memory of the African diaspora outside of Africa itself . . . Valongo was understood as a location that encapsulates memories of pain and struggle for survival in the history of the ancestors of Afro-descendants.

The death and discarding on land and sea of millions of Africans was for most Europeans an acceptable by-product of profiting in billions of pieces of gold.

BONE CRUSHERS

Dawn broke over the Suriname River. The water ran slack and flat. The midmorning wind was yet to stir. At first light the locals were heading to work, crossing the broad river by ferry, carrying shopping baskets and pushing mopeds to scoot off to the office back on the other bank.

Alannah, Kramer, and Kinga were commuting in the opposite direction, scouring the seabed off Suriname's fertile forests. Somewhere out there Leo Balai was certain lay the resting place of the long-lost *Leusden*, a Dutch trader sunk with the greatest loss of enslaved life in the history of the Netherlands. Blinding silver rays of sun lit up the water. Maybe it was a good omen from the spirits of the past.

In a narrow, motorized barge, the dive team slowly traveled upriver, away from the Atlantic Ocean. The Suriname River is vast. The explorers felt like insignificant specks caught between forest and water.

Leo Balai took the opportunity to remind the team about the *Leusden*'s final hours. "The ship was stuck on the sandbank and water came in. They tried to mend it, to prevent the water from coming in, but it didn't stop. The captain decided the ship was lost. He also decided that the 'cargo' was lost. The captives were of no value anymore. The 664 Africans who perished could have survived, but the captain had a different idea."

Diving With A Purpose was heading away from the sea inland to try and make sense of the best-case fate of the *Leusden*'s African captives if they had made it to Suriname alive. They would see where and how the Dutch manufactured huge profits.

"I want to show you what was supposed to be the final destination of the enslaved Africans on board the *Leusden*," Balai explained. "Around this whole territory there were slave plantations. And such a creek was essential to take the sugar and the coffee to the river and then to Paramaribo and transport it to the Netherlands and Amsterdam to sell."

Looking at the waterway running over the horizon, Kinga started to visualize how these shores once bustled with plantations. "So, these were the highways basically?" she asked.

Not only were these waters highways, Leo Balai confirmed, but what looked like a river was actually a canal hand dug by thousands of slaves over a hundred miles all the way to the Atlantic Ocean.

"If you look around you can't imagine that there were thousands of Black people living over here, died over here, were massacred sometimes over here because they had to make sugar and coffee," Leo observed. "Sugar was the curse of Black people, because Europeans wanted sugar."

The creek started to narrow. Branches hung over the water, keeping outside eyes away from the secrets abandoned in the interior. The riverbank was densely overgrown. Nature had reclaimed the past. A boa constrictor watched the divers sweep by, uncurled its body, and licked its lips but could not be bothered to move out of the sun and grab a juicy meal.

"So, nature is covering up the crime," Kramer whispered.

The team pushed deeper into the outback, bent over to stop being hit by trees overgrowing the creek.

Leo pointed out that once "This place was flatland, with sugar canes. Thousands of slaves working day and night."

"This was all flat, clear, no jungle?" a shocked Kinga exclaimed.

"No jungle," the Dutch scholar confirmed. "The slave owners were so inventive to stop the slaves from running away that they planted cactuses around the plantation so you couldn't get in or out."

The Suriname Trade

By the time the *Leusden*'s captain bolted down its hatches to deny the African captives any chance of escape, the once mighty Dutch West India Company was a shadow of its former glory. Its powerful grip over the Africa trade had crumbled. The battle for colonies and endless wars against Spain and Portugal in the Atlantic had exhausted the company's capital and took it near to bankruptcy. All Dutch commerce with Africa was opened to free traders from October 1734.

With the loss of New Brazil, Suriname was key to a range of agricultural wealth. Only in Suriname, Berbice, and Essequibo in Guiana did the West India Company hang onto its monopoly. In particular, it was contracted to deliver at least 2,500 slaves a year to the plantations owned by the Sociëteit van Suriname, a corporation run by the city of Amsterdam, the Amsterdam Chamber of the West India Company, and the aristocratic Van Aerssen van Sommelsdijck family. The company managed to ship 60,800 Africans to Suriname between 1674 and 1740.

By 1713, in its 171 factories, Suriname grew a wealth of tropical goods, not just sugar, but coffee, cacao, and cotton. By the late eighteenth century, the colony was one giant factory inhabited by five thousand European masters and seventy-five thousand slaves.

To feed the isolated colony, North America was a vital lifeline, sending four thousand ships to Paramaribo over 112 years. US traders sold building materials, household supplies, sheep, pigs, and geese to Suriname. Horses, needed to turn the heavy stones that crushed the sugarcane, were a vital overseas commodity. Six hundred horses were shipped to Suriname every year from New York, Connecticut, Massachusetts, and Rhode Island at the time when the *Leusden* sank. The American supply ships were known as "horse jockeys." Sadly, 36 percent of the horses died during the crossings, washed overboard from upper decks.

Sugar remained the king of Suriname's exports for two centuries, reaching twenty million pounds a year in the 1720s. By the time the *Leusden* set sail on its final voyage, the coffee beans first cultivated in Suriname rivaled sugar. Exports averaged more than 1.5 million pounds in the 1730s.

Silent Witness

The narrow barge veered down a tight creek off the Suriname River, just a few meters wide. The water was completely flat, the trees and bushes untamed. It felt as if no one had traveled these waterways for decades. All Alannah could make out were capuchin and red howler monkeys hooting, grunting, and jumping between trees. The wild jungle felt menacing. Humans had no right to be here. Kramer peered into the thick green wilderness and wondered what he was doing miles away from the sea where he should be searching for the *Leusden*.

The divers made landfall in the middle of nowhere. A pale green katydid sat patiently awaiting its next dinner of flies. The friends strolled uncertainly down an earthen snake track, nervously keeping their ears peeled for the forest's crocodiles, lancehead snakes, panthers, and jaguars. A mysterious wind blew through the leaves, sending shivers down the travelers' spines. Leo Balai sliced away foreboding undergrowth with his machete.

The cactus fence that Dr. Balai had mentioned, guarding the rainforest's interior, started to thin out. In the middle of the jungle, Diving With A Purpose stumbled onto what Leo brought them away from their ocean prize to see. The intended final destination of the *Leusden*'s 664 drowned captives.

Two ruined brick columns veered out of the wild forest undergrowth. Emerging out of the jungle, the team were suddenly confronted by giant, rusting monuments to a now dead age. Nearby, iron wheels that once turned a sugar mill stood rusting in the open air. Collapsed roofs and walls littered the ground next to an overturned oven.

"This is huge! What is it?" Alannah asked.

Leo Balai rested a soft hand on the mill teeth and explained that it was part of an abandoned sugar factory. "These are silent witnesses of an enormous crime," he continued. "You had hundreds of people working over you; some of them at the plantation to cut the cane. And then you have the people who work in the factory to process the cane. Imagine yourself being a slave over here, then you can see how horrible it was. Get up in the morning, work eighteen hours a day, seven days a week. Every mistake you make, the whip comes out."

The team could almost hear the cries of the enslaved Africans. Somebody had spent a small fortune investing in this factory of death and profit. Suriname's sugar estates, divided into squares, covered five hundred to six hundred acres. Some were staffed with up to four hundred slaves.

Kramer stared in disgust at the atrocity, failing to process the sense behind such brutal architecture. Anger and sadness coursed through his veins. A grim look crossed his face. What was worse, drowning on the *Leusden* or being led to a harrowing life making sugar?

Kramer knew all too well the fate the exiled could expect. Just to make sure, he asked, "So the life expectancy of an African here was about eight years?"

Leo confirmed that slaves forced to work on Suriname's sugar plantations lived an average of eight to ten years. And then it was over. Another 14 percent did not even make it, dying at sea in the hands of Dutch slavers.

Kramer, sensing the horrific living conditions of the ancestors, tried to control his emotions bubbling to the surface. "Alright, I am trying to imagine this, right?" he thought out loud. "You get captured in Africa and then once you are here . . ."

"You get branded," Leo added, tight-lipped but wanting to paint the full picture.

Kramer closed his eyes and took slow breaths before continuing in a soft whisper. "You get branded, right, bought and then tortured for eight years in a sugar plantation, and then you die."

All around the divers' feet lay scattered the debris of despair and destruction, the loose change left over from the eighteenth century's biggest moneymaker. Iron wheel cogs no longer turned, the oven was cold, and the pistons pumped no more. But the bitter taste of the sugared savagery still felt raw.

Kinga pulled the discussion back to the here and now. She needed help understanding the physical ruins at her feet. "What did all of this look like?" she asked. "What are all these pieces? We are looking at skeletons."

By the 1730s two great arm-shaped regions greedily enveloped the northern and western reaches of the Suriname River. A map drawn in 1734 shows an astonishing spiderweb of five hundred Dutch plantations clustered between the town of Paramaribo and along the Suriname and Commewijne Rivers. The estates bore Dutch, German, and French names, many perverse in hindsight. The slaves who broke their backs in the plantations of La Paix, La Liberté, and Nieuwe Hoop enjoyed no "peace," nor "freedom," nor chances of "new hope."

Alannah, Kramer, and Kinga walked past the engine, which lay shattered on the ground. Nearby was the oven that once melted cane juice. The most important part of the factory was the press. It was into this crusher that raw sugarcane was fed by armies of enslaved Africans until its juices ran free. This was a dangerous piece of equipment, especially if your hand got trapped inside.

DANGERS OF SUGAR MILLS

From Captain J. G. Stedman, *Narrative, of a Five Years' Expedition, Against the Revolted Negroes of Surinam, in Guiana . . . from the Year 1772 to 1777 . . . Volume I* (London, 1796). "So very dangerous is the work of those negroes who attend the rollers, that should one of their fingers be caught between them, which frequently happens through inadvertency, the whole arm is instantly shattered to pieces, if not part of the body. A hatchet is generally kept ready to chop off the limb, before the working of the mill can be stopped. Another danger is, that should a poor slave dare to taste that sugar which he produces by the sweat of his brow, he runs the risk of receiving some hundred lashes, or having all his teeth knocked out by the overseer. Such are the hardships and dangers to which the sugar-making negroes are exposed."

"When your hand gets stuck in the machine," Leo Balai was forced to spell out, "the only thing they did was to chop it off. Because they couldn't, wouldn't, stop the machine . . ."

Far away from London, Amsterdam, Lisbon, Paris, and Madrid a 24/7 world had developed to feed Europe's great capitals with coffee sweetened with must-have sugar. Nothing was allowed to get in the way of profit. Lost limbs were all in a day's work. The next victim in line simply walked forward, risking life and limb.

"There was always someone around here with a machete," Leo told the team.

"Someone stood here with a machete, just in case that happened," Kinga understood.

"Just in case, and it happened often because the people worked sixteen to eighteen hours a day and you get tired. And a mistake with such a machine often happens. That is the price of sugar, of course," Dr. Balai concluded.

Alannah saw the big picture. The Africans enslaved on the *Leusden* were in a lose-lose position. Death at sea or die worked to the bone? "And the Africans on the *Leusden*, they didn't even give them this chance to come here or try and live their eight years of life expectancy or to get away. They were murdered because the captain took a wrong turn. They weren't even worth the chance."

Alannah's voice trailed off. After seeing the workplace expected of African slaves in Suriname and hearing about their living conditions, the divers were even more desperate to track down the lost Dutch slaver and expose its horror story.

SWEET TOOTH

Transporting millions of slaves across the Atlantic took a tremendous amount of resources and money. How did these gigantic logistics make financial sense to Europeans and how did they balance the books? The answer lies in the bottom of a coffee cup.

In the first half of the seventeenth century, a commercial craze shook the civilized world. The humble berry discovered by an Ethiopian goatherder after his flock turned frisky chewing the bean in the wild became a $100 billion annual industry. After coffee at first stopped worshippers from falling asleep in mosques, coffeehouses opened across the Near East from Cairo to Constantinople. Sipping bitter black water was an expected sign of Turkish hospitality. By 1630 coffeehouses were go-to places for people from all walks of life to gossip, talk news, and make business deals across the Ottoman Empire.

The exotica of the "Orient" caught on fast in Britain after Parliament allowed Turks and Jews to trade in the kingdom. London's first coffeehouse, its doors opened in 1652, was the brainchild of a Christian Turk called Pasqua Rose who immigrated to London with an English merchant. Everyone loved Pasqua's coffee. So he set up a stall in a shed in the churchyard in St. Michael, Cornhill. Business boomed, and the shed was replaced by the capital's first coffeehouse just around the corner from the Royal Exchange in Saint Michael's Alley, the heart of commerce in the City of London. Overnight, copycat shops appeared. By 1663 London's punters could choose from eighty-three coffeehouses, and 550 by 1740. The forest-fire spread of coffee drinking was helped by Oliver Cromwell, the Lord Protector of Britain's war on fun. His Puritan party frowned on the theater, beer, and wine, and stooped as low as to ban Christmas. But Cromwell allowed coffee drinking as a diversion from all the other losses.

Coffee may have been prohibited in the Ottoman East for its drug-like intoxication, and King Charles II of England unsuccessfully tried to ban the drink in 1785 too, but Pope Clement VIII gave it a divine blessing. When Italian merchants presented him with a cup in 1581, he was hooked. As much as his priests pointed out that it was invented by infidel Muslims, the leader of the Catholic Church conveniently replied that "This Satan's drink is so delicious that it would be a pity to let the infidels have exclusive use of it. We shall cheat Satan by baptizing it."

Instead of profits flooding into Saracen pockets, England's East India Company started promoting tea over coffee, which it could better control. Tea was already being sipped in London by the 1650s, but mainly as medicine for the elite pockets of the famous, like the diarist Samuel Pepys. British tea drinking exploded after 1704 as scientists, medical experts, and fashionistas heralded the genius of taking a tea break. By 1767 Britain had seven million pounds of tea in its warehouses.

The obsession with tea created one of the most extraordinary social and cultural revolutions imaginable. Leaves shipped 10,000 miles were blended with sugar exported 5,000 miles. The sweet white crystals had been processed by Africans trafficked against their will 3,790 miles across the Atlantic.

Into bottomless cups serving coffee, tea, and cocoa, mountains of sugar was poured. All four addictive must-have products were shipped west through the hands of African slaves sweating in Brazil and Suriname. Sugar's volume and profit are hard to visualize. Addiction to the sweet tooth began on the side tables of the high and mighty. A French ambassador described the teeth of sugar lover Queen Elizabeth I as "very yellow and unequal . . . Many of them are missing so that one cannot understand her easily when she speaks quickly."

Bad teeth and sugar were not just a British complaint. Louis XIV of France, the Sun King, ruled without a tooth in his head. All of them had fallen out by the age of forty. The French were said to heap so much sugar into their coffee cups that spoons could stand up on their own. By 1800 sugar was one of life's pleasurable essentials.

The chain of manufacture that started with seizing and trafficking humans in West Africa was a vital cog in the making of the modern world, and the coffee shop was at its center. The insurance industry was born on the banks of the River Thames in Lloyd's Coffee House. Coffee shops doubled up as libraries and became places to read newly invented newspapers and discuss the politics of the day at a time when the Puritains' thought police were everywhere.

Coffeehouses were much more than places to drink: they were places to socialize, share information, read, and make deals. Sugar and coffee spawned modern polite society in spaces that broke down social barriers. Rich and poor rubbed shoulders. For the price of one penny, any man could enter and enjoy. And so coffeehouses became known as "penny universities." Playwrights and writers like Jonathan Swift and Samuel Pepys favored certain establishments. Men of fashion and young adventurers had their favorites. Families had their own local coffee shops.

Coffee was not to everyone's taste. Some women hated what the bean did to their men, complaining that "we poor Souls sit mopeing all alone till Twelve at night, and when at last they come to bed smoakt like Westphalia Hogs-head we have no more comfort of them, than from a Shotten Herring or dryed Bulgrush; which forces us to take up this Lamentation." The lobbyists demanded coffee be banned to make sure of a "return of old strengthening Liquors of forefathers and Lusty Heroes to improve women's interest and replenish the race." Men seemed to prefer coffee and manly fellowship to making babies. Other women made hay on the back of coffee and sugar, running and working in shops. Moll King's café became an infamous den of prostitution.

Ironically, it was on the tea tables of elegant ladies, a centerpiece for intimate meetings and polite discussion, that the tide against sugar and the slave trade turned. *An Address to the People of Great Britain on the Utility of Refraining from the Use of West India Sugar and Rum*, written by William Fox in 1791, stirred the waters by claiming that ladies' sugar-sweetened tea was tainted by the blood of African slaves. The accusation hit a raw nerve.

Fox, a publicity genius, warned his genteel audience that each pound of West Indian sugar contained two ounces of African flesh. His pamphlet sold over 250,000 copies in more than twenty editions. The poet and opium addict Samuel Taylor Coleridge angrily denounced the murder of colonial slaves so that "fine Ladies and Prostitutes' might be fashionably out-fitted as they gathered around the British tea table."

After reading Fox's broadside, around half a million British abstained from sugar taken in coffee and tea and eaten in desserts, bread, porridge, and puddings. Sugar and the slave trade had turned sour.

DEAD SILENCE

On the Tiger Bank at the entrance to the Suriname River, Jerzy Gawronski and Steve Moore had managed to nail down a set of coordinates as the potential location where the *Leusden* was wrecked and its human cargo of Africans drowned. Suriname may be blessed with no winter, a strong attraction for its pale Dutch overlords, but that did not make these waters any more alluring. The swirling ocean still looked pea soup green rather than tropical blue.

On a digital map, Jerzy and Steve had plotted a red grid around part of the Tiger Bank where the Aquascan magnetometer registered a big spike above something unnatural, something metallic on or under the seabed.

"We can see here the target we just got," Steve pointed out on a graph, taking off his glasses to peer at his laptop screen. "There's two passes here, identical! So that is a definite hit." The team surveyed the area repeatedly to make sure their eyes did not deceive them.

Jerzy looked on, hand on chin, wondering whether he could dare to dream. Leo Balai was tight-lipped. Nobody on earth had researched the *Leusden* as deeply. In his mind's eye he could imagine the ship's last hours and the panic onboard as the African captives realized they were being abandoned. Finding the *Leusden* would be epic, the crowning achievement of his life's work. For the first time in days, the mood lifted over the heavy weight pressing down on the divers' shoulders. Was the *Leusden* finally ready to give up its ghosts?

As ever, Kramer was figuring the angles, wondering what could positively identify the wreck. "I don't want to get ahead of myself," he cautioned, "but we do know that the *Leusden* dropped more than one anchor, and it was carrying a number of cannons." These kinds of sunken artifacts were exactly what could register metallic hits like Steve and Jerzy had found.

Steve's experience matching magnetic targets to wrecked finds told him the team was on the right track. "That's definitely something iron, an anchor, a few cannons, a cluster of shackles," he tried to convince the crew. "It could be something really big and really deep or it could be something not so big just under the surface."

Kinga was sold. "Okay got it. So, we're in the right place," she hoped. "Finally, we have a definite target."

Steve's energy was sky-high. "Yes, the right target, the right signal, the right everything."

Diving With A Purpose started preparing their gear. Their date with destiny had arrived. This was why they crossed the Atlantic and spent days surveying miles of ocean in search of a small patch of wreckage of immense historical importance. Kramer strapped his buoyancy vest to a white dive tank: even if the water was murky, his friends surely would be able to spot him.

Kinga checked her dive computer. If the visibility was poor, she would need to rely on it to make out north from south.

As the senior diver on the expedition, the plan was for Kramer to head down first. You did not need to be a master dive instructor to appreciate that these waters were incredibly dangerous. Kramer would need to overcome strong currents, low visibility, and then hope not to come face to face with venomous stingrays feeding on the riverbed. He had drawn the short straw. Still, scouring the seabed was a duty, he felt. He owed it to the *Leusden*'s drowned voices.

Kramer pulled on his signature gray-and-black-hooped wetsuit. Somewhere down there, Captain Joachim Outjes and his crew locked up 664 Africans and threw away the key. Now the divers were back to pick the lock.

Alannah spelled out what Kramer had signed up to. "During the dive, there will be no direct communication between Kramer and us," she explained. "So, a rope is attached to him and, in case of an emergency, we can pull him up."

Diving With A Purpose was going old school. The conditions were too hazardous for everyone to dive. They could all get lost in the soup or swept away by the fast-running currents. Everyone knew what the security alarm of a rope meant. The topside team would need to pull Kramer out of the Maroni River fast if he ran into trouble like being menaced by those stingrays or getting tangled in fishermen's nets.

Kramer was focused on the task at hand. "It's just me, but it's not. I am sensing the souls of six hundred-plus and I want to find them," he said out loud. There was no way he was going to back out, come hell or high water.

Steve Moore had devised an old-school communications system using the rope line. "Kramer, let's just go over the signals," he said. "One long pull: return the signal, 'I'm okay, are you okay?' Two pulls: 'I am coming up.' Or four pulls: 'There's a problem, coming up,' or 'We have a problem, get me up.'"

Kramer was only half listening. He was desperate to come up with good news, to tell the team, "They're here. We've found them; we've done what Dr. Balai called us for." Then Diving With A Purpose, Leo Balai, Jerzy Gawronski, and Steve Moore could try and give the lost Africans peace and hopefully, on some level, a proper burial.

The shallow-bottomed barge bobbed precariously from side to side like a drunken sailor as Kramer gingerly clambered over a blue steel ladder in the stern. Along the side, the boat's name was written in black paint, *Maranatha*, a biblical reference to 1 Corinthians: "Our Lord has come." Would the *Leusden*'s 664 enslaved get divine justice today?

Just as Kramer was about to drop into inner space, Steve added more insult to the danger of the dive. "Kramer, this is for sweeping on the bottom for any stingrays," he said, dropping a wooden pole down to him. The lead instructor for Diving With A Purpose had the lowest form of tech to protect him. Kramer followed the line of the *Maranatha*'s hull to the bow and then dropped down.

Time stood still. Kramer's air bubbles vanished. Everyone held their breath.

In his mind, Leo Balai played out the West India Company ship's final minutes. The *Leusden* had hit a sandbank and was sinking in the river mouth. At that moment the captain made a fateful decision. He ordered the sailors to nail down the hatches, in an instant signing the death warrant for 664 humans. To make sure, the sailors sat on the hatches all night.

By morning, all the Africans below deck were dead. They could easily have been saved. Instead, they drowned in shallow waters in sight of land. The captain and crew took to the lifeboats and made it safely to shore. Leo Balai shuddered. The screams of the forgotten souls haunted his dreams.

Why did the *Leusden*'s crew choose death over life? Why not simply unlock the hatches and let the enslaved make a run from the sinking ship? What did the captain have to lose?

The fateful decision of 1738 made little financial or humanitarian sense. If the West India Company planned to cash in an insurance policy on the ship's "cargo," letting the Africans sink may have had a despicable logic. It would have meant less paperwork and no need to organize a costly and dangerous posse to hunt them down in Suriname's rainforest.

Because they were classed as "valuable and perishable" cargo, slaves were insured in Genoa, Rome, and Barcelona from the fifteenth century and Antwerp and Holland by 1592. Private Dutch companies like the Middelburgse Commercie Compagnie insured hulls and cargo separately. General maritime insurance policies signed in Amsterdam covered losses caused by unexpected events at sea, such as storms, fire, and piracy. But when slaves escaped or revolted, marine insurers often refused to pay out claims. Just uncontrollable perils were covered. Slave insurrections were thought to be preventable.

In any case, the West India Company did not insure its captive human cargos. The *Leusden*'s hull was insured for ten thousand Dutch guilders and its goods for forty thousand guilders. The captain knew that the ship was old and that he could recoup most of its losses anyway. More to the point, his aim may have been to save his own hide. If he let the enslaved swim for it, they might have overpowered the crew, or worse. But he wasn't looking for a solution, not even for the children.

INSURING THE SLAVE TRADE

The question of "damage" caused by slave uprisings was heavily debated in Amsterdam. On December 17, 1750, the enslaved Africans on board the *Middelburgs Welvaren* revolted after the African coast was no longer in sight. To put down the revolt, the crew locked down the captives in the ship's hold and closed all openings to limit their view. As a result, 231 Africans suffocated.

When the ship returned home to Middelburg in 1751, an insurance claim was issued. The failed revolt led to an angry debate between the insurer, Servaas Bomme, and shipowner Jan De Munck. Rather than question the morality of the mass murder, Bomme and De Munck argued about "the damage," the reimbursement per murdered African, and who was responsible. In the end it is believed the insurer paid out.

After half an hour, Kramer slowly surfaced. Relief flooded the *Maranatha*.

Steve could not contain his hope. "How was it?" he asked.

"All blacked out . . ." Kramer said, his mouthpiece hardly spat out. As he slowly climbed up the boat's ladder, he shared his experience. The team pressed close to catch his breathless words. "Can't see a thing down there. I was feeling around, to see if I could feel something down there. Really didn't feel anything, right . . . just sandy and black."

Back onboard, Kramer started his return from the past to the present. He popped off his face mask and turned it backward. Even with eyes in the back of his head there was no seeing anything in the Maroni River's zero visibility. Sand from the Atlantic Ocean and the same soils where sugar and coffee once grew washed down from the rainforest, mixed together into an impenetrable gloom.

Thinking back to the sea bottom, Kramer told the team, "This is a murder scene and the souls of over six hundred Africans are down there. So, on some level, you want to feel like you can hear them calling to you, right? But it was just silence. Dead silence."

Skies and seas were overcast and not going to improve any time soon. The only way to ground-truth if the magnetometer had truly found the *Leusden* would be to dredge the seabed and uncover what lay below. If Diving With A Purpose was at the right spot, they might end up disturbing and bringing up the bones of the dead from the river bottom.

Directly below them they felt in their own bones the final resting place of the murdered and unnamed 664 Africans. Collectively, the team decided against dredging. The best decision was to let the dead rest. The divers and archaeologists would come again. Hope for better conditions.

As the *Maranatha* returned back to shore, Alannah found one image spinning around and around in her mind. Had the Africans been set free to flee into the surrounding jungle, could they have survived?

Before moving onto the next slave wreck, Leo Balai had one more secret to share with the team.

FREEDOM FIGHTERS

Leo Balai did not want the hunt for the *Leusden* to end on a low. The story of all Africans trafficked between West Africa and Suriname did not end badly. Thousands took their fate in their own hands. Leo also wanted to show the divers, show the world, that if the captain of the *Leusden* had shown enough compassion to unlock the hatches and let the captives swim for it, they could have sought asylum deep in Suriname's forest.

A red dawn shone down on the bones of the *Leusden*. The rising sun shimmered off the flat water. Palm trees stood motionless and trusting. The dive team's mood was subdued but they had high hopes for the future. The atrocious tale of the *Leusden* was out in the open, remembered.

Leo Balai was taking the team to one final place, called Akalikondre in the region of Marowijne, a Maroon village, fifty-four miles east of Paramaribo. "There is something more I want to show you," he winked.

"And the Maroons are escaped slaves?" Kinga asked.

"I call them 'freedom fighters,'" Leo corrected, "because they fought the plantation owners, killed them, went away, took people with them. Went into the woods and started new communities."

The deeper the river barge chugged down the creeks, the more canoes and people the team spotted along the banks. Behind a picture-perfect tropical sandy beach, hidden behind the trees, wooden shacks appeared, home to descendants of slaves who escaped Suriname's plantations. Long after the Dutch went home, the Maroons stayed on, carving out an existence in one of the transatlantic slave trade's great survival stories.

The Maroons got their name from the Spanish word *cimarron*, meaning "cattle gone wild in the bush." Fed up with miserable living conditions and sexual exploitation, Suriname's enslaved Africans often rose up in rebellions, strikes, suicides, and sabotage. The freedom fighters who escaped built remote villages above waterfalls in terrain that Europeans could not reach, but reminded the captives of their tribal homelands. Every year the Maroons cut down and burned part of the forest, then replanted the charcoal-fertilized soils with rice, corn, yams, plantains, beans, peas, sweet potatoes, okra, peppers, and sugarcane. There the six tribes of Saramaka, Ndyuka, Matawai, Paramaka, Aluku, and Kwinti worshipped Nana the god of creation, the ancestors, and the serpent, sky, and bush spirits.

DUTCH CRIME & PUNISHMENT IN SURINAME

From Captain J. G. Stedman, *Narrative, of a Five Years' Expedition, Against the Revolted Negroes of Surinam, in Guiana . . . from the Year 1772, to 1777 . . . Volume I* (London, 1796).

"Not long ago . . . I saw a black man suspended alive from a gallows, by the ribs, between which, with a knife, was first made an incision, and then clinched an iron hook with a chain; in this manner he kept alive three days, hanging with his head and feet downwards . . . Another negro . . . I have seen quartered alive; who, after four strong horses were fastened to his legs and arms, and after having iron sprigs driven home underneath every one of his nails on hands and feet . . . As for old men being broken on the rack, and young women roasted alive chained to stakes, there can nothing be more common in this colony."

"The first object which attracted my compassion during a visit to a neighbouring estate, was a beautiful Samboe girl of about eighteen, tied up by both arms to a tree, as naked as she came into the world, and lacerated in such a shocking manner by the whips of two negro-drivers, that she was from her neck to her ancles literally dyed over with blood. It was after she had received two

hundred lashes that I perceived her, with her head hanging downwards, a most affecting spectacle. When, turning to the overseer,
I implored that . . . might be immediately unbound . . . but the short
answer which I obtained was, that to prevent all strangers from
interfering with his government, he had made an unalterable rule . . .
always to double the punishment, which he instantaneously began
to put in execution: I endeavoured to stop him, but in vain . . . Thus I
had no other remedy but to run to my boat, and leave the detest-
able monster, like a bird of prey, to enjoy his bloody feast, till he
was glutted."

About 250 of Suriname's 60,000 slaves ran away each year. In 1690,
the slaves there unleashed "a general terror" on the plantation of Immanuel
Machado on a tributary of the upper Commewijane River. In 1693, they
did the same at the plantation Providence, along the Suriname River. By
1749, 6,000 Maroons were on the run. Around 1,500 new freedom fighters
joined them every year. Between 1750 and 1759, fifteen revolts broke out.
The Maroon Wars would last two hundred years, until 1862.

To punish the rebels, the Dutch dispatched waves of warships from
Texel in Holland. Most troops ended up dying from disease, running
out of food and being forced to eat monkeys, marching around in circles
scared witless by nighttime drums, or ending up decapitated on wooden
spikes. This was the Maroons' revenge for their own people being hanged
on meat hooks, broken on wheels, sexually assaulted, roasted alive, and
beheaded on plantation estates. Following the British model in Jamaica,
the Dutch eventually sent a hundred soldiers up the Saramacca River in
October 1749, destroyed 415 Maroon houses, and only then set about
negotiating peace. In recognition of his people's newly won independence,
Captain Adoe, chief of the Seramica, was gifted a large cane with a silver
pommel engraved with heraldry of Suriname.

The Dutch-born Scottish soldier John Stedman wrote sympatheti-
cally about his experiences hunting the rebels from 1773 to 1777. In his
memoir, *Narrative of a Five Years Expedition Against the Revolted Negroes
of Suriname* (1796), he writes:

Some Afric chief will rise, who scorning chains,
Racks, tortures, flames, excruciating pains,
Will lead his injur'd friends to bloody fight,
And in the flooded carnage take delight;
Then dear repay us in some bloody war,
And give us blood for blood, and fear for fear.

On the shore of the Maroon village of Akalikondre, the air was thick with anticipation and nerves as various cultures, untrusting for centuries, were about to meet. Three men emerged out of the forest, cautious but relaxed. At center strolled the captain of the village wearing a camouflage hat and a vintage purple Chelsea Football Club shirt. A large silver cross swung protectively around his neck.

The groups stood apart and aloof, not quite sure how to act. The captain smiled gently and stared intently at the foreigners. Should he trust them or turn on his heels?

They all shook hands. The ice melted. The strangers made their way into the heart of the village. Chickens grubbed around the beaten earth in front of a wooden shuttered house painted sky blue with brick foundations, the same style of architecture used in Paramaribo centuries ago. Other homes were painted yellow or had fallen down. Tree roots slithered across the ground in a thirsty search for ground water. A curious youngster stuck her head out of the front door of a shack wearing a Sex Pistols T-shirt, still rebelling after all this time. Bare-chested Maroon men wondered what all the fuss was about.

The divers and villagers sat down stiffly in a circle. Before chatting, the village captain made a blessing and poured a libation of rum into the ground to appease the ancestors.

"Spirits in the ground we are begging you," he prayed. "Stand for us, small ones who are left behind today. Make the world see we are here. Here is where I grew up. Here is where I was raised. Here is where I was fed. I give you my thanks, Father. You are not here anymore, but your name is still here. Mothers, come and accept our gifts. Mother Bakalobi, mother Nali. Please accept this mother Lena, mother Mijeso, and mother Malo. Accept our gifts. Grandmothers and grandfathers, great-grandparents, great-great-grandparents. Please accept our gifts and stand with us. Yeeha."

MEETING A MAROON REBEL

A description of a rebel African slave in Suriname from Captain J. G. Stedman, *Narrative, of a Five Years' Expedition, Against the Revolted Negroes of Surinam, in Guiana . . . from the Year 1772, to 1777 . . . Volume II* (London, 1796).

"This rebel negro is armed with a firelock and a hatchet; his hair, though woolly, may be observed to be plaited close to his head, by way of distinction from the rangers . . . his beard is grown to a point . . . The principal dress of this man consists of a cotton sheet, negligently tied across his shoulders, which protects him from the weather, and serves him also to rest on . . . The rest of his dress is a camisa, tied around his loins like a handkerchief; his pouch, which is made of some animal's skin; a few cotton strings for ornament around his ancles and wrists; and a superstitious *obia* or amulet tied about his neck, in which he places all his confidence. The skull and ribs [also worn] are supposed to be the bones of his enemies, scattered upon the sandy Savannah."

The prayer finished, the captain drank to the bottom of the glass and poured the dregs of the rum over his hands, wrists, and face. The ancestors permeated into his very being.

Kramer watched, captivated. Diving With A Purpose would dive on ships where hundreds of Africans perished faceless, nameless, voiceless. Theirs was an ephemeral fate written in water. In Akalikondre he sensed overwhelming pride. The Maroons lived a meager existence, he noticed, but they were happy and proud because they fought and won their freedom. Kramer, searching for his own lost African ancestry, felt a warm affinity with these forest people.

Kinga had more immediate thoughts on her mind as she watched a village wife prepare a delicious-smelling communal meal over the fire, steaming the food under a banana leaf.

"This is cassava," Leo Balai explained. "We call it Tomtom. It is peanuts with rice."

The woman started frying up chicken and stock. Her friend watched on, clad in a black T-shirt emblazoned Smile.

The divers realized that even though the freedom fighters had struggled for liberty a couple of hundred years ago, the Maroons and their children, and the future generations, were fully aware of their tumultuous past. They remember and still teach their history.

Kramer beamed, joyful. He felt a release, uplifted that even in the midst of such historic brutality the Maroons' pride and the fighting spirit of African people won out.

Before serving up their chicken and rice, the village women dressed Alanna and Kinga in traditional blue, red, and white checked skirts and scarves. It was a mark of respect. They also knew this was hearty, messy food. The laughter spread. Leo Balai smiled on. The divers may not have uncovered the *Leusden* but they had come face-to-face with living descendants of Africans trafficked from Angola and Ghana, thousands of miles across the Middle Passage. These people had beaten the odds. Lived to tell the tale.

Looking around at the simple village existence so full of vitality, Alannah could not help but wonder. The African captives on the *Leusden* could have shared this life.

Kramer agreed and muttered out loud, "What if? What if they hadn't been murdered? What if they hadn't nailed down the hatches? If they hadn't sat on the hatches to make sure that they drowned and killed every last one of them. They could have saved themselves. It could have been another Maroon village."

As the new firm friends made their way back to the creek, back to their boat, Paramaribo, and the next slave wreck dive, Alannah asked the captain's right-hand man, "Baisha, do you know what country in Africa you're from or where everybody is from?"

The captain's translator explained how it is said that their tribe came mainly from Ghana. Alannah had heard about the mighty fort of Elmina on Ghana's Gold Coast, where hundreds of thousands of captive Africans were pushed through the Door of No Return, the African women raped in its loathsome chambers.

"Okay. How do they know?" Alannah checked.

"Their ancestors. From their grandparents. The other told the other and so on. As slaves they come from there," the captain told the divers.

"Baisha, have you ever been to Africa?" Kramer asked. He had not.

"Do you want to go?" Kramer followed up.

Baisha confirmed he did, smiling. He knew, though, it was a distant dream.

"If you did get the chance to go, would you call that home? Or is this home?" Alannah pressed.

"When we go there, I come back to here. This is my home," Baisha let everyone know.

The Americans, Dutchman, and Maroons all laughed. They came from different ends of the globe but shared the same roots, the same sense of identity, never forgetting the past. They were all survivors.

Down at the water's edge the rebels and divers shook hands and embraced. They would never forget this day. Hours ago, they never knew of one another's existence. Now by giving voice to their trauma, fighting for their rights and winning, everyone felt exuberant, inspired.

It was time to push on. More slave wrecks lay out there, their stories and the voices of the lost Africans needing raising from the deep.

Slaves to Profit

The transatlantic slave trade is not some irrelevant story that happened centuries ago, of no consequence to our sophisticated twenty-first-century ways. In Brazil, today, on the ruins of the Valongo's wharves, where hundreds of thousands of Africans arrived, their descendants hold religious ceremonies commemorating the deaths of Black senators. An ebo steer has been sacrificed on its paving stones and ritual charms spoken over the excavated finds to appease the ancestors clamoring for justice. A ritual of redemption poured flower-scented water over the quay and dedicated a large heart made of red roses spelling the word PEACE in white roses. The Valongo is now consecrated by law as sacred ground.

Still, Brazil is a country of great inequality, crime, and poverty. Slavery persisted until almost the twentieth century and its effects haunt the present. The city's Afro descendants have the least opportunities for studying, earn the lowest wages, and are forced to live in the most dangerous and degrading conditions. The roots of this social depression all started when their ancestors landed in Rio, were enslaved, and treated as inferior beings. The shackled stigma of inferiority is hard to break.

As sincerely as Rio de Janeiro has sought to give the city's Black community ownership of the Valongo past, across the Atlantic in Portugal, a planned memorial to honor the African dead under Lagos's mini-golf course is sunk in bureaucracy. Portugal is full of monuments to conquerors and explorers but is accused of trivializing its role in the slave trade. Slavery existed long before Portugal got involved, Lisbon pleads. Portugal, like Spain, is yet to apologize for the role it played.

The Maroons of Suriname are also still fighting. From Canada to Argentina, every nation in the Americas has given special legal protection to its Indigenous populations. The one exception is the Republic of Suriname, whose government insists the Maroons have no special rights. Their precious land can be ripped away whenever the government wants. Suriname shows no respect for history or the peace treaties signed with the Dutch in the 1760s that gave autonomy and territorial rights to the Maroons.

To the displaced Africans, the treaties are legitimate to this day. Suriname's government rejects them as out-of-date colonial trivia. The Maroons may be the majority population of the country's interior at 10 percent of Suriname's people, but they are treated as a minority taking up prime land for mining bauxite and gold, cutting timber, dam building, and ecotourism. To many city slickers, Suriname's Maroons are a Stone Age people without meaning to the modern world. Slavery was abolished in Suriname, in 1863. For the Maroons, the battle continues.

RATIONALIZATION

When a vessel arrived to conduct us away to the ship, it was a most horrible scene; there was nothing to be heard but rattling of chains, smacking of whips, and groans and cries of our fellow men . . .

—Quobna Ottobah Cugoano, *Thoughts and Sentiments on the Evil and Wicked Trade of the Slavery and Commerce of the Human Species* (1787)

THE OLDEST SLAVER

Mylor—Cornwall, England

The tragedy of the *Leusden* happened when the slave trade was in full gear. Now the investigation team was confronting the start of the trade 7,300 kilometers (about 4,500 miles) away in the English Channel. This is where the transatlantic slave trade first went truly global. London took over from Portugal and Spain in the late seventeenth century and built a monstrous machine in human trafficking. From the goods exported to buy Africans; to captains' contracts; the seizing of humans from Senegal, Gambia, Ghana, Benin, Nigeria, and Angola; and the handling of the ships that took them, nothing was left to chance. The slave trade was a meticulously planned evil.

Somewhere out there off southwest England, the earliest slave ship in the world had been discovered. This was a unique chance to get up close and personal with what the trade looked like in its early years. This would also be by far the team's most dangerous operation.

The sea calmly licked the stone harbor wall at Mylor in Cornwall, the first landfall for ships returning to England from Africa and the Caribbean. The early morning sky was crystal clear. It was going to be a fine autumnal day to dive. The English Channel is the opposite of the tropical calm of the Florida Keys, Diving With A Purpose's home base. More often than not, forbidding gray skies hung over churning waters.

In the later seventeenth century, England was the master of the slave trade. Between 1640 and 1807, 3.1 million Africans were shipped to the Caribbean plantations in English hulls. Around 400,000 died in the Middle Passage between Africa's Gold and Slave Coasts and the backbreaking plantations of Barbados and Jamaica. Together, England and Portugal were responsible for 70 percent of all Africans trafficked throughout colonial history. Britain, though, was the dominant player in eight of the thirteen decades from 1681 to 1807.

The shores of England were a launchpad for an inexplicable evil that jars the modern mind. Why did London "industrialize" the greatest enslavement history ever witnessed? How did its merchants manage the trade and what was life like for the enslaved? To make sense of unfathomable numbers and statistics, Diving With A Purpose—Kramer Wimberley, Alannah Vellacott, and Kinga Philipps, now joined by Joshua Williams—and helped by British specialist deep divers, Richard Stevenson and Kieran Hatton, would have to head seventy kilometers (around forty-three miles) offshore. And then somehow descend 110 meters to scrutinize a wreck codenamed Site 35F.

There was one major problem. No human had ever dived the wreck before. Only a handful of scientists had even locked eyes on its secrets using an unmanned remotely operated vehicle (ROV). Dr. Sean Kingsley, an English marine archaeologist, was one of the few. The team had come to Mylor to meet Sean, hear how the rare wreck came to light, what they might find, and to figure out how to crack the lost ship's secrets.

Hellbound

Looking out to sea toward a frightening ship lost beyond the sight of land, Dr. Kingsley pulled no punches. The project was ultra-dangerous. The risks were high, the rewards great.

From royal warships to floating treasure chests, French pirates and Nazi submarines on secret missions, the English Channel shatters dreams for kicks. It respects nobody, neither prince nor ship's cook. These Narrow Seas were Britain's communications highway centuries before planes, trains, automobiles, and the World Wide Web. From here fleets set out into the Atlantic in search of wealth, land, power, and people.

This highway to hell was invaded seven times every century over the last nine hundred years. Mostly the weather, not brilliant commanders and heavily armed warships, forced enemies into retreat. The brave few who did make landfall—Julius Caesar and the Roman Empire in 55 B.C.E. and Norman invaders from France in 1066—changed the course of history. Down the centuries, thirty-seven thousand ships sank off England's deadly waters.

Diving With A Purpose would need to head to a place where the mouth of the English Channel meets what captains called the Western Approaches. These are perilous seas: battered by wind and wave, beyond the sight of land, and deep. The team had better get a good night's sleep, Dr. Kingsley warned, because this was not just another dive. This was extreme marine archaeology.

The team learned how, in the late seventeenth century, half a day from returning to home base in London, the unidentified ship, now given the bland discovery name "35F," got into trouble. Its wooden walls were whipped by mountainous waves. Sails, rigging, and crew whistled overboard. The anchors were useless, manning the sails and resisting the wind pointless. After two years at sea, the crew was doomed.

This was not how it was supposed to end. The hard graft was over, the cargos bartered half a world away safely secured in the hold. In the last weeks, all the crew had dreamed about was how they would spend their hard-earned gains.

The end came suddenly. After months in tropical Caribbean waters, the patched-up hull was rotten, attacked by armies of shipworms, the silent assassins of the seas. Water poured through cracks between planks. Part of the cargo was slung over the side in a last-ditch effort to pay the devil for salvation. The carpenter and cook made a run for it, throwing themselves into the charging "white horses," white crested waves. They were never seen again.

The captain manned the helm till the bitter end. Then a colossal wave sucked him down into the abyss. With his final breath, he must have wondered if he should have done the right thing and unbolted the hatches leading below deck. His paymasters in London would have been disgusted by the very idea. The captain must have pushed the thought to the back of his exhausted mind. Rattling chains and the screams of the few enslaved heading to serve Britain were probably the last sounds the slave trader heard.

Narrow Seas

The world's oldest slave ship was found by a high-tech yellow robot called Zeus, an intrepid new generation of deep-sea explorer designed to beat the odds. The seven-ton robot runs on fiber optics and electricity, not oxygen, and is the eyes and hands of archaeologists where it is too deep to dive. The most sophisticated archaeologically tooled robot in the world could boldly swim through high waves and strong currents to places no human had gone before and stay there as long as needed.

Site 35F came to light by chance during the world's biggest deep-sea sunken search run by Odyssey Marine Exploration. Somewhere out there between England and France was dazzling Spanish, French, and English treasure. The Americans were determined to hunt it down. They had hit pay dirt before. For example, they had recovered 51,000 gold and silver coins from the Civil War–era shipwreck of the SS *Republic*.

Off the coast of Gibraltar they also discovered the *Nuestra Señora de las Mercedes,* a Spanish ship blown up by the Royal Navy in 1804, whose treasure of 14.5 tons of silver coins was said to be worth a cool $500 million today. The Odyssey boys flew the booty to Tampa to claim it in the courts, but the bet backfired. When the Spanish government moved in on the find, Odyssey was forced to hand it back to Madrid. A few years later they netted 109 tons of silver ingots, 4,700 meters deep off southwest Ireland, from the British India steamship the SS *Gairsoppa*. This time they got to keep it.

Site 35F was a double crime scene. First, it was an ancient echo of the slave trade. Secondly, it had been ransacked in the modern day. When the wreck was first discovered by Odyssey, side-scan sonar images showed disturbing lines running through its heart. Mega-trawlers raking the seabed for shellfish had crushed the delicate cultural remains. Site 35F had been put through a shredder. History's hard drive had been wiped to put fish and chips on dinner tables.

WRECK SITE 35F

- Royal African Company merchant ship
- London to Ghana, Caribbean, and England
- Keel 26.1 meters long, 600 tons capacity, and crew of 70 (?)
- 48 iron cannons for protection and sale
- Sunk *ca.* 1672–1685, Western Approaches to England
- Depth 110 meters
- Cargo: elephant tusks, manilla copper bracelets, stacks of copper basins, sugar, slaves, and gold (?)
- Small finds: English wine bottles, tobacco pipe, ceramics, wooden folding ruler, cannonballs, galley bricks, lead hull sheeting, and concreted iron rigging

Site 35F is not the *Titanic*. It does not stand proudly above the seabed defying time. It has been flattened into a low mound. No more than forty centimeters of its crushed decks are left today. Enough survives to reconstruct the old ship, its stern to the northeast, the bow to the southwest. Underwater surveys had shown that 35F was once a force to be reckoned with. The sea floor around it is littered with forty-eight iron cannons, bits and pieces of ceramic pots, wine bottles, tobacco pipes, a pile of copper basins, elephant tusks, and round copper bracelets used as currency in Africa.

Elephant tusks and copper "manilla" bracelets are extremely rare among the world's three million shipwrecks. They are monstrous artifacts exclusively used in the African slave trade that make the hairs on the back of explorers' necks stand up—immortal memories of Europe's trade in ivory, gold, and humans. There was no doubt about it, Site 35F stank of guilt. But could they prove that it was a slave ship and, if they could, would they be able to identify its nationality and owners? The detective work began in earnest.

The Odyssey team and Dr. Kingsley realized this was a big vessel, perhaps six hundred tons, and manned by a crew of around seventy. Here and there, a few wooden planks were spotted with signs they had been patched up with a double layer of wood. This naval technique, known as "furring," was a kind of protection used in tropical waters to slow down shipworms feasting on hulls. Furring was a European method for ships that sailed in warm tropical waters. This ship had undoubtedly worked the Americas before the early eighteenth century. If it was a slave ship, it would be the earliest ever identified. If it was English, it would have belonged to the Royal African Company, a London trading company set up in 1672 by the royal family. The company gave itself a national monopoly over the slave trade for almost two decades.

RED GOLD

Legend has it that manilla bracelets were first made in West Africa from copper bolts salvaged from wrecked ships. They were manufactured by the millions but are rare finds on just a few wrecks off France, Spain, England, Bermuda, Cape Verde, and Ghana.

The scale of the manilla trade was colossal. By 1635 up to 763 tons of copper were being shipped to West Africa a year in Dutch, English, and French ships. Portugal's copper was mainly mined in Flanders (modern Belgium), but was also bought in Venice and Morocco. At the end of the fifteenth century, 80 percent of the manillas shipped out of Lisbon—seventy-one thousand bracelets—went to the fort of Elmina in Ghana.

Traders started looking for ways to make manillas more cheaply and boost profits. In the 1720s, Robert Morris of London thinned the copper by mixing every ton with half a ton of lead. The Cheadle company in Greenfield, Warrington, the Forest Copper Works in Swansea, and Thomas Williams's Holywell Works in Flintshire soon jumped on the bandwagon. When Bristol turned into the leading port for the English slave trade in the 1710s, Thomas Williams became known as the Copper King.

How many manillas were manufactured by Europe to buy Africa's elephants, gold, and people is not recorded. The numbers were staggering. In 1949, when authorities forced Nigeria to move to a monetary economy after World War II—not one based on cowrie shells and copper bars—32.5 million manillas were handed over.

In the early surveys of the site, nine tusks, each up to 1.4 meters long and weighing twenty-four kilograms (over fifty pounds), were identified scattered over the bows, a fraction of the cargo once rounded up in West Africa. No doubt the rest had been harvested in fishermen's nets, now scattered to the four winds. Over a quarter of a million tusks left West Africa, mostly in English and Dutch holds, between 1699 and 1725. At its peak, sixty-one tons reached London every year.

Underwater, bright green bracelets shone forth from the seabed among the sand and gravel as if they were desperate not to be forgotten by the future. Each bracelet measured around 9 x 7 centimeters and weighed up to 140 grams (about five ounces). They were tiny finds with a huge impact. Slave traders called them manillas, from the Latin word *manus* (hand) or *monilia* (necklace or neckring).

Manillas were a sinister cog in a machine designed to get West Africa addicted to Western goods. European merchants had noticed how African women wore their money on their arms and legs in the form of copper bracelets. At market, they used this currency to buy and sell. By imitating their design, the West settled on a cheap way to get Africa to part with its brothers and sisters. Manillas made in Europe were specially designed as a currency to buy gold, elephant tusks, and humans.

MANILLAS IN AFRICA

Since manillas became the currency of trade, West Africans were very particular about their quality. Dr. Dapper's *Description de l'Afrique* (*Description of Africa*) showed in 1668 how, "Along the river of Kalbaria [Calabar, Nigeria] the white races . . . trade with the inhabitants, and in exchange for slaves offer rough grey copper armlets, which must be oblong with a rounded curve and very well made, since the natives are very particular on these points and frequently will reject two or three hundred out of one barrel . . . the armlets brought there by white men, which they call Bochie, are used solely for money."

What could a manilla bracelet get you? Portuguese merchants at Calabar in Nigeria could buy an African for eight to ten copper manillas in 1505. By 1517, a plantation slave cost fifty-seven manillas. An ounce of gold cost eighty manillas in 1556. In 1681, around the time when 35F sank off the Western Approaches, the Royal African Company merchant John Thorne was buying one slave for two hundred bracelets.

Company ships headed to Africa with thousands of "manilloes black" and "manilloes bright" made of copper and brass. The Royal African Company's copper came from Sweden, Germany, Hungary, and Morocco. At first, in 1673, one ton of manillas was used to test the waters in Africa. Then the floodgates opened. By 1700, a colossal forty-six tons had reached the Gold Coast.

35F's nationality is a crucial question. The glass wine bottles on the wreck looked like the goods made in John Baker's glasshouse in London's Vauxhall until it was demolished in 1706. But bottles like this were also made in Holland and France. The smoking gun turned out to be a lucky strike. A sliver of rectangular wood preserved by pure fortune, etched all over with marks, letters, and numbers, was one half of a two-foot wooden folding ruler. Rulers like this were kept handy in carpenters' chests to work out mathematical areas and volumes of timber to be sawn into ship-building parts. It worked like a slide rule with a pair of dividers. Folding rulers are rarer than hen's teeth and this was the oldest "pocket calculator" found underwater. The best brains dated it to the 1670s or 1680s.

It was a tiny detail in the ruler that in the end gave away the ship's nationality. Dutch, German, and French carpenters all used slightly different units of measurement. 35F's folding ruler was designed using the inch measuring 2.54 centimeters. Only one nation stubbornly preferred this formula: England.

The final fragment of the puzzle slotted into place. 35F was an English merchantman returning from a trading voyage to West Africa and the Caribbean, only to end up decimated by a storm half a day from home, probably between 1672 and 1685.

The forensics pointed to an inescapable reality. When it sank, the ship was in the service of one of the darkest merchant monopolies English history witnessed: the Royal African Company, run by the king's brother, James, the Duke of York. The company was in the business of buying massive amounts of gold, elephant tusks, and captives all along the coast of West Africa. At the height of the trade a ship left London, Bristol, or Liverpool to hunt for slaves every second day.

BIRMINGHAM MANILLAS

W. J. Davis, *A Short History of the Brass Trade* (1892): "it will perhaps not be uninteresting to mention that many ton of Manilla money are annually cast in Birmingham. This is a species of ring money used in Africa and on Spanish settlements in Calabar. It was first made of alloy of copper and lead, and hardened with arsenic. Nearly thirty years ago the black mint master of the African tribe visited Birmingham to inspect the pieces. It is said that the degree of rank in this tribe is determined solely by the possession of these articles: those having the most being the wealthy members, and, as a consequence, have proportionate sway. Livingstone, Stanley, and other travellers tell us, that when about to penetrate into the interior of the dark continent, they had to provide themselves with cloth, beads, looking glasses, and brass wire, to be used as a medium of exchange with the natives, as much as would make good loads for 40 or 50 natives to carry. These things afterwards served the double purpose of personal finery and money. Orders for wire for this purpose amount to many tons a year. Rings or 'Bangles' made of thick solid wire, or tube, or even cast, are also made here, and sent in large consignments for the adornment of African swells and belles. One order amounted to 20,000 dozen of rings, 3½ inches in diameter, weighing 23 tons."

Mission Impossible

Investigating 35F would be a dangerous challenge for Diving With A Purpose. It was a gamble. Dr. Kingsley could not even guarantee anything of the ship survived. The wreck had not been looked at in years. It was 50/50 that fishing trawlers had bulldozed its remains so catastrophically that nothing was left to bear witness to the thousands of English slave voyages that once crossed the Western Approaches.

"No one has put eyes on this wreck for ten years now," Dr. Kingsley told the team. "We don't even know if it still exists. So your mission is to get out there, try and rediscover the site and see what other bits of information we can extract to add to our story."

"And by the way," the scientist who would not be going offshore warned, "when there is a storm here, it's the perfect storm."

The team was left to chew over the risks ahead. The odds were stacked against them. They needed the notorious British weather to behave for just one October day. Not even English warships went out in this weather. If you were caught on the high seas in October, you got what you deserved, King George II's commanders used to say. This was perfect storm time of year.

With their mission impossible set, the nervous team pored over sea charts with Sacha Hall, who would lead the dive boat in search of 35F. Sacha had seen it all in these waters. He pointed out on a map how the wreck lay in a danger zone where the wide Atlantic tightens into a funnel between the two narrow arms of England and France. It was a natural choke point. Here the waves grow in height and the seas get more ferocious.

"To dive the site, the conditions have to be good, calm, perfect, and flat," Sacha shrugged. "For all those factors to come together, we'll need a small window of opportunity."

The team would need a minor miracle. The next stop was the middle of nowhere, the cruel Narrow Approaches, to explore what African voices could be brought back to life from a shipwrecked grave.

The team felt a heavy burden of responsibility.

KINGDOM OF LOANGO

Today, most of the natural and cultural landscapes where Europe's traders bartered and trafficked Africans would be unrecognizable to a time traveler from the seventeenth, eighteenth, or nineteenth century. Concrete urban jungles have replaced sprawling forests. Traditional villages built of wooden poles and mud walls have left no traces for archaeologists to explore. The African kingdoms' art was hoovered up by pith-helmeted English, French, German, and Austrian explorers. One unique area, though, retains a feel of times gone by, an opportunity to visualize—and rationalize—the landscapes and cultures from where the trafficked millions were dispossessed.

The kingdom of Loango is a rare exception. Stretching from Cape Lopez in the north to the Congo River in the south, the 460-mile coast now spanning Gabon, Angola, and the Democratic Republic of the Congo was dragged into the transatlantic slave trade around 1660. Unlike much of West Africa, where heavy industry has stripped the forests bare, a thin slice of times past endures. Gabon in particular, at 88 percent rainforest, is the second most forested country on the planet. Miles of dense trees run deep inland and down to the coast.

Gabon also remains a rare sanctuary for over 60 percent of Africa's forest elephants. The snaking Ogooue River in Loango National Park, flanked by forbidding dense forest, once offered a convenient way to paddle upriver to tribal villages. Equatorial Guinea and Cameroon lie to the north and the Democratic Republic of the Congo runs to the east. The Ogooue River drains the whole of Gabon down to a wide estuary before pouring out into the mighty Atlantic Ocean. Green savannah and sandy shores replace haunted forests. It is not hard to sense the slave trade and imagine wooden slave ships bobbing menacingly close to shore. For centuries, enchained Africans and tusks, sawn off butchered elephants, were trafficked down these river highways to hell.

Even today, keeping elephants free to roam in their natural habitat has to be closely protected by eco-guards, who put their bodies on the line fighting poachers. The war that slaughtered millions of these gentle beasts since the sixteenth century is still raging. Gun battles between rangers and poachers break out every month, just like in the slave days. Now, however, they are feeding a demand mostly driven by East and Southeast Asia, where ivory is regarded as an amulet and a status symbol. Selling ivory may be illegal, but it still brings in $2,000 a kilogram on the black market.

It was here that the first transatlantic slaving voyage departed the Congo River, the southern boundary of the Loango Coast, with a captive cargo in 1514. The Portuguese ship picked up 237 Africans, mostly destined for Vigo in Spain; 69 died in the sea crossing. In centuries gone by, people were marched for three months from the interior down to the slave ships, while others were paddled down in canoes. Along with humans, forty kilograms (about eighty-eight pounds) of tusks and ebony wood were dragged to the shore. Either way, the Atlantic was the end of the line.

In the slave trade days, this historic landscape was the heart of the kingdom of Loango, which by the late eighteenth century was the backdrop to half of all slave transports from West Africa. Europe's superpowers prized open trade routes deep inland to exploit the rainforest's riches, including African men, women, and children.

Portuguese traders at first bought palm cloth, redwood, ivory, elephant tails, and copper, which was used to barter for slaves in Angola. In exchange, they introduced cloth, iron goods, alcohol, guns, ammunition, and beads into the region. The trade in humans took off in Dutch holds in 1651, followed by British dominance between 1721 and 1740, the French until 1790, the Portuguese from 1811 to 1850, and finally the Americans for the last thirteen years of the trade. At least 475,000 slaves entered the transatlantic slave trade through the ports of the Loango Coast between 1660 and 1810, and another 1.3 million from 1811 to 1867.

Slave traders expected to spend four months in Africa securing their human cargo. Corralling them onboard ship took one and a half months. The cost of slaves varied between the equivalent of £17.5 and £26.9 between 1681 and 1750. The value of a Loango Coast slave peaked at £77.9 around 1790.

Most of the prisoners were channeled through the Valley of the Slaves to be shipped out of Africa by way of the Iguela Lagoon, eighty-five achingly beautiful square miles studded with tiny islands. Before the captives were shipped and shackled for the Americas, they were given a last supper. After all, it was in the traders' best interests to keep the slaves functioning and healthy. Strong slaves meant bigger profits.

In the Iguela Lagoon European merchants could keep their captives well fed and cut costs at the same time. In these tranquil bays the archaeologist Dr. Richard Oslisly recently turned up traces of the mind-boggling scale of slave trafficking in millions of discarded oyster shells. The lagoon has always been rich in nutritional oysters. Over time the last suppers fed to the enslaved built up a whole island whose foundations were made up solely of oysters—two and a half thousand acres of shells piled up to four meters high. Each discarded shell symbolizes the death of hope.

AMERICAN SLAVERS ON THE CONGO

A March 2, 1860, description of American slavers on the coast of Congo in the *New York Times* described how "they sail boldly in, anchor, and in two or three hours are filled with negroes, who are carried off to them in canoes. The refractory ones are clapped in irons, or made drunk with rum; and in this stupefied condition they are carried aboard, stowed in a sitting posture, with the knees drawn up so closely that they can scarcely breathe, much less move.

"Now their sufferings become dreadful—horrible; indeed, human language is incapable of describing, or imagination of sketching even the faint outline of a dimly floating fancy of what their condition is—homesick, seasick, half starved, naked, crying for air, for water, the strong killing the weak or dying in order to make room, the hold becomes a perfect charnel house of death and misery—a misery and anguish only conceivable by those who have endured it."

For most of the enchained Africans seized deep in the forests, this was the first time they saw the ocean, let alone those strange floating trees called ships. Families were torn apart and cultures destroyed for 351 long years until 1865 when the *Cicerón*, a Liverpool steamship, sailed from Cadiz to the Congo River and took a last group of enslaved Africans.

What were conditions like for the dispossessed forced to sail the Middle Passage? In 1667, Capuchin priest Dionigi de Carli left behind a rare early account after boarding a Portuguese ship loaded at Luanda in modern Angola on the Loango Coast. On a fifty-day voyage to Brazil, he matter-of-factly reported in his *Curious and Exact Account of a Voyage to Congo*, how

> The Ship I went onboard . . . was loaded with Elephants Teeth and Slaves, to the number of 680 Men, Women, and Children. It was a pitiful sight to behold, how all these People were bestow'd. The men were standing in the Hold, fastned one to another by Stakes, for fear they should rise and kill the Whites. The Women were between the Decks, and those that were with Child in the great Cabin, the Children in the steeridg, press'd together like Herrings in a Barrel, which caus'd an intolerable heat and stench.

Where the Ogooue River meets the Atlantic Ocean, the light changes from the somber overcast darkness of the forests to a glaring yellow horizon shimmering off the water. The enormity of the world opens up. The big slave ships stood at anchor awaiting their human cargos. From an isolated shore, feared even by Europeans for its mighty surf and underwater earthquakes, a future in chains and sleepless days breaking your back in the fields was only weeks away. The moment the inland Africans saw the ships for the first time, all hope ran out and was replaced by absolute terror.

Two hundred years ago, this tropical paradise was hell on earth. Next stop was Brazil, Cuba, the United States, England, or the bottom of the ocean.

OUT OF AFRICA

S asha's *Severn Sea* research ship plowed through the English Channel. The team was not bursting with adrenalin and excitement like on most wreck dives, but was silent, deep in reflection. They were sailing treacherous waves in search of the world's most perilous trade. When you think about the slave trade, the horrors can be imagined but kept at arm's length. Physically seeing man's shame is raw, emotional.

Each of the Diving With A Purpose dive team was battling their own personal journey. Alannah Vellacott's father was British, but her mother came from the Bahamas, a descendant of slaves trafficked from Africa. She was straddling two conflicting ancestry lines, trying to make sense of who she was.

There was plenty of time to prepare for whatever lay below. The wreck was marooned five hours offshore. On the way out the team caught up on the backstory of the Royal African Company and how one of its ships ended up lost half a day from home.

Black London

35F began its final voyage in London, the headquarters of the Royal African Company. African House had pride of place between Fenchurch and Leadenhall Street, a few minutes' walk north of the River Thames. Company ships docked between the awe-inspiring majesty of the Tower of London and London Bridge. Here the captain of 35F anchored among a forest of ships' masts and hurried past the king's Customs House to pick up his sailing instructions from the lords of the Royal African Company.

By the 1670s Black slaves were an exotic but common sight on London's streets from the royal court to private houses. Most people had no clue where they came from. They were either Black-skinned, what the Portuguese called *negro* (from the Latin word for black), or the color of moors (from the dark brown fields of Europe). Londoners found it easier to lazily call all captive Africans "blackamores."

Africans served in a range of positions, from a royal trumpeter to a sea diver, laundresses, soldiers, needle makers, and goldsmiths. Africans were so fashionable in London by 1680 that it was callously said a lady of fashion was almost obliged to "hath two necessary implements about her; a blackamore and her dog."

Absolutely nothing is known about where these displaced peoples were born, their fears and hopes. Only a few of their Western names survive. The odd medical record remembers how "Polonia the blackmor maid at Mr Peirs" suffered from "a fever . . . faint heart full of melancholy" in 1597. "Nicholas a Negro of unknown parents . . . at the age of 3 yeares or thereabouts" was baptized in St. Margaret's Westminster in 1619, while "Anthony, a poore ould Negro aged 105 yeares" died in Hackney in 1630. "Black Lucy" was forced from slavery into prostitution. What these people's parents called their children when they were born has vanished into thin air.

The architect of Black London and the slaves sent to backbreaking work cultivating the sugar and tobacco plantations in the Caribbean was the Royal African Company. The company had the kind of connections you did not mess with. Through its governor and chief backer, James, Duke of York, and future king of England, it enjoyed a cartel-like monopoly. King Charles II gave the company his royal approval on September 27, 1672. The Duke of York's men were bulletproof in its first three decades. Its charter gave it the exclusive trade rights to five thousand miles of the West coast of Africa from Morocco to the Cape of Good Hope in South Africa. Never mind that the same land occupied for millennia by Indigenous communities was never theirs to give away. The company's aim was to export cheap trifles in exchange for gold, elephants' tusks, wax, wood used for dyeing textiles, and humans, and maximize profits.

ROYAL AFRICAN COMPANY: TRUTH IN NUMBERS

Between 1672 and 1690, the widest dates when the Site 35F ship sailed, the Royal African Company made 279 voyages to West Africa. The company took most Africans in these years in Whydah (67 voyages), Calabar (southeast Nigeria, 40), West Central Africa and St. Helena (35), Gambia (24), New Calabar (eastern Nigeria, 22), the Gold Coast (22), the Bight of Biafra, and Gulf of Guinea Islands (10).

In this period the company signed charter contracts for the purchase of 65,411 Africans. In the end, 67,723 Africans were taken (3.5 percent more than chartered). Twenty-one percent died crossing the Middle Passage. The main Caribbean and American ports where the enslaved were disembarked from Company ships were Barbados (96 voyages), Jamaica (93), Nevis (36), Virginia (11), and Antigua (8).

The Site 35F trader could be any one of fifty-five ships documented in the company's archives as wrecked or fate unknown. Just two are listed as specifically "wrecked" or "destroyed," the *Providence* of 1679 and the *Lindsey* of 1686.

The *Providence*, Theodore Tyler captain, sailed from London to West Central Africa. The crew started buying Africans on May 23, 1679, and left for Jamaica on August 16, 1679. The ship was chartered to take 330 Africans, but shipped 223, including 24 women. Forty-three people died in the crossing.

The *Lindsey*, James Butler captain, sailed from London for West Central Africa on October 22, 1685. Five hundred captives were chartered for shipment to Barbados; 528 were eventually taken. On November 23, 1686, 458 reached the plantations, and 70 died en route.

Whether Site 35F is the *Providence* or the *Lindsey* may never be known. The archaeological evidence has been too heavily destroyed by fishing trawlers.

Before heading for West Africa, company ships picked up a department store of goods in London's African House to sell: everything from

British cloth and Swedish and German iron and copper to French brandy and glass beads sourced in Holland and Venice. Muskets and pistols were eagerly snapped up by West African rulers to get an edge fighting neighboring kingdoms.

Gold bartered mainly in modern Ghana was shipped to the Royal Mint in London, where it was turned into guinea coins stamped with the logo of the Royal African Company, an elephant with a castle on its back, symbols of profit and power. Around 548,000 gold guineas were cast from African gold between 1673 and 1713. Tusks were more expensive than humans and were mostly bought in Gambia and today's Ivory Coast between Ghana and Liberia. About 215 tons were imported into London every decade.

When creaking hulls could take no more enslaved Africans, elephant tusks, and gold, crews set out across the loathsome Middle Passage on the second leg of the triangular trade between West Africa and the Caribbean. Sometimes the whole proceeds from slave sales were paid in bills of exchange, a kind of check, stuffed into a wallet. Sailing home weighed down by unsold goods or just ballast was bad business, though, which most skippers tried to avoid. Barbados, Jamaica, and Nevis were famous for that rapturous, exotic, mouth-watering commodity—sugar. In 1677 alone, forty-three Royal African Company ships carried Caribbean sugar to London, each stocked with thirty-two tons of white crystals.

Sugar and humans' sweet tooth drove the transatlantic trade's engine from the very start. All in all, the Royal African Company sent over five hundred ships to West Africa between 1672 and 1713, from small boats of less than fifty tons to mega-traders of over four hundred tons.

The Middle of Nowhere

Five hours after setting out, the research ship *Severn Sea* finally reached the Site 35F wreck site. The research ship shut down its engines, a tiny speck beyond the view of England or France in the middle of nowhere. The team moved like clockwork. The target's coordinates were roughly known from Odyssey's previous robotic investigation, but hunting down this needle in a soggy haystack would still take time. And time was precious and expensive on a large boat far out to sea, where the weather window could change in an instant.

Even the planet's most skilled divers can spend no more than thirty minutes at a depth of 110 meters, so a Cougar XT remotely operated vehicle would be sent to try and locate the old ship. The remote-controlled robot was equipped with cameras, sonar, and sensors to let the crew scrutinize the seabed. Live images would be fed up to the research ship's control room from where the robot would be flown using a joystick. ROVs are the world's most expensive video games.

Six divers crowded around the television screen in breathless antici-pation as the ROV ended its five-minute commute down to the seabed. Plumes of algae cascaded sideways through the water column. Staring at the deep for too long made you dizzy. Slowly the team's eyes adjusted to the marine environment. A flat seabed was cut by low sand ripples, interrupted by the odd rock, crab, and conger eel.

There was little life down there and no sign of ancient wreckage. The ROV systematically searched the abyss. Time passed and the team shrugged. Maybe the entire wreck had been lost to fishing trawlers. Or was it all covered up by sand? Today, it seemed, was not going to be the day.

When hope was fading, a bright spot lit up the ROV's sonar. Any-thing bright-colored was material sticking up above the seabed. The next few minutes would tell whether it was natural geology or cultural remains.

The bright spots suddenly turned into lines, and the sonar shined like a Christmas tree. The sides were too straight to be made by Mother Nature. Then, on the live video stream, a cannon appeared out of the gloom, and then more, coated in thick concretion formed around the rusted iron submerged for so long.

The ROV headed for a closer look, all eyes glued to the screen. This was what Diving With A Purpose had crossed the Atlantic to see. The cascabels from the back of the guns, where fuses were lit to hurl iron cannonballs at enemy decks, could be clearly traced. The seabed was a forest of iron guns. This was no random artillery jettisoned by a passing warship. No doubt about it, X marked the spot of an historic wreck.

The ROV hovered over the wooden hull, cannonballs and concretions containing who knew what. Then a curved length of something made of bone snapped into focus, almost completely camouflaged on the seabed. Seaweed growing off its back danced in the current. The object looked out of place, not part of the natural habitat. The divers gasped when its true nature became clear. Far from home, it was a tusk from an elephant that once roamed free in the wilds of West Africa. A graceful creature murdered in the slave trade cycle to feed England with gold, African captives, and ivory.

The tusk's jagged ends were sharp, not waterworn. It had been freshly snapped off, desecrated by passing fishing trawlers. Elephant teeth were exactly what Royal African Company slave ships carried as homebound cargo. This living memory was once stored next to African captives in the wooden hull, perhaps the very ancestors of the team captivated by the images beamed up from the deep. The divers were relieved to have rediscovered the wreck. They had met the ancestors. At the same time, they were angry and confused.

Time was precious and emotions had to be set aside to deal with practicalities here and now. Should the tusk be recovered or left untouched as a silent gravestone memorializing human history's darkest times? So little survives of Site 35F. Its very existence is endangered, like the people the Royal African Company once trafficked and the slaughtered elephants whose teeth were ripped out by the millions. The suffering seems never to end.

The team was united about the right way ahead. "Bringing this tusk up is going to be raising the voices of people who didn't have a voice," Alannah stressed. "That tusk was worth maybe hundreds of lives of slaves. It's giving people like you and me an artifact to connect to. That tusk is a symbol of the pillaging of Africa. It can help a lot of people identify with that."

"Absolutely, we should do it," Kinga Philipps agreed. The question was how to lift it in the safest way? Recovering the tusk was going to be a major hurdle. For reasons that make little sense, English marine law forbids mechanical devices like ROV robots from touching cultural artifacts underwater. Which meant there was only one way to save it. If Diving With A Purpose wanted the tusk, they would have to go down and get it.

Diving so deep is a massive risk. Qualified tech divers like Kramer Wimberley can get down to forty meters. Site 35F was almost three times deeper. Richard Stevenson, the project's senior diver, was one of few people in the world to have mastered the art. Rich is daring but calculating. He sucked in the salty sea air to collect his thoughts and told the team, "It is deep but there is a way we can do it safely with rebreathers and mixed gases. For that, everything needs to be aligned perfectly. We need perfect conditions, good dive planning, and a great support team."

The group would never get this chance again. It was now or never. As Site 35F decays and eventually vanishes, the preservation of this crucial piece of history relied on the team's decision right now.

Kinga summed up the team's feelings. "Our options are either tell the story or walk away. And unless we bring something up, we're only really telling a portion of the story." The friends nodded in agreement.

"So, from what I'm hearing, we're going for it," Kramer smiled.

The deep dive for the voices of the African slave trade was a go. The *Severn Sea* was headed back to shore to gear up and leave nothing to chance. The divers had locked eyes on the scene of the crime, a ship like the thousands on which millions of African men, women, and children were stacked like cattle and sold into captivity. How had they ended up caught, enslaved, and sold? What experiences did ships like 35F have in West Africa and how were such unthinkable numbers seized?

35F was the earliest Royal African Company slave trader ever discovered, maybe the earliest slave ship in the world. Diving With A Purpose planned to plant a flag on the dark side of the ocean. They were sending the first human being down to explore its decks.

ABOVE: The Dutch slaving headquarters of Fort Zeelandia at Paramaribo in Suriname. By Gerard Voorduin and Jacob Eduard van Heemskerck van Beest, 1860–1862. *From Creative Commons.*
BELOW: In Paramaribo, Suriname, Diving With A Purpose discuss, with Dr. Leo Balai and Prof. Jerzy Gawronski, the Dutch West Indies Company slave ship the *Leusden*. The ship sank in 1738. Six hundred sixty-four enslaved Africans were drowned when they were locked into the hold by the European crew.

ABOVE: Prof. Elena Moran and Simcha Jacobovici examine photos of the remains of enslaved Africans found in a mass grave in Lagos, Portugal, where the African slave trade began in the sixteenth century. A mini-golf course was built over the excavated cemetery. BELOW: Kramer Wimberley diving in the murky waters of Tiger Bank at the mouth of the Marowijne River, Suriname, in search of the *Leusden* shipwreck.

From the mid-sixteenth century onward, millions of enslaved were shipped to sugar plantations in Recife, Brazil, to cut sugarcane.

ABOVE: Ruins of the Valongo wharf in Rio de Janeiro where millions of enslaved Africans were landed in Brazil. *From Creative Commons.* BELOW: Traveling to an abandoned plantation in Suriname.

ABOVE: In the jungle with Dr. Leo Balai, exploring the rusting remains of an abandoned Dutch colonial sugar factory, once manned by enslaved Africans in Suriname. BELOW: Alannah Vellacott hears about their heritage from Captain Akoloi Kandre in a Maroon village in Suriname. These people's ancestors were runaway slaves who fought for and won their freedom in the eighteenth century.

ABOVE: The dive team watching the ROV robot locate the late seventeenth-century Site 35F wreck of a Royal African Company ship in the English Channel. BELOW: Divers in the English Channel. From left to right: Richard Stevenson, Kieran Hatton, Alannah Vellacott, Kinga Philipps, and Kramer Wimberley.

ABOVE: Elephant tusks wedged under an iron cannon on the Site 35F wreck, Western Approaches to England. BELOW: Copper manilla bracelets from the Site 35F wreck, Western Approaches. *Both images from Seascape Artifact Exhibits Inc.*

ABOVE: Elmina Castle on Ghana's Gold Coast. Over half of all Africans trafficked in the transatlantic trade passed through this fort and were held in its dungeons. BELOW: Diver Kramer Wimberley holds an elephant tusk recovered from the 110 meter-deep Site 35F wreck. During the slave trade, ivory was worth more than a trafficked African.

ABOVE: Bust of Kazoola in Africatown, Alabama. He was the last survivor of the *Clotilda*, the last slave ship to land on US soil in 1860. *From Creative Commons/Amy Walker.* BELOW: Mural of the slave ship the *Clotilda* in Mobile, Alabama. *From the Alabama Historical Commission and Alabama Tourism Department.*

Grammy Award–winning musician, Rhiannon Giddens, performs a song at the Kazoola Club in Mobile, Alabama. The banjo originated as an African, not Western, instrument.

ABOVE: Young Bribri divers get ready to dive the *Fredericus Quartus* and the *Christianus Quintus*, two Danish slave ships that went down in 1710, off the coast of Costa Rica. Some of the divers may be descended from the 751 enslaved Africans who made it to shore. BELOW: Youth diver Esteban Gallo preparing to dive the *Fredericus Quartus* and the *Christianus Quintus* with other Bribri divers.

ABOVE: Discovering Danish yellow brick ballast from the *Fredericus Quartus* and the *Christianus Quintus*, Cahuita National Park, Costa Rica. BELOW: Chef Matthew Raiford picks organic herbs at his farm on Jekyll Island, Georgia. In 1858, the *Wanderer*, the second to last slave ship to arrive in America, landed at Jekyll Island. Enslaved Africans brought their food traditions and culture with them.

ABOVE: The DWP dive team searches and records the galley area of the *Niagara* steamship, wrecked in Lake Michigan in 1856. As part of the Underground Railroad, runaways from the American South, masquerading as staff, made their way to freedom in Canada on the *Niagara*. BELOW: The Fisk Jubilee Singers perform the encoded slave resistance song "Wade in the Water" in the Fisk Memorial Chapel in Nashville.

ABOVE: Kinga Philipps in the bell tower in Saint John's Church in Cleveland, Ohio, where runaway slaves hid along the Underground Railroad before "freedom boats" took them on the last dangerous leg to Canada. BELOW: *Empire Sandy* is a topsail schooner similar to the *Home*, a freedom boat involved in the Underground Railroad, and identified at the bottom of Lake Michigan.

ABOVE: The wreck of the *Home* schooner in Lake Michigan, commanded by Underground Railroad abolitionist Captain James Nugent. It sunk in 1858. It is the first boat positively identified as a "freedom boat" that repeatedly smuggled African Americans to freedom. BELOW: Divers taking a reggae break while diving the pirate city at Port Royal, Jamaica.

ABOVE: Preparing to use magnetometers to search for remains of the slave ship the *London*, washed ashore in Rapparee Cove, Ilfracombe, in 1796. BELOW: Heading offshore to search for the wreck of the *London* at Ilfracombe, UK.

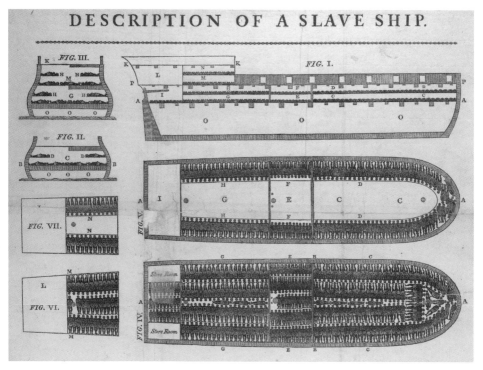

A diagram of the *Brooks* slave ship, which transported enslaved Africans to the Caribbean. The drawing showed the world how 609 Africans were tightly packed at sea in an area ten inches high, often chained or shackled together. The diagram appeared in newspapers in England in 1787 before being published around the world. It was instrumental in turning public opinion against the slave trade.

LEFT: Olaudah Equiano was an enslaved man who bought his freedom and wrote compellingly about his experiences. He was a prominent figure in the British abolitionist movement. *From Creative Commons.*

BELOW: Antietam National Cemetery. The Battle of Antietam (September 17, 1862) remains the bloodiest day in American history, with 22,717 dead, wounded, or missing. It was a turning point in the Civil War.

ABOVE: In 1791, Captain John Kimber of Bristol tortured to death an enslaved teenage girl who refused to dance naked on the deck of the *Recovery*. Kimber was tried for murder. Though he was found "innocent," this cartoon by Isaac Cruikshank led to growing opposition to the slave trade. BELOW: Concrete busts of enslaved Africans made by Ghanaian sculptor Kwame Akoto-Bamfo for his Ancestor Project. His art helps humanize the anonymous millions of trafficked Africans.

ABOVE: Diving With A Purpose ready to explore the Spanish slaver the *Guerrero* off the Florida Keys. The ship sank in 1827, illegally trafficking 561 enslaved people from West Africa to Cuba. BELOW: Divers Alannah Vellacott, Josh Williams, and Kinga Philipps examine human leg shackles from a slave ship discovered off the Florida Keys.

ABOVE: An iron anchor believed to be from the British antislavery patrol ship HMS *Nimble*, off the Florida Keys. It was lost in 1827, while chasing the illegal Spanish slaver the *Guerrero*. The slave trade had been abolished in England in 1808. BELOW: Marine archaeologist Corey Malcom finds a Spanish-style bar shot, a type of cannon projectile believed to be from the slave ship the *Guerrero*.

Samuel L. Jackson, Prof. Lee White, and archaeologist Dr. Richard Oslisly looking at millions of oyster shells spanning 2,500 acres in Loango National Park, Gabon. This food was a "last supper" for Africans prior to being forced to board European slave ships and trafficked across the Middle Passage to plantations in the Americas.

Alannah Vellacott and Kramer Wimberley's hunt for European slave ships ends by meeting the late civil rights leader and congressman John Lewis in Washington, DC.

I rise!

ENCHAINED

Back on firm ground, air tanks were filled, buoyancy vests checked, dry suits fussed over for the tiniest of holes, and the ROV system taken apart and cleaned. The team was as prepared as it would ever be. The next day they steamed out of Mylor at the crack of dawn. Nobody likes heading to work at 4:00 A.M. The night-lights were still twinkling across town. Southwest Cornwall, home to the wizard Merlin, looked magical. Nobody had slept the night before. The team felt hungover. For the best chance of getting in and out before the punishing waves started rolling, this was the only window of opportunity.

The *Severn Sea* research ship had gone ahead to send the ROV over the side, relocate the wreck site and lay the groundwork. The team was on a speedboat in hot pursuit. The sea was seriously choppy. The tech divers tied down their equipment so it would not fly overboard. Others put their heads down to stop themselves being sick.

Richard Stevenson and Kieran Hatton rested as best they could and started visualizing the challenge ahead. They are two of the best rebreather divers in the world. Some say it's crazy, the dangers too great. Rebreather divers need to be as cool as a cucumber and obsessive-compulsive to make sure technology, mind, and environment are perfectly in tune. Deep divers go down with multiple backup systems—belts and braces. Like a parachute, everything has to be tested time and time again. There are dozens of diving fatalities every year. Many involve rebreathers.

Getting down would be the easy bit. By the time they would be ready to ascend, their bodies would be saturated with gas. To safely decompress, they would need to stop every three meters for one minute on the way up and then hang suspended at six meters below the surface for an hour. Ten minutes down. Three hours to get back. Crawling home from 110 meters and 340 years of time travel. All in a day's work.

Still the weather worsened. A heavy wave crashed over the deck. The speedboat was lifted high out of the sea and crashed down into the ocean valley before the next wave hit. The team hugged their raincoats tightly and pushed on toward the Western Approaches. Nobody was having any fun. This time warp reminded the team what the captain, crew, and enslaved Africans on 35F must have felt in their final minutes—pure terror.

If the weather was mean halfway out, conditions were atrocious over the wreck. The *Severn Sea* had made it and called in with bad news. The ship was being pounded by waves. The sea state was too heavy to launch the ROV. The team ran the risk of becoming the Narrow Seas' latest victim. Rich took the painful decision to can the dive. The perils were just too great.

The divers headed back to port empty-handed. The great storm Sean Kingsley had warned the team about had rolled into town with a vengeance. Waves the size of houses broke over Mylor's harbor sea wall. All Diving With A Purpose could do was batten down the hatches, wait out the storm, and daydream. The wreck was jealously guarding its historic secrets.

The weather reports promised this was just the beginning of a major storm front. The forecast was for at least four days of rain and havoc. The clock was ticking and the window of opportunity to dive Site 35F closing fast. The team could only pray for a lull between storms and then make a run for it. They had come too far not to prevail.

Raiding & Trading

The life and times of the sunken Royal African Company trader haunted the team's waking hours and dreams. How did a cargo of elephant tusks end up on this merchant ship? Were the copper manilla bracelets used to buy and enslave people in West Africa? The history behind the finds told a spine-chilling truth.

The Royal African Company acted like lords on the Gold Coast, even though England's powers had practical limits so far from home. To make sure Western society could start the day with two lumps of sugar in their tea and coffee, take hot cocoa in the afternoon, and so men could relax at night with a pipe filled with tobacco, meant fueling the plantations of the West Indies with a factory treadmill of manpower. The African trade flowed through a string of fourteen English forts, some ferocious, others mere "thatched hovels" with little defense. Finding and loading ivory could take 90 days, slaves 120 days. The forts were less about protection. Day-to-day they were giant holding pens.

Even in Africa, few captains had a clue where the human cargos they enslaved came from. Fort governors raised their eyebrows at the many languages the Africans spoke and that some were scarred with marks on their faces and bodies. They did not appreciate how they were cultural markers of different tribes and cultures. The capture of Africans took place far from the eyes of Europeans in the hands of West Africa's rulers.

The harsh reality was that everyone was to blame for the slave trade. Everyone had blood on their hands, including the English, Dutch, French, Portuguese, Spanish, Danes, Prussians, and even Africans. It was brought about by Europe's consumer greed. Without the West's obsessive needs, Africa's human population would have been left in peace.

Africans ended up trapped by many foul and deceptive ways. Ship captains dealt directly with African kings, rulers, and their brokers. If they were given advance notice, castle governors could guarantee slave cargos were already locked up and ready to sail as soon as favored customers made landfall, all for a handsome fee.

Most adventurers believed enslaved Africans were the spoils of wars between tribal kingdoms. In the years of feuding, as in 1681, an English captain could buy three hundred captives overnight "for nothing besides the trouble of receiving them at the beach in his boats" after enemies dragged captives "from the field of battle, having obtained a victory over a neighboring nation, and taken a great number of prisoners." When the inland country was at peace in 1682, the French failed to find a single captive to buy after three days of searching.

In his book *Description of Guinea* (1732), John Barbot, a French trading agent from Paris, similarly understood that

> Those sold by the Blacks are for the most part prisoners of
> war, taken either in fight, or pursuit, or in the incursions they
> make into their enemies territories; others stolen away by their
> own countrymen; and some there are, who will sell their own
> children, kindred, or neighbors.

Other native peoples were imprisoned by lies and treachery. After being hired to carry goods to the coast like leather hides and elephant teeth, many innocents ended up taken and sold at the tip of a spear. Men, women, and children might be stolen by neighboring kingdoms if they were caught alone on the open road or tending corn fields. At times of famine, some families had no option but to sell themselves or starve. Nothing in this chain was possible without the approval of the local rulers. Today, raiding and kidnapping, not wars, are thought to have been the main source of slave trafficking.

The kings of Accra in Ghana raked in fortunes from gold and slaves. In 1785 a Danish scientist visited an inland ruler who showed him a gold nugget so large it took four men to lift, so the story goes. Around 22 percent of all slaves exported to the Americas came from the Bight of Benin, where one million captives were sold in Whydah. In the 1680s, Barbados's plantation owners preferred workers from Ghana's Gold Coast, especially the River Gambia. Some estates paid £3 or £4 more per head for the Papa Africans of Whydah. The enslaved shipped from nearby Ardra in the Bight of Benin were also especially popular on sugar plantations, being, according to their owners, "lusty, strong, and very laborious people."

Deals were sealed a number of ways. In the Bight of Benin, captains were welcomed by 1,200 armed men dancing on the shore. Porters carried ships' officers to Ardra in hammocks for the price of four manillas a day. Negotiations began at Little Ardra when ship's agents called "supercargoes" gifted a king three or four pounds of fine coral, cloth, and silk. The Europeans then paid the kings the value of fifty slaves in imported goods in return for the right to trade. At Whydah, the price of captives was reckoned according to the number of a ship's masts. Three-mast ships paid rulers the equivalent of twenty-one slaves in European goods. Women cost a fourth or a fifth less than men. When the negotiations were sealed, the town crier announced that every subject in the kingdom was free to trade with the supercargo. European slave traders set off in canoes along the shore in search of willing sellers.

In other towns, after a king reached terms, an iron bell was rung and captives dragged in and sold on the spot. A surgeon would carefully examine the captives, force them to jump up and down and stretch out their arms "to see that they were sound wind and limb." The doctor would gape into the captives' mouths to check their teeth and age and "our greatest care of all is to buy none that are pox'd [diseased], lest they should infect the rest aboard."

In New Calabar in eastern Nigeria, Royal African Company merchants received kings on their ships. One ruler dressed in a worn-out scarlet coat laced with gold and silver, a fine hat, and walking barefoot was saluted with seven cannon shots when he came onboard an adventurer's ship in 1699. The ruler was presented with a new hat, a firelock pistol, and nine bunches of beads. When negotiations were over, the king's public crier blew a trumpet made from an elephant tusk to announce permission to trade. Elsewhere, in Angola, deals might be made in front of a prince seated on a great chair, shaven-headed and naked under a black cloak and slippers. King and merchant shared palm wine served in a silver cup.

Captives were bought using the local currency, copper and brass manillas, or the thirty-six copper bars for a man and thirty for a woman paid by the supercargo of the *Arthur* in 1678. The captain of the *Hannibal* paid one hundred pounds weight of cowrie shells for one slave in 1693.

In the eyes of the Africans, Europeans were all-powerful, with their ships and guns. It was natural for African chiefs to barter with them for prisoners. At first it never occurred to these chiefs that the people sold into slavery would be regarded as chattel, property, less than human. By the time kingdoms, like the Ashanti, realized what the Europeans were up to, it was too late. They were complicit in an economic system that traded European goods for African resources—gold, ivory, and people.

THE DOOR OF NO RETURN

After four days of waiting for the weather to break, the sea finally fell calm, a short relief before winter rolled into Cornwall with a vengeance. This was the last chance saloon. The orange-red sun rose over the Narrow Seas, lighting up the waters like a gift from above.

Once again, Diving With A Purpose and rebreather divers Rich Stevenson and Kieran Hatton raced toward Site 35F. The signs looked promising. The only bad omen was Kieran, who realized that he had forgotten to put on his lucky underpants that morning.

Alannah was excited. She could see the end of the tunnel. "I never would have imagined this opportunity to give a voice to the silenced, breathing new life into people of color who are still living with questions unanswered," she said, sharing the team's feelings.

The *Severn Sea* made it to the wreck site and called in a sea state report. Conditions were good. The dive was on. The ROV was safely lowered overboard and its lights turned on. Soon after, the dive team arrived and suited up.

Rich and Kieran's rebreather kit, four air tanks attached to their backs and sides, looked like something from a Hollywood sci-fi fantasy. They stepped into inner space and immediately plunged down a shot line dropped by the ROV, their only link between surface and seabed. Time was precious. There was no room for error. Getting lost could be fatal. A one-inch-thick piece of rope would be their only guide. The divers' lives hung on a wire.

Unlike open-circuit scuba, where every time you exhale you lose a lungful of gas, Rich and Kieran's rebreather tanks would re-loop the gas to turn it back into fresh air. Rebreathers let divers breathe the same lungful of gas over and over again. Their efficiency lets them dive deeper and longer. Even the Darth Vader noises of a scuba mouthpiece disappear. Rebreathers are so silent fish think divers just are bigger fish. They cannot hear you coming.

At 110 meters the water is like ink. An eternal night enveloped Rich and Kieran. Making out where you are, up or down, is impossible in this inner space. The divers had no benefit of sea-to-surface underwater communications speakers. They were isolated between the devil and the deep blue sea.

Getting to the wreck was a ten-minute commute with just a flashlight for company to show the way. The good news was there are no sharks in these seas. The bad news was the punishing cold. Deep diving is as much a state of mind as a physical activity. Finning ever deeper, like sportsmen visualizing a win, they got into the zone, thinking about the job at hand, what they needed to achieve and foreseeing any glitches. The rest of the team was geared up and on standby at the surface, ready to rush down extra oxygen tanks if trouble hit. Two thirds of diving fatalities happen in under three meters.

After seven minutes, faint beams of light from the divers' flashlights flickered on the ROV's video feed. Rich and Kieran had made it to a place no human had been before. A lone sea bass swam across the wreckage, unflustered by the alien invaders.

Within fifteen meters of the seabed the whole wreck opened up in a panoramic bird's-eye view. The ship's wooden sides had flattened out long ago like a filleted fish. A cluster of eight cannons welcomed Rich and Kieran, even though cut marks in their sides told a sad tale of fishing boat scallop dredge teeth still bulldozing the precious remains. The guns had been scrambled too, worryingly thrown around like matchsticks by fishing trawler gear since the last time robots visited Site 35F. Shredded parts of the wooden ship and strange concretions hiding invisible secrets lay all around.

Stubbornly refusing to give in to the inevitable, part of the fragile keelson—the ship's backbone—sat above the seabed as if it hoped one day to take off and sail again. There was little time to take in the glory. Rich and Kieran had just ten minutes to find the tusk, prepare it for lifting, and get out of there.

Tainted Blood

How did it come to this? Why did the Royal African Company and the West find it reasonable to treat human beings like cattle? In 1651, the Guinea Company instructed Englishman Bartholomew Howard to sail for West Africa and "buy and put aboard you so many negros as y'or ship can cary, and for what shal be wanting to supply with Cattel." Africans were reduced to the status of cargo and beasts of burden with no human rights.

Oxygen was first breathed into this hateful mindset in Spain. In Toledo, any hope that Africans converted to Catholicism might one day escape bondage, was shattered. In June 1449, a set of laws based on the "purity of a human's bloodline," the Sentencia-Estatuto, was signed by the magistrate of Toledo, Pedro Sarmiento, on behalf of the city cathedral. The legislation was meant to ferret out Jews and Muslims who had been forcibly converted to Christianity. After all, once they became Christians, technically speaking, there were no obstacles to their advancements.

So the new laws, for the first time in Europe, differentiated between people not on the basis of faith but blood. From now on what mattered was birth. Whether you were a Jew, a Muslim, or an African was one and the same. You were foreign, other, and stained. Only Christian Spaniards from a pure and uncontaminated bloodline, where all four grandparents were Spanish Christians, could work for the government, religious orders, or join guilds.

The new creed got the ultimate blessing. Pope Nicholas V signed a public letter in 1452 giving Spain's chief ally, Portugal, the right to enslave sub-Saharan Africans. The Church elders insisted slavery was a natural and righteous Christian way to stop the spread of barbarian behavior. And so King Afonso V of Portugal was given a green light to

> invade, search out, capture, vanquish, and subdue all Sara-
> cens [Muslims] and pagans whatsoever, and other enemies
> of Christ wheresoever placed, and the kingdoms, dukedoms,
> principalities, dominions, possessions, and all movable and
> immovable goods whatsoever held and possessed by them
> and to reduce their persons to perpetual slavery.

People with the wrong blood coursing through their veins could also be reduced to "perpetual slavery," even if they were Christians. The pope and king of Spain had unfurled the world's first racial profiling based on bloodline. Bad ideas can go a very long way. In the 1670s the Royal African Company latched onto Spain's thoughts on Africans as perpetual slaves. If it was good enough for the pope, it was good enough for King Charles II.

SLAVERY THROUGH THE AGES

Slavery has been a constant part of human history from Europe to the Middle East and China. It still persists today in places like Mauritania, Sudan, and India, where it is estimated that over fourteen million people, including women and children, are enslaved, working in quarries, farms, and brick kilns.

In biblical times, slavery was permitted but a master's power over a slave was restricted. As the Book of Leviticus puts it, "You may buy male and female slaves from among the nations that are around you. You may make slaves of them, but over your brothers, the people of Israel, you shall not rule, one over another ruthlessly." Nevertheless, activists like the prophet Nehemiah scolded wealthy Israelites for owning local slaves. The entire theme of the biblical narrative is antislavery.

The central story of the Hebrew Bible is the exodus and the emancipation of the Israelites from slavery in Egypt. Hebrew slaves had to be let go after six years and provided with the means of being free. Slaves—Hebrew and non-Hebrew—were also offered relief on the Sabbath. These innovations were without parallel in the ancient Near East. Non-Hebrew slaves were considered permanent acquisitions and never had to be freed. However, the Rabbinic Talmud argues that this does not give one the right to humiliate them: "Rabbi Samuel said: I gave them to you for work, but not for humiliation." The great Jewish philosopher Maimonides elaborated further how to "be compassionate and pursue justice, do not excessively burden slaves, nor cause them distress."

The Hebrew Bible is so powerfully antislavery—Moses is, in effect, an abolitionist leader—that slaves in the nineteenth-century American South were given Bibles that omitted most of the Old Testament. The so-called Slave Bible told the story of Joseph's enslavement, for example, but left out the parts where Moses stands up to authority, stating, "Thus says the Lord, the God of the Hebrews: Let my people go!" (Exodus 9:1). Because of this, many antislavery spirituals, such as "Go Down Moses," explicitly reference the Bible for inspiration.

Rome ran the largest slave society in the ancient world. Captives were enslaved from empire-wide wars as far as Britannia and the Balkans. In Roman Egypt around 15 percent of city residents were slaves and as many as two million across Italy. Slaves did not come cheap: an unskilled rural laborer might cost one thousand daily wages. The enslaved toiled in fields as estate managers, field hands, domestic staff, craftsmen, miners, clerks, teachers, doctors, midwives, potters, and entertainers.

Slaves could be kept in chains, turned into gladiators for entertainment, abused, and used for sexual services. Some did work their way up to positions of power, wealth, and freedom. Those who were granted *libertus* by their masters became citizens. They could vote and play a role in politics. Other freedmen became wealthy, such as the brothers who owned the fancy House of the Vettii in Pompeii, one of the city's most magnificent houses. It was a freedman who designed Pompeii's amphitheater. The ex-slave Trimalchio, who organized the finest dinner parties in the Roman world in Petronius's book *The Satyricon*, ended up inspiring the lead character in F. Scott Fitzgerald's *The Great Gatsby*.

Rome's fluid society was a far cry from the two centuries leading up to the American Civil War. Slavery may have been abolished in America, but Black people in the Southern states were still subject to segregation and oppression. Integration remained an impossible dream well into the twentieth century. Fundamentally, the difference between antiquity and colonial Europe was that the special brand of racial segregation seen in the transatlantic trade was not a feature of earlier civilizations. The customs of earlier cultures may have been abhorrent, but ancient empires did not industrially mine an entire continent like Africa to enslave its people.

England added a dark religious spin to justify its actions. According to the Church of England, Africa was condemned by God Almighty. Why? Because Africans were descended from the Biblical Ham and his son Canaan. In the Book of Genesis (9:25), Noah's son, Ham, made the disrespectful mistake of looking at his father's nakedness. For this sin, Noah raged against Ham and his son Canaan: "Cursed be Canaan; a slave's slave shall he be to his brethren." By declaring Africans "Hamites," the Church of England was saying that Africans were destined for "eternal servitude."

The End of the Line

Over three thousand years after Noah's curse was recorded, his words were used to justify one of the greatest atrocities in human history. Once captured, Africans ended up enchained in the dungeons of castles like Cape Coast and Elmina in Ghana, West Africa's most powerful forts. The captives were locked in what the British described as spacious mansions, which were really dungeons "cut out of the rocky ground, arched and divided into several rooms; so that it will conveniently contain a thousand blacks, let down at an opening made for the purpose," explained Jean Barbot, the French trade agent-general, in 1682.

In these dungeons, newly taken Africans were shackled in collars and branded over their hearts with the initials DY, standing for their new owner, the Duke of York and governor of the Royal African Company, or the initials of the ship's name or captain. The captives and masters are now long gone, the cries of anguish faded into thin air. The memories, though, are still with us.

Very few African voices record the atrocities. Quobna Ottobah Cugoano, born in the Fante village of Ajumako in 1757 and kidnapped at the age of thirteen, is one of the exceptions. Cugoano was traded to England, rechristened John Stuart, and ended up writing a diary about his scarring experiences, *Thoughts and Sentiments on the Evil and Wicked Trade of the Slavery and Commerce of the Human Species* (1787).

The youngster had been sold into bondage in Cape Coast Castle, where he was petrified the English planned to eat him. He was locked up in the dungeon for three days where he "heard the groans and cries of many . . . when a vessel arrived to conduct us away to the ship, it was a most horrible scene; there was nothing to be heard but rattling of chains, smacking of whips, and groans and cries of our fellow men . . ."

On their forced march to the shore, many Africans dug their nails into their home soil. Crews kept them shackled between the forts and ship holds and while they were in sight of the coast of Africa. This was where captives tried their hardest to escape or mutiny. At times, captains cut the legs and arms off the most rebellious Africans "to terrify the rest, for they believe if they lose a member, they cannot return home again."

Twelve captives trafficked to the English ship the *Hannibal* in 1694 refused to go quietly and accept a future worse than death, so its captain wrote:

> The negroes are so wilful and loth to leave their own country,
> that they have often leap'd out of the canoes, boat and ship,
> into the sea, and kept under water till they were drowned . . .
> they having a more dreadful apprehension of Barbadoes than
> we can have of hell . . .

The English and other Europeans may have lived behind silk curtains, and dined off silver plates, but civilization had long deserted these shores. In both Cape Coast and Elmina Castles, the governors' bedrooms led by a secret passageway to the women's dungeons. Female slaves would be picked out for the governor's personal "inspection" and raped. Life was cheap and governors made merry while they could. Nobody stopped them. Nobody wrote about the violations. They were kept out of governors' and captains' logs. What happened in Africa stayed in Africa. Besides, if the women became pregnant, all the better. There would be another child to sell at journey's end.

Elmina Castle, with its gleaming whitewashed stone walls, was the last sight the enslaved saw of their homeland. Ahead waited the fearful Middle Passage between West Africa and the West Indies, the plantations, and eternal slavery. Crossing these seas, 1.8 million enslaved Africans would die.

At Elmina, captives were held in an airless hole in the ground. To enter you had to pass the castle's church, acknowledging the all-seeing Christian God and bend over in surrender to almost crawl through an arched passageway. This dark, dirty space was the end of the line, the end of freedom.

A small sliver of light shone through the chilling Door of No Return, guarded by an iron gate, at its center a cross, the sign of Christ's compassion. Thirty thousand slaves a year were prodded, one by one, through this one-way door. Once the enslaved passed this point, it marked the end of their culture. Their names would be changed. They faced a life of forced labor and their children and children's children would be born into slavery. More than half the Africans trafficked in the transatlantic trade passed through Elmina's sea gate.

THE ELMINA SHIPWRECK

The approaches to Elmina Castle in Ghana saw many disasters. In the 1580s, Portuguese galleys attacked a French fleet, sinking the *Esperance*. The British brig *James Matthews* was lost off Elmina in 1766. The crew and six slaves escaped to shore, only to be stripped naked by the locals. A reef running eight hundred meters offshore was a natural ship trap to be approached with great caution.

A mile and a half off Elmina, an armed Dutch ship was lost in sight of the castle stocked with remains of a rich cargo ready to trade: 34 stacks of brass basins, brass pins, over 3,800 glass beads, 636 manillas, pewter basins, and cowrie shells have been found. The ship is thought to be the Dutch West India Company's *Groningen*, lost in 1647 after catching fire when a cannon exploded during a salute to Elmina Castle.

A letter written by Hendrick Caarlof, the governor of Elmina, on March 5, 1647, describes how "the ship Groeningen . . . wished to fire 5 shots, as is customary, had caught fire from the last cannon, which had burst . . . The hatch of the orlop flew overboard; but the worst of all was that the blow took its chief force downwards . . . The descending fire progressing so strongly caused the crew, through sheer amazement to get into perplexity . . . 11 seamen and eight soldiers perished in the fire. In the blowing up of the ship some goods flew up and got into the hands of the Blacks, part of which has been taken from them, and some fished up by dredging, which we will continue to do . . ."

When the Dutch West India Company was founded in 1621, its directors at first refused to trade in humans as immoral. The Dutch changed their mind by the mid-1630s and committed to the slave trade. From 1674 to 1730, the company signed 383 slave trade ventures.

Today, the hatred has flown from the white walls of Elmina. The English have gone home, along with the rest of colonial Europe. Since then, Britain has apologized for the slave trade. The Netherlands, Germany, and America have apologized. So has the pope, the Church of England, the Bank of England, and the world's biggest insurance company, Lloyd's of London. West Africa, Benin, Ghana, Nigeria, and Uganda have also apologized for their role in the slave trade. South Africa has apologized. But are apologies enough? They slam the lid shut on the dark past, rather than seeking creative ways to make sure the world never forgets.

The Royal Bubble Bursts

The Royal African Company's cozy deal did not last long. The organization that sent the 35F ship to West Africa was a blazing financial comet. It burned brightly before fizzing out. The company turned out to be a monster with sprawling overheads and ambitions that it could not sustain.

The company had to fight to keep its royal rights. Few liked the powers wielded by the pro-French Catholic Duke of York, the governor of the Royal African Company and heir to the crown. England was a land for Protestants. The company behaved like a divinely sanctioned bully, far too big for its boots. Branding any English ship trading independently a pirate spread unease across the British Isles.

Little wonder skippers skimmed profits by smuggling extra slaves and cargos. The company's finances were a nightmare to juggle. The king's men were required to maintain the string of Gold Coast forts for Britain's foreign interests. But they were not given anywhere near enough government funds for the upkeep of bricks, mortar, guns, and officials.

Cash flow was a problem. The company sold slaves to its Caribbean colonies on credit. The floating debt was never easy to recover from far-off planters. The Royal African Company was a bureaucratic nightmare as well. Independent traders could complete two journeys to Guinea and back in the time it took London to get a single ship readied.

War with France made safe passage tricky, as enemy corsairs from Saint-Malo preyed on English merchant shipping. The Royal African Company managed to lose 114 ships from 1689 to 1708 to storms, wrecks, and the enemy, raking up losses of £124,652 or $18.3 million today.

The biggest nail in the company's coffin was the feeling of unfair play. To the great coastal cities—Liverpool, Bristol, and Lancaster—the royal monopoly violated the natural human right to free trade, the very bastion on which Britain was built. Corporations like Bristol's Society of Merchant Venturers sent petitions to London demanding change.

After just twenty-six years of trading, the Royal African Company was beaten. The Act to Settle the Trade to Africa signed in 1698 opened up Africa to all adventurers for a small fee: "Any Subjects as well as the Company may trade to Africa between Cape Blanco and Cape Mount, paying £10 per Cent. for Goods exported; And £10 per Cent. on all Goods, &c. imported into England or America, from Africa." Now everyone could get into the African trafficking business.

Facing the Atlantic on England's southwestern shore, Bristol was perfectly placed to knock London off its arrogant slave-trading perch. After 1698 the city played a major role in the transatlantic slave trade. Its merchants backed over two thousand voyages trafficking more than half a million enslaved Africans to the Americas. By the 1730s, thirty-six slave voyages left Bristol a year, rising to fifty-three at the end of the decade. Bristol had got its hands on 40 percent of Britain's slave trade.

With its forest of ships' masts bobbing in the channel down to the sea, Bristol was built on the back of enslaved Africans. The whole city gladly took an economic shot in the arm—shipbuilders, merchants, tradesmen, manufacturers, bankers, and small-time investors. Prosperity snowballed. The city made and sold guns, brass goods, booze, cloth, hats, and fancy goods for the Guinea trade. The Warmley Brass Company exported cooking pots. The Bristol Brass and Copper Company cast manilla bracelets.

Newly docked sugar had to be refined, tobacco and indigo processed, and chocolate manufactured from cargos of cacao. Thousands worked for the slave trade machine, which gave birth to Bristol's first banks, whose profits landscaped the city with the finest architecture from warehouses to churches. Bristol, the metropolis of the West, enjoyed a golden age.

Despite the depth of slavery's influence, the finger of blame is pointed today at one man—Edward Colston. His name is everywhere in the city—Colston's Almshouses, Colston Tower, Colston Street, Colston's Girls' School. The Colston bun, a sweet bun made of yeast dough fla-voured with fruits and spices, still honors his legacy. How did Britain's most hated historic figure of recent memory, who got rich from human suffering, become so famous and then infamous?

Colston's cash was bloodstained from his inside trading as a fixer, enforcer, and in 1689 deputy governor of the Royal African Company. In the years he worked for the company, 84,500 enslaved African men, women, and children were branded and sold in the Caribbean and Americas. Up to 19,300 died crossing the Middle Passage.

Back in the day, everyone loved Edward Colston, who was one of the country's great philanthropists. In his lifetime he donated £63,940 to charities, including hospitals, almshouses and churches. He left another £71,000 to grand causes when he breathed his last in 1721 ($22.1 million in modern money). Everyone revered and respected the humble Colston, a man who refused to marry and left instructions to be buried in a simple grave. When people sniggered behind his back at his lack of a bride, he quipped that "every helpless widow is my wife and her distressed orphans my children." He doled out cash to old helpless sailors. When he died, aged eighty-four, the bells of Bristol rang for sixteen hours straight. Colston's obituary called him "the highest example of Christian liberality that this age has produced, both for the extensiveness of his charities and the prudent regulation of them."

In the twenty-first century, Colston's reputation lies in tatters. As we now know, his "Christian liberality" was made possible by his involvement in the slave trade. The grand statue the city set up in his honor was ripped down and slung in Bristol harbor at the height of England's Black Lives Matter protests in 2020. A new conversation is now underway about Britain's guilt in the transatlantic slave trade and how it should remember and mark past evils.

Bristol's conflicted history is perfectly summed up today by the poet and educator Lawrence Hoo's *Inner City Tales*:

> *Now Edward Colston is held as the beacon for this trade. When the reality is that through it, Bristol was made.*

> *Bristol profited so many ways, to name them all would take us days.*

> *But trade, commerce, and stature is to name just a few. On the power of the African people's suffering, Bristol grew.*

> *Imagine not being allowed to speak in your natural tongue. Imagine not being allowed to educate your young.*

> *Then, over time, your ways are lost and your history is forgotten, and you become a part of a world where you belong at the bottom.*

> *The people who did it said they're the civilized race. They keep rewriting history to make their case.*

> *But if we look at the facts and the facts alone. Who was uncivilized and savage is easily shown.*

By 1701 the Royal African Company's share in the slave trade had plummeted to 8 percent from a high of 88 percent in 1690. Bristol had disrupted and overtaken London's position as Britain's top slave trading city. Profititing from trafficking innocent Africans was no longer an elite pursuit. Rather, it was now in every Englishman's economic interest.

White Gold

Kramer waited, suspended in the shallows of the English Channel. Had Rich and Kieran found one of the wrecked elephant tusks and would it see the light of day, safe and sound? *Those two gentlemen are in a place where no one else has ever been*, he thought. Josh was struggling to make sense of past and present. He knew he was literally free diving above a sunken graveyard that may have entombed his ancestors, who were anything but free.

Time passed painfully slowly. The divers had spent just twenty minutes on the sea bottom. The tiptoe ascent would take another two and a half hours of decompression. You can fly from New York to Miami in the time Rich and Kieran would need to claw their way back from the sunken past.

Finally, telltale jellyfish-shaped air bubbles rose from the oblivion below. Diving With A Purpose had set up a final decompression station six meters below the surface. Emergency gas tanks filled with 100 percent oxygen were tied to the sides of a bar Rich and Kieran could hang onto and start to relax. They were too exhausted battling strong currents to celebrate. All they could do was wait for the inert gas their bodies had absorbed to be released. Another hour of decompression to go.

When their bloodstreams returned to normal, the divers clambered gratefully onto their speedboat. Rich peeled the hood off his dry suit and blinked, pasty looking, in the midday sun. It would take time for the ancient dust to settle. It was too soon to make sense of where they had been, what they had achieved. Rich sighed, humbled by the history-making dive, and told his friends that "to be enlightened is my motivation to spend four hours in the freezing water. That's my personal reward."

The living were safe. It was time to check in with the ancestors. On the seabed, the elephant tusk had been liberated from its sandy tomb by light hand fanning and secured in a custom-built padded lifting basket. The team took turns hauling up by hand the tusk attached to the rope line. Their muscles ached in sympathy with the pain the Africans trafficked on this Royal African Company ship felt toiling in Caribbean plantations.

The 340-year-old tusk pillaged from Africa, along with millions of Africans, was hauled over the side of the *Severn Sea*. The team stared in wonder, shock, and anger. Seaweed and sand covered the artifact, but it was clearly a curved elephant's tusk. The hard dentin of its tooth had preserved it for all time, a fossil of England's role in the slave trade.

Europe's lust for what it called luxurious white gold took a heavy environmental toll. The greed for luxury and profit was a pandemic that spread from the savannah grasslands of Ghana to the streets of London, Paris, and Amsterdam. As time went by, the majestic sight of elephants faded from the map. Today, the long shadow of the ivory trade has reached the end of the line, too. Three and a half million elephants once roamed wild. Seventy percent are now gone. Africa's elephants are on the edge of extinction and it all started with English and Dutch ships like 35F in the seventeenth century.

WHITE GOLD

Three million elephants ended up slaughtered and their tusks stowed in European slave ships. White gold was a high-end luxury used to make statues, medallions, and fancy furniture. Ivory's soft, satiny surface was perfect for cutting tiny details for portraits and busts paid for by high society's deep pockets.

Ivory carving was a popular fashion in London, Germany, and Dieppe in France. Queen Anne, King George I, Sir Isaac Newton, Christopher Wren, and Samuel Pepys sat for ivory busts made by David Le Marchand, a Frenchman who fled religious persecution to London. In 1639 the German master craftsman Marcus Heiden created the wonder of the age for his Saxon duke masters: a drinking vessel perched on an elephant and topped with a ship under full sail.

Tusks could be turned into a dizzying selection of exotic goods, from combs and knife handles to keys for clavichords and medical syringes. If you could afford it, from the 1700s you could buy lifelike ivory eyeballs, prosthetic limbs, false teeth to spare your mouth's rotten immodesty, artificial legs, noses, and, for the challenged male, even ivory penises.

Raw emotions hidden deep in the divers' souls bubbled to the surface. Private emotions for Kramer, Alannah, Josh, and Kinga. But most of all, emotions for the ancestors. Voice could finally be given to the enslaved.

For Alannah, the tusk symbolized the full circle of hundreds of years of suffering. She could now touch and sense the enslaved trafficked on hundreds of ships like this. Every captive had a mother, a father, a name, all ripped away from them. "They were people," Alannah choked emotionally. "I can't imagine being taken away from my family. I cannot fathom being taken across oceans I didn't even know existed. And then to be beaten and thrown about and be yelled at in a language I don't even understand and be told to do things I do not want to do."

For Kramer, this was just the start of righting injustice. "If it's the final resting place of some of my ancestors, then it's a burial ground," he told the team. "But it's also a crime scene because they were taken. There was an injustice that took place, and no one has ever been brought to account for that. I want justice for those people."

"It always bothers me to use the language 'slaves' on the ships," Kramer went on. "People speak in terms of the Africans in the ships as if they started out as slaves. They weren't slaves, they were Africans who were *enslaved*. There are generations who think that African history started with slavery. African history didn't start with African slavery. African history was interrupted by African slavery."

The profound shift from chasing gold and tusks to hunting slaves in the mid–seventeenth century struck a fatal blow for West Africa's destiny. Its economy and industry were held back for two hundred years. While the West raked in cash, Africa was locked in one of history's darkest ages. Feeding Europe's sweet tooth and smoking pipes opened the door to centuries of warlords that divided Africa, and still does in some regions.

The team took turns holding the resurrected tusk. It had traveled out of Africa on an English ship that sold most of its captives on the plantation islands of Barbados, Jamaica, and Nevis. Then it headed to London, possibly accompanied by a few slaves held back for the local market, the unsold outbound manillas, additional elephant tusks and almost certainly sugar and maybe gold. As the divers held the tusk, they felt a victory of sorts; free people holding ivory that was once worth more than the lives of their ancestors.

NEW WORLD CULTURES

We lookee and lookee and lookee and lookee
and we doan see nothin' but water.
Where we come from we doan know.
Where we goin, we doan know.
De boat we on called de Clotilde . . .
De water . . . It growl lak de thousand beastes
in de bush . . .
Sometime de ship way up in de sky.
Sometimes it way down in de bottom of de sea . . .
    —Kazoola remembers in Zora Neale Hurston,
Barracoon: The Story of the Last "Black Cargo" (2018)

SANCTUARY

Down a twisting road, Alannah, Kramer, and Kinga wound their way along the coast of Costa Rica in blue and white Land Rovers. To the left rolled the Caribbean Sea; to the right rose mountains and dense tropical rainforest. The landscape was the wildest that Diving With A Purpose had confronted so far. The Land Rovers plunged and rocked through fjords swollen by winter rain and jangled over rickety wooden bridges. Monkeys and alligators glared at them. Locals on motorbikes swerved dangerously across the road. Women sliced jackfruit off trees with sharp machetes.

The divers' destination was Aditibri Suretka, several hours inland in southern Costa Rica. Today this land lies in the territory of the Bribri, an Indigenous people who have lived here for centuries. The Bribri are one of the most isolated of Costa Rica's eight Indigenous groups. Their thirty-five thousand people grow their own crops and have kept their language and culture alive.

The team had come to Costa Rica to meet a local group of young Bribri divers who believe Africans are a central part of their past. This time Diving With A Purpose were not investigating the deaths of those who never made it. They were investigating a group that may have beaten the odds and survived.

Most people will tell you the Bribri are descended from Mayans. But there is a another twist to the tale. As the Land Rovers cautiously headed uphill to Aditibri Suretka, Alannah told the team how "Their folklore tells of slave ships that were wrecked on the Costa Rican shoreline and of Africans who came ashore to make a new life for themselves in the forests. But their African ancestry has always been considered to be a mere tribal legend."

The human rights activist Maria Suárez Toro had invited the dive team to a Bribri feast to try and help the Bribri community reclaim the truth about their past by helping local teens dive slave ships off the coast. The Land Rovers parked among simple houses with corrugated roofs scattered among banana trees. After the introductions were over, and the feast underway, Maria took to her feet to talk about the legend of Africans arriving among the Bribri much earlier than previously thought. Just looking at one another's faces, these Bribri have often wondered about their color and wavy hair, glancing east across the Middle Passage to Africa.

Don Alejandro Swaby, a Bribri elder, may have been clad in his Indigenous group's traditional embroidered shirt but he told the visitors, "I have Black ancestry and I am proud of that. And that is the history we pass on to our kids. And it's the history that should be written for the future."

Kramer thanked the villagers for sharing their story and added that "On some level, I'm jealous because my question is always 'where do you come from?' And the answer to that for me is always 'I don't know.' I don't have a connection to my home or my people. So, to be able to assist in answering those questions is a connection for me."

Standing quietly on the side lines, Laura Wilson, an expert in local folklore, watched with great satisfaction as the descendants of Africans living far apart rubbed shoulders. Alannah asked Laura to share the locals' story about what happened on the slavers supposedly wrecked off Costa Rica.

Laura explained that "What we have heard of those ships that are at the bottom of the sea: Africans came to our area. These Africans came on a boat that gets wrecked on a beach where they know no one. You know, it's disastrous. You don't know where you're going. You don't know where you went to sleep."

Alannah found it hard to visualize being uprooted in this way. "I can't really imagine. You've just wrecked up in the middle of nowhere. You have no idea where you are. You look to your left and it's just ocean.

And then you look to your right and you see dark forest and you have to make a choice. Do you try and go back to the wreck or do you go into the rainforest? That must have been absolutely terrifying."

Laura shuddered. "This story is bringing me back to horrible things," she admitted. "You know, slavery was very horrible. Taking you out of your own homeplace and you don't know where you're going. There was nowhere else but to go but to adapt themselves with the Bribri and the other Indigenous folks that we had around here. As a kid in school, they didn't teach us that."

"They went into the rainforest and the Bribri adopted them. That's an amazing story," Alannah replied, before moving the story along. "From time to time, teenage divers have seen artifacts offshore. If we can connect them to slave ships, we will be able to back up the legends with hard evidence."

To the escaped captives, the tropical climate of the Mosquito Coast's lagoons, savannas, and rainforests must have felt very much like parts of West Africa. Into the modern day, many words used along the Mosquito Coast still have African roots. The enslaved carried their language into exile where they entered modern speech. Sweet potato yams spread West with the Fulani people. Gumbo, a culinary calling card of Louisiana, is borrowed from the Bantu *gumbos*. The cockroach takes its name from the West African *cacarootch*. Honeybees are believed to come from the Yoruba *honi*. *Todi* and *babuun* gave the West the frog and monkey. Jonathan Swift claimed to have invented the word *yahoo* in *Gulliver's Travels* in 1726 for a race of brutes, although it sounds surprisingly close to—and twisted from—a West African devil, *yahue*.

Legends of Danish Slavers

Most people in Costa Rica do not take the folklore about the Bribri's Black ancestry seriously. Sounds too much like a tall tale. But marine archeologist Andreas Bloch thinks differently. He may even have identified the precise ships the legends talk about. Clues back home in the archives in Denmark set him and his fellow researchers on a remarkable journey.

CHRISTIANUS QUINTUS & FREDERICUS QUARTUS

- *Christianus Quintus*, 35.9 meters long, 7.9 meters wide
- Named in honor of the Danish king, 1670–1699
- Built in Larvik, Norway
- Commanded by Captain Hans Hansen Maas, Jost van de Vogel, and later Anders Pedersen Waerøe
- Traded for gold, slaves, and ivory on the Gold Coast in 1699, 1703, and 1709
- *Fredericus Quartus*, 43.8 meters long
- Named in honor of King Frederik IV, 1699–1730
- Built in Copenhagen
- Commanded by Captain Dirk Fijfe
- Both ships carried twenty-four cannons and were manned by sixty men
- On their final voyage, the frigates left Denmark in December 1708 with cargos of sheets, guns, knives, Norwegian and Swedish iron, and cases of gifts, including cowrie shells and copper manilla bracelets
- Burnt and scuttled at Cahuita, Costa Rica, March 1710

Maria Suárez Toro, Kramer, Kinga, and Alannah met Andreas down by the shore near the Punta Cahuita. In this idyllic setting, the waves softly crashed onto the shore. Roosters crowed in the undergrowth. Andreas was poring over ancient cargo lists and comparing old maps of the region with aerial photos of the landscape today.

From her wreck dives so far, Alannah knew all about the history of England, America, Spain, and Holland in the slave trade. But she told Andreas she had no idea Denmark was also involved in trafficking Africans.

Andreas has researched lots of finds, from the Vikings of Denmark onward. He admitted, though, that even experts know little about Denmark and the slave trade. "Actually, I didn't know how large scale we were involved in the slave trade. I couldn't believe when I started looking at what had been written. Scholars believe that two specific slave ships made it to this coast. I think they're right."

"Looking at the material, they left Copenhagen in 1708. *Christianus Quintus* and *Fredericus Quartus*," he continued. "They're going to go to West Africa, to get slaves, and then transport them to the West Indies. When they leave West Africa, they are in bad weather conditions. They're completely lost in open waters for days and days. And they end up about here," Andreas ended, pointing toward the shore.

The *Christianus Quintus*, commanded by Captains Hans Hansen Maas, Jost van de Vogel, and later Anders Pedersen Waerøe, and Captain Dirk Fijfe on the *Fredericus Quartus*, sailed from Copenhagen in December 1708, each with a crew of sixty men. The frigates were owned by the Danish West India Guinea Company, part of its fleet of twenty slavers. Denmark usually sent two ships together—safety in numbers—to cover risks of mutiny, storms, and piracy. In the three decades from 1698, around 9,300 slaves were trafficked on Danish ships to the West Indies.

The frigates were contracted to deliver Africans to the company's vice commander, Jochum von Holten, on the small Danish island colony of Saint Thomas in today's US Virgin Islands. On their arrival at Cape Three Points in West Africa in March 1709, the captains' run of bad luck began. Relations had soured between the Akwamu empire in Ghana and Denmark's governor in Fort Christiansborg at Accra. The *Christianus Quintus* and *Fredericus Quartus* could not find enough captives locally. So, they were forced to hunt people and ivory as far east as Whydah in the Bight of Benin, two hundred miles away.

DANISH FORT CHRISTIANSBORG, GOLD COAST

Sweden built Christiansborg in 1652 to lodge staff and store goods. Denmark bought the land under the lodge from the local Ga Paramount chief, Okaikoi, for 3,200 gold florins ten years later. They upgraded it into a stone fort and called it Fort Christiansborg after

King Christian IV. Enlargements transformed the building into a castle with storage and living space, as well as impregnable defenses.

Christiansborg contained a courtyard, cistern, chapel, "mulatto school," storerooms and living quarters, a bell tower, and twenty-eight defensive cannon. In the castle lived the governor, bookkeeper, physician, and chaplain, protected by a garrison of Danes and Africans. Christiansborg Castle became Denmark's headquarters on the Gold Coast. The Danish transatlantic slave trade ended in March 1792 but was only enforced in 1803. The Danes claimed to be the world's first nation to abolish the trade. Denmark sold Christiansborg to the British for £10,000 in 1850.

Onboard the *Christianus* was an outbound cargo of 2,400 copper manilla bracelets, cloth, metal wares, and weapons to barter for goods. In the lower hold building materials were destined to repair and enlarge the Danish fort on Saint Thomas. The *Fredericus* was stocked with thirty chests of sheets, eight chests of "Dane-guns" especially loved by local rulers, two casks of knives, 1,170 bars of Norwegian and Swedish iron, and nineteen cases of curiosities. Four chests of blue paper would be used to pack West Indies sugar for the home crossing. For the long triangular voyage, the ship's stores included twenty-five thousand pounds of hard bread, three thousand pounds of soft bread, and twenty-two pounds of salted pork.

DANISH ST. THOMAS ISLAND, WEST INDIES

The Virgin Islands were "discovered" in Christopher Columbus's second voyage in 1493. Denmark colonized St. Thomas Island—half a mile long and two and a half miles wide—in 1672, the intended destination of the *Christianus Quintus* and *Fredericus Quartus* frigates' African captives. In 1673 the Danish West Indies Company sent a ship to Guinea to take 103 captives to work the island's cotton, sugar, and indigo plantations and kill-devil rum factories. By 1691 the island had a population of 212 men and women, 177 children, and 555 African slaves. Eighty-seven ships landed captives between 1687 and 1754.

In 1705 the *Cron Printzen* left Fort Christiansborg in Ghana for St. Thomas with 820 Africans, the largest Danish shipment from Guinea to St. Thomas. Smallpox killed many, then a fire broke out in the gunpowder room in the Gulf of Guinea and the ship exploded. Only five men were saved. Two overcrowded Danish slavers reached St. Thomas in 1793, only to be destroyed by a hurricane at the harbor entrance. Nobody survived. The *Frederick III*'s 630 enslaved trafficked in 1696 was the island's largest successful "shipment."

Pirates were a more constant danger than shipwrecks. In the years when the *Christianus* and *Fredericus* sailed, St. Thomas was one of the Americas' most feared pirate lairs, where the likes of Henry Morgan, Henry Avery, William Kidd, Jean Hamlin, and George Bond raided and traded. The colony's early Danish governors cut deals with the pirates to let them use the port and warehouses. Denmark was politically neutral at the time. St. Thomas became a major slave market for all nations across the West Indies.

St. Thomas's harbor in Long Bay was one of the finest of the American islands, at times sheltering two hundred ships. The five-story-high Fort Christian was built in 1689 to house a hundred men. Its four bastions were armed with four cannons. Flag Tower and North Tower looked far out to see for trouble and trade. The governor lived inside the fort "like a viceroy," along with his government and privy council. The island was home to three towns, Charlotte Amalie, the Brandenburgery, and the so-called Negro Village.

At Little Popo in modern Togo, the curse struck again. The *Christianus* was loading captives and elephant tusks when a canoe capsized in the surf, killing the captain, a priest, and a trader. The first mate died soon after from a tropical illness. The inexperienced Anders Pedersen Waerøe, aged in his twenties, was left in command.

The *Fredericus* was also in trouble. The frigate had been delayed so long that the ship's stores were running dry. While boarding captives from Fort Prinsensten in Keta in Ghana, the malnourished and restless Africans broke free of their shackles and attacked their captors on the night of September 13, 1709. The rebellion did not last long. The hands of the mutiny's leader were cut off. Then he was decapitated, his body hanged from the rigging to scare the rest of the Africans into obedience.

PUNISHMENT FOR RUNAWAY SLAVES, DANISH ST. THOMAS

A Danish Royal Council decree, dated January 31, 1733, to stop slaves escaping from St. Thomas (now the US Virgin Islands): "The leader of runaway slaves shall be pinched three times with red-hot iron and then hung. Each other runaway slave shall lose one leg, or if the owner pardon him, shall lose one ear, and receive one hundred and fifty stripes . . . A slave who runs away for eight days, shall have 150 stripes, twelve weeks shall lose a leg, and six months shall forfeit life, unless the owner pardon him with the loss of one leg . . . A slave meeting a white person, shall step aside, and wait until he passes; if not, he may be flogged . . . Witchcraft shall be punished with flogging . . . All dances, feasts, and plays are forbidden unless permission be obtained from the master or overseer."

After months of searching the coast, the *Christianus* took onboard 373 captives (49 percent men, 46 percent women) and the *Fredericus* embarked 433 Africans (52 percent men, 36 percent women). They paid 52–54 silver rix-dollars for a male and 36–40 rix-dollars per woman. The ship was divided into four rooms, twenty-five feet for cargo, and three others separating the men, women, girls and boys, measuring forty-five feet, ten feet, and twenty-two feet, respectively. In these tight spaces, the captives' skin fell off at the elbows, hips, and shoulders rubbing on the deck plank as the ship swayed from side to side.

A temporary wooden space to house the Africans on deck was lashed together from mast to mast. Rigging spars were covered with light matting to let a breeze blow through the makeshift jail, protecting the Africans from sun and rain and stopping them jumping overboard. Near the main mast the crew built a *barricado* from wooden boards, eight feet high, running from port to starboard. Cannon-sized portholes were cut into the barricade, ready for the crew to fire blunderbusses and prevent mutinies if they needed to retreat and protect themselves.

On the deck the captives were exercised, whipped, and forced to dance to music and drumming. The women were given beads to string as a diversion. The crews were under strict orders from the Danish Company directors to treat their captives like small children with regular food, fresh air, and singing and dancing. The Africans were washed and groomed daily to remove vermin, their quarters fumigated with Scandinavian juniper berries. Sexual abuse was supposedly forbidden.

Because they failed to round up the commissioned size of cargo, the ships topped up their hold with one hundred marks of gold and eight thousand pounds of elephant tusks. The troubles hounded them after leaving West Africa in October 1709, when the captains hoped to take on supplies on the Portuguese island of São Tomé. Bad weather made landing dangerous. The ships were forced to head to French-held Cape Lopez in Gabon. When word reached them that France and Denmark were at war, they lifted anchor at once and left without stopping for the West Indies with dwindling rations and many captives ill from malnutrition.

End of the Line

The Bribri teenagers, members of a local dive club, joined the team's discussions, eager to hear what Andreas thought about the legend of their African ancestry. The name of this spot, past and present, was a major clue.

"One of the reasons that we note the two ships could be here," Andreas explained, "is because in the Danish archives the name Carato is mentioned. That was where they ended up, close to the port of Carato. But that doesn't exist. So Carato sounds a lot like our Cahuita, and that is one of the reasons that it could be here. From the historical records, we know that the crews of the *Fredericus* and the *Christianus* anchored the ships close to shore and then mutinied against their captains."

"The conditions on board were horrendous," Andreas went on. "There was no food, no water. And they were afraid to die. The *Fredericus* was set on fire and the crew on the *Christianus* cut the anchor and the ship ran aground. The objects on board sank with the ships and scattered across the ocean floor. Most of the Africans were set ashore. So, these might be some of the first Africans coming to this area and populating it."

Eighteenth-century maps called the area where the jumbled wreckage lies off Cahuita "Pt. Carrett" and "Point Carata." Andreas, Diving With A Purpose, and especially the Bribri youth were hoping that a name sounding like "Cahuita" was not just a coincidence.

In local folklore, the African captives took to the forests. Many were never seen again. Fast-forward half a century to 1757 and Captain Robert Hodgson, the English superintendent on the Mosquito Coast, wrote a different version of the story:

> The natives, or Mosquito people, are of two breeds; one are the original Indian; the other (who are called the Samboes), a mixture of these with negroes, occasioned, so far as can be learned, by two Dutch ships full of them being cast away some years ago to the southward of Nicaragua, from whence the negroes travelled to the Mosquito country, where, after several battles, they had wives and ground given them; since which their posterity are become as numerous as the others, and there is now no distinction either in their rights or customs.

In the Bribri clan system, if a woman had a Black child, it was accepted by everyone and was considered Indigenous, neither Black nor African. The father's ethnicity or skin color made no difference. The Bribri divers were hoping the wreckage off Cahuita and Captain Hodgson's account beat a path to their existence in the here and now.

Salvador van Dyke, one of the Bribri teenagers, had noticed lots of artifacts of all ages off the local coast. He wanted to know, "How can we link all these objects to that time period in which these ships actually shipwrecked here?"

Andreas explained the plan to dive and find clues linking the artifacts by date or origin to the two lost Danish slave wrecks.

Kinga was intrigued by the spidery writing covering a particular historical document open in front of where Andreas was sitting at a table by the shore. "This looks like a cargo list. Is that correct?" she asked, pushing her sunglasses onto the top of her head. Everything stocked on the *Christianus Quintus* and *Fredericus Quartus* was meticulously logged before the ships left port.

"It is," Andreas confirmed. "We can see there's loads of different stuff here. There's pieces of canvas, and there's clothes, handguns, timbers, and bottles of wine and brandy."

"What key pieces of information and evidence do you have in these records that would connect them to these two wrecks?" Kinga inquired.

"There's a lot of artifacts that would survive. The ceramics would survive, the glass bottles that are very specific in this period would survive. That's what we focus on."

Alannah was itching to try and crack the mystery of the ancient cultural debris off Punta Cahuita. "Sounds like we need to go diving!"

SIN CITY

Three and a half centuries ago, Port Royal was the Las Vegas of the Americas. Pirates, cutthroats, and the meanest criminals on the planet squandered up to three thousand "pieces of eight" a night in Sin City on the island of Jamaica. Port Royal was a mecca for selling and exporting goods, making fortunes on the island's 246 sugar plantations, and partying like there was no tomorrow.

Strolling along the quays, newcomers were stunned by the hundreds of ships in harbor; markets full of fresh fish, fruit, and meat; and a hundred ways to be entertained by bear gardens, cockfighting, billiards, music houses, and "all manner of debauchery." "Vile strumpets and common prostratures" beckoned buccaneers from the entrances of alehouses. Goldsmiths, artisans, and traders worked out of two hundred buildings up to four storys high. Every drink imaginable was available in the town said to have a tavern for every ten of its 6,500 residents. Port Royal was the largest and richest English town in the Americas, rivaled only by Boston. Rents were higher than in London, wages three times greater.

Port Royal was everything Europe's rulers feared. Yet its mayhem was all authorized by royal approval. The governors of Jamaica encouraged pirates to frequent the harbor to scare off Spanish and French attacks. The Sodom of the New World grew dirty rich by raiding Spanish shipping. It became the wickedest city in the world. But it also helped create a New World culture.

All along the docks and in the taverns, a unique sight in these unjust times were Black sailors laughing and partying alongside white crews. Jamaica was a bizarre contradiction. The forty-five thousand slaves from mostly Ghana and Nigeria sweating on the sugar plantations by 1703, rising to three hundred thousand by 1800, were the cornerstone of the island's riches. And yet former African captives and escaped African slaves made up 25–30 percent of pirate crews. On the docks of Port Royal, the most unlikely of human experiments played out: equal rights for fellow man, and damn where he came from.

Next to human captives, slave ships carried gold, ivory, and untold exotic wonders. Slave ships were big investments, and the lure of their booty attracted pirate attacks. Pirates started ransacking European trade along the coast of West Africa in 1683. Their disruptive powers peaked during Queen Anne's War between France and England from 1702 to 1713. Around six hundred pirates chased glory off West Africa, taking more than one hundred slave ships.

Many of the great pirate boats started out as slavers. Blackbeard's flagship, armed with forty cannons, the *Queen Anne's Revenge*, had been a French Guinea trader from Nantes heading to Martinico called the the *Concorde*. In its hold Edward Thatch (aka Blackbeard) found 516 enchained Africans from Whydah in Benin. Black Sam Bellamy's own flagship, the *Whydah Gally*, had sold six hundred Africans and Jamaicans and was heading home to London with its payout of gold, silver, and jewels when the pirates seized it. John Bowen's *Speaker*, a former five-hundred-ton, fifty-cannon French warship, was a slave ship before he took it in Madagascar.

Pirates lived outside the law. Some ran away from slavery; others fled the fear of being forcibly press-ganged into Europe's navies. In common they refused to be treated like disposable objects. Sam Bellamy especially hated "snivelling Puppies, who allow Superiors to kick them about Deck at Pleasure." In Charles Johnson's *The History of the Pyrates* (1728), Captain Mission set out the pirates' vision from the deck of another seized slave ship:

> That no Man had Power of the Liberty of another . . . That for
> his own part he had not exempted his Neck from the galling
> Yoke of slavery, and asserted his own Liberty, in order to
> enslave others. That however these Men were distinguished
> from the Europeans by their Colour, Customs, or Religious
> Rites, they were the Work of the same Omnipotent Being,

and endued with equal Reason: Wherefore he desired they might be treated like Free men (for he would banish even the name of Slavery from among them).

Captain Mission was a fictitious pirate who founded the ultimate pirate democracy on the African island of Libertalia. The real Libertalia was Madagascar in eastern Africa, beyond the Cape of Good Hope, frequented by Henry Avery and Captain William Kidd and where pirates found sanctuary and married local women.

On the decks of the pirate ships of Samuel Bellamy, Edward England, Blackbeard, and Olivier La Bouche, up to one third of the crew members were Black—eighty-eight Africans among Bartholomew "Black Bart" Roberts's crew of 368, and 60 Africans in Blackbeard's crew in 1717. Blacks like Diego de Los Reyes, Ipseiodawas, John Mapoo, and Diego Grillo earned enough respect from crew members to be voted leaders of pirate ships. Abraham Samuel worked as a quartermaster, and Caesar, a former slave owned by Tobias Knight of North Carolina, was a Black officer with Blackbeard.

The counterculture born on the decks of pirate ships made them the most color-blind places in the world. Crews like on the *Whydah Gally* included English, Irish, Scottish, Welsh, French, Dutch, Spanish, Swedish, Native American, African American, and African men, all enjoying revolutionary liberty, equality, and fraternity. Black pirates had the right to bear arms, voted with the rest of the crew—one man, one vote—got an equal share of treasure and, when caught, were hanged next to their brothers in arms.

Many of the Golden Age of Piracy's big names—Henry Morgan, Calico Jack Rackham, Anne Bonny, and Mary Read—cut their teeth in Jamaica. Near the entrance to Port Royal, Rackhams Cay remembers the spot where he was hanged at Gallows Point. Calico Jack was left in a cage as a warning to would-be copycat offenders. And somewhere in its waters lies Bartholomew Roberts's pirate ship the *Ranger*, sunk in a hurricane of 1722.

It was in Jamaica, among the vice dens of Sin City, that enslaved Africa helped plant the first seeds of democracy in the Americas.

AFRICATOWN

Africatown—Near Mobile, Alabama

People were not all that was brought from Africa during the trans-atlantic slave trade. Their knowledge came with them. Knowledge that helped give birth to the world we live in, even though few recognize the roots of so much musical, culinary, and mathematical inspiration. The talents, traditions, and memories of the enslaved Africans helped create the culture of the New World in fresh ways that we are only now beginning to fathom.

Today, Africatown looks like many sleepy places on the western coast of Alabama. Kids play pickup basketball games in backyards behind wooden-shuttered one-story homes. Look carefully and something unusual stirs. On the approach between the town and the port city of Mobile, a mural of a ship welcomes visitors along Bay Bridge Road. The white-hulled schooner with three masts skimming over choppy blue seas is the *Clotilda*.

Africatown was started from scratch by captives forcefully trafficked on the *Clotilda*, the last illegal slave ship to arrive in America in the summer of 1860. Five years after 110 men and women were stowed in its swift hull—on the back of a bet—the end of the American Civil War set them free. Without the money or support to make their way home, they started the first purely African town in America.

In the heart of Africatown, a bronze bust proudly celebrates the tough life of Cudjo Lewis, one of its founders. Cudjo lived through times of monumental change in America, World War I, and the Great Depression. His defining challenge was being trafficked at age nineteen from his home among the Yoruba people in Benin on the *Clotilda*. Cudjo was born Kossola (Kazoola)—meaning "my children do not die any more"—in the town of Bantè in Dahomey. Kazoola was the last human to be locked into America's last slave ship and died in 1935, one of the crossing's last survivors. He had gone from being the grandson of an officer of a king in Africa, singled out to train as a "special ops" soldier, handling his town's justice and security, to being forced into the lowest state of being, slavery in America. Kazoola was the last survivor of a group of people who were born in Africa, trafficked to the New World, enslaved, liberated and experienced Jim Crow laws in the American South.

People always talk about the transatlantic slave trade as if it is ancient history. But it is living memory. Black-and-white photos of Kazoola wearing his Sunday best still exist. Piecing together the traumatic exodus of most slave ship captives, taken in tribal raids, crossing the Middle Passage, and forcibly settled in the Americas is a tall order. Few wanted to remember or knew how to write about it.

Fragments of oral memory endure for the millions sold into slavery and their descendants. The surviving stories of a few successful Africans—Olaudah Equiano, Ottobah Cugoano, and Venture Smith—can be counted on one hand. Next to nothing is known about the lives and hopes of the ordinary millions. Which makes the *Clotilda* crucial to US and world history. A tremendous amount of information came from the trials of the *Clotilda* Africans in their own words.

America's Last Slave Ship

Timothy Meaher thought he could laugh at the law all the way to the bank. Which is exactly what he did. America banned the transatlantic slave trade on January 1, 1808. Decades later, plantation owners and speculating merchants were still busting open loopholes to keep Africa's forced labor flowing.

The Meaher brothers moved to Alabama from Maine to strike it rich in Mobile, the second greatest exporter of white gold—cotton—in America after New Orleans. The city's steep profits were earned from a single moneyspinning product. As a Massachusetts journalist wrote of Mobile in the 1850s, "People live in cotton houses and ride in cotton carriages. They buy cotton, they sell cotton, think cotton, eat cotton, drink cotton, and dream cotton. They marry cotton wives, and unto them are born cotton children . . . It is the great staple—the sum and substance of Alabama."

Meaher and his brothers James and Burns had fingers in the whole supply chain: a plantation, shipyard, and steamships. Throughout the 1850s, Mobile had been the slave-trading emporium of Alabama, a slave society at the center of the South's internal slave trade. After the ban on slavery came in, the state's fields ran the risk of being emptied of muscle. Mobile needed to find cheaper workers faster. Male African slaves already working in America were selling at an all-time high of $2,400 in 1860, about $49,000 in today's money, a 100 percent hike on prices a decade earlier.

Timothy Meaher did not believe the ban on the transatlantic slave trade could hold. He put his money where his mouth was, betting "a thousand dollars that inside two years I myself can bring a shipful of n-----s right into Mobile Bay under the officers' noses." He just laughed when his friends warned he would end up hanged.

THE *CLOTILDA*

- The *Clotilda*, the Americas' last slave ship
- One-deck schooner, two masts, copper-sheathed hull, twelve-man crew
- 26.2 meters long, 7.0 meters wide, 120 tons
- Owned by William Foster
- Normally used in the timber trade
- Commissioned for the slave trade by Timothy Meaher

- Left Mobile Bay, Alabama, in March 1860, carrying $9,000 in gold to buy slaves
- Reached Whydah, Bight of Benin, May 1860
- Loaded 110 captives, returned to Mobile Bay, July 1860
- *Clotilda*'s captives founded Africatown, 1866

Meaher supposedly invested $35,000 in the *Clotilda* and commissioned William Foster, its original owner, to give it a thorough makeover. Tall masts and broad sails were added to turn the schooner into more of a racing yacht, able to outrun pirate ships and the Royal Navy. Water, rice, beef, pork, sugar, flour, bread, and eighty casks of "n----r rum" were stored in the lowest hold to feed the twelve-man crew for four months and, on the way back, up to 130 Africans, for eight weeks. The "slave food" was hidden under a cargo of timber ready to be turned into platforms, partitions, and beds for captives in Africa. Foster was handed $3,500 in trade goods and $9,000 (about $185,000 today) in gold to buy 125 Africans. The captain sailed off with false papers and the flags of various nations to hide the ship's true intentions.

Meaher no doubt read with great curiosity in the November 9, 1858, edition of the *Mobile Register* how "The King of Dahomey was driving a brisk trade in slaves, at from $50 to $60 each, at Wydah." King Ghezo of the Fon people may have had his arm twisted by British forces to sign a treaty abolishing the slave trade, but the cash brought in from local palm oil was small potatoes. Cuba's hunger for illegally trafficked Africans persuaded Ghezo to rip up the 1852 peace treaty. And so the *Clotilda* headed for Whydah in Dahomey at the heart of the Slave Coast in July 1860, anchoring offshore six weeks after leaving Alabama.

The ship's timing was lucky for the Americans. King Ghezo was shot dead while on a military campaign the year before. His son, King Glèlè (named Badohun, which meant "terror in the bush"), sacked enemy towns with his twelve-thousand-strong army to avenge his father's death. Anyone trying to flee through town gates was decapitated, their heads hanged on the belts of Fon warriors, Kazoola remembered. The rest of the captives of the massacre were "yoked by forked sticks and tied in a chain," then marched three days to Whydah near the Bight of Benin and locked up in wooden pens.

William Foster offered the "ebony prince" in charge of trade in Whydah $100 each to buy 125 people. Eight days later, permission was given. America's last cargo of illegal Africans were farmers, fishermen, and traders mostly captured by the Dahomey army. The rest were refugees and victims of kidnappings. Some worshipped Islam, others tribal Vodun, Orisha, or nothing. They came from Benin and Nigeria. All the different cultures, histories, religions, and languages were locked up in one slave pen. The strangers were as foreign to each other as the countries of Europe are today. They all spoke different tongues.

The identities of the enslaved were taken away. Their heads would have been shaved to stop outbreaks of lice at sea, a humiliating cultural violation. Africans' hair—sculpted, shaved, twisted, braided, rolled, woven, and adorned with beads, gold, silver, feathers, grass, combs, pins, seeds, and shells—were windows into identity. Hairstyles marked at a glance ethnicity, family, social status, and professions. The captives' names were taken away, too. Gumpa from the Fon tribe became Peter Lee and Kanko of the Yoruba, Lottie Dennison.

Crossing the Middle Passage took forty-five days. The captives remembered that the loud banging of the water against the *Clotilda*'s hull and thunderous wind in the sails sounded like "a thousand beasts" in the bush. The Africans felt that the ship was constantly rolling high up to the sky and then to the bottom of the ocean. Only after thirteen days in the Middle Passage were the cramped captives eventually allowed on deck to stretch their legs.

The arrival of the illegal slaves in Mobile was an open secret, a daring raid that made Alabama proud. The *Macon Daily Telegraph* told its readers how the *Clotilda* "moved 110 Africans onto a steamboat and headed up the river." A Louisiana newspaper, the *Delta*, reported on the "secret landing" behind the islands in Mississippi Sound near the lower end of Mobile Bay. A tug pulled the schooner to Twelvemile Island.

There the Africans were transferred onto the steamboat the R.B. *Taney* and taken up the Alabama River to a plantation below Mount Vernon. Eleven days later the captives were marched onto the steamer *Commodore* and taken down to where the Alabama and Tombigbee Rivers met and where Burns Meaher had a plantation. The Africans were separated into two long rows, men in one, women in the other. Some couples were bought together and taken to Selma. The rest were divided between the Meaher brothers and Foster. The slaves were then set to work.

Timothy Meaher was arrested and accused of illegal slaving. Under oath he swore he never sailed on the *Clotilda*, which was technically correct, even if he owned the ship and was the brains behind the scheme. Meaher was released on bail with little fuss. Judge William G. Jones was a friend, after all, in whose honor Meaher had even named a steamer. Meaher laughed about his adventures for years to come, just as he had predicted. Meaher and William Foster became local heroes.

After slavery was abolished, the *Clotilda*'s slaves started saving up enough cash to buy the land they were renting from Meaher and other local plantation owners. The men sweated in sawmills and the railroads. The women grew and sold vegetables in Mobile. The dream of Africatown, a haven away from white supremacy, became a reality in 1866. As the only African nobleman and courtier, Gumpa—now Peter Lee—was chosen to lead the new community.

How many Africans were illegally imported into America nobody can say for sure. Figures vary wildly from fifteen thousand to one million. The Meaher family still owns huge swathes of property around Mobile, valued at over $25 million. They never admitted their role in America's last transatlantic slave crossing. To many, the voyage of the *Clotilda* was nothing more than a hoax.

Keeping Tune

In Africatown the *Clotilda*'s former slaves grew their own food and built their own community, not in the American way but based on their homeland traditions. The community had everything it needed; a grocery store, a doctor, school, and entertainment. Africatown was a proud town of twelve thousand people. Today just two thousand remain, the *Clotilda*'s descendants scattered far and wide in the big cities.

Now the local community is reviving Africatown. If you head down to Kazoola Eatery & Entertainment on Dauphin Street, the soul of Africa lives on in food and music. Bare brick warehouse walls remember the area's commercial cotton past. Kazoola is a place to inspire, to remember the story of a community that endured so much.

Just as Africatown does not run from its past, Kazoola questions what we think we know about America's cultural inheritance from Africa. If you are lucky you might pick up Grammy Award–winning Rhiannon Giddens making the banjo sing in a late-night session. Most people think the banjo was an American instrument plucked on veranda porches by white hillbillies spitting tobacco. Folklore credits Joel Sweeney from Appomattox County in Virginia as its inventor in the early 1830s before he gave the first public performance and toured Europe.

Rhiannon Giddens has a very different take. She grew up seeing white people play the banjo and finding it cool, but not part of her culture. Later she came across musical recordings of Black musicians playing the same instrument. The more she dug into the banjo's background, the more she realized it had an ocean-spanning legacy. Long before the modern banjo became a metallic instrument to play bluegrass, it was an African and then an African-American instrument. The very emblem of being Black was the banjo.

It was only in the 1820s and 1830s that white folks started getting tuned into the banjo and paid a backhanded acknowledgement of its inspiration in blackface performances. For sixty years, blackface minstrel shows entertained middle-class America. Much earlier, the banjo, bluegrass music, and the do-si-do danced to it were brought to America by African captives trafficked on slave ships. Black folk music and musicians would inspire and teach the first generation of minstrel banjoists, including Sweeney, Billy Whitlock, and Dan Emmett, who made the song "Dixie" world famous.

Early travelers saw the banjo in its original setting in Africa as early as 1621, where it was "made of a great gourd, and a necke thereunto fastnd." A slave dealer named Nicholas Owen heard an instrument made of wood and played by the people of Sierra Leone in the mid–eighteenth century that sounded "like a bad fiddle . . . called a Bangelo." The "banza" or "banjer" was already the instrument of choice on slave plantations from Martinique to Virginia in the 1670s and 1680s, especially after the drum was banned by estate owners as slaves' potentially warlike call to arms.

Early America found the banjo greatly fascinating. On Sundays at "Negro Balls," "these poor creatures . . . generally meet together and amuse themselves with Dancing to the Banjo. This musical instrument (if it may be so called) is made of a Gourd something in the imitation of a Guitar, with only four strings and played with the fingers in the same manner. Some of them sing to it, which is very droll music indeed," wrote Nicholas Creswell of Maryland in 1774. To white ears, the rude African banjo grated. In Richmond, Virginia, Thomas Fairfax felt in 1799 that the banjo's "wild notes of melody seem to Correspond with the state of Civilization of the Country where this species of music originated."

Banjos and fiddles left a deeper impression on Mary Livermore, a governess on a Virginia plantation around 1847, who never forgot a Black dance and the lyrics chanted to accompany it:

> Now all dis week will be as gay As am de Chris'mas time;
> We'll dance all night, a' all de day, An' make de banjo chime;
> Wi' 'nuff t' eat an' 'nuff t' drink, An' not a bit t' pay!
> So shet youah mouf as close as def
> An' all you n-----s, hol' youah bref,
> An' hear de banjo chime!

Today the *Clotilda*'s descendants still celebrate the banjo being played in Kazoola's bar in Africatown. Rhiannon Giddens and her fellow musicians never forget this place's historical and cultural link to the last ship sent over to America. Most African Americans have no idea where their families came from," Rhiannon knows, "but musically, I know my lineage," she says. "There's more than one way to be connected to who we are as a community. It's not just blood."

Just as the banjo's African inspiration is increasingly appreciated, the truth behind America's last illegal slave voyage is now undeniable. The wreck of the *Clotilda* was finally discovered in 2019 near Twelvemile Island, just north of the Mobile Bay delta.

The ship really existed. It was no hoax. The whole world can now understand its plight.

CAHUITA'S CARPET
OF TREASURE

The Bribri teenagers were decked out in shorts, flip-flops, baseball caps, and gold earrings. Theirs, though, was a unique blend of African and Central American identity and culture. From their inland hideaway they set out to show Alannah, Kramer, and Kinga the shore where they believe their African ancestors were wrecked and waded to a new world. The ships may have sunk, but the captives found sanctuary.

In the shallows of Punta Cahuita on the east coast of Costa Rica, the Bribri youth had noticed a perplexing carpet of treasures that might shed light on where they came from. They wanted to understand how these far-flung goods got there and what they tell us about the sunken past.

"We are searching to discover how my ancestors came here. And to know where we came from," Anderson Rodriguez told the Florida dive team.

Kevin Rodriguez Brown added that "Trying to find these ships means a lot to us because we will get to know the history these people brought. And that history becomes our culture."

Salvador Van Dyke also hoped that whatever was out there in the Punta Cahuita could finally give a voice to the escaped African ancestors.

Guided by the Bribri teenagers, Diving With A Purpose started snorkeling around Cahuita Bay to get familiar with the underwater terrain. Everyone needed to swim carefully. This stretch of the southern Caribbean is protected. Cahuita National Park controls 2,732 acres of land and 55,200 acres of sea. On land, sloths blink at white-headed capuchin monkeys watched by kingfishers and toucans. Underwater, five hundred species of fish and orca whales make merry. Cahuita was the most stunning and least spoiled waters where Diving With A Purpose had chased slave ships so far. White beaches poured into the Caribbean's turquoise sea.

Alannah, Kramer, and Kinga had joined up with some of Diving With A Purpose's founding figures. In orange shorts and cap, the skipper of the *Gumbe* pulled the throttle. The *Sinac* motored alongside. It was a short commute: the dive site turned out to be just a few hundred meters offshore.

Kinga expected Cahuita to be an easy and fun dive. Gently undulating water in the warm Caribbean, mildly overcast skies, and a shallow seabed. What was not to like? The problem was that the survey area was huge and for more than three hundred years tides and storms had mixed artifacts lost over the centuries all over the reefs. What could have slipped off the Danish frigates, and not English or American ships, needed to be expertly picked apart.

Shafts of light lit up the top layer of Caribbean water like a chandelier, but even in just three meters' depth, swirling algae and silt made detecting any wreckage challenging. Kramer could not help but worry whether the hunt for the *Christianus Quintus* and *Fredericus Quartus* would turn into another *Leusden*.

"We can barely see anything down here. The visibility is so bad," Alannah told the surface team after a quick snorkel. The team persevered, flashlights in hand. Above the waves it was day. Below an eternal night enveloped the sunken secrets.

Kramer focused on making the most of what visibility existed. After the horrendous conditions of the English Channel and Suriname's Maroni River, this was still a breeze. He reminded the team of the prize. "Our job is to discover if there are any remains of two Danish slave ships left behind."

Whether the folklore was true or just a tall story, whether the *Christianus Quintus* and the *Fredericus Quartus* ever made it to these shores, depended on what wreckage Diving With A Purpose could find. The very identity of a group of young people depended on it.

The Wrong Turn

In 1709, the situation on the Danish frigates had gone from bad to worse. They left the Guinea coast in September 1709. The plan to take on supplies in Barbados before starting the final outbound leg to St. Thomas was abandoned after the *Christianus* and the *Fredericus* missed the British colony by sailing three degrees too far north. By November, provisions were dangerously low. Panic was setting in when an island was spotted. A boat from Jamaica fishing for sea turtles told the crew the island was Providence, modern Santa Catalina between Jamaica and Nicaragua.

More bad news. Providence was the base for English pirates and their Mosquito Coast Indian allies slave raiding the coasts of Costa Rica and Nicaragua, 125 miles away. The notorious pirate Henry Morgan had used Providence to raid Panama in 1670. If the present band of pirates heard about two shiploads of African slaves, the Danish crews could expect a sticky end. The ships had made landfall 300 miles from their intended destination. Lacking cash for supplies, they made do with turtle meat the Jamaicans gave them and got the heck out of these waters on February 19, 1710.

A new plan was hatched. St. Thomas was forgotten. Instead, on February 19, 1710, the captains set course for Portobelo in Panama. Strong currents and bad weather soon made a mockery of this plan, too. The frigates missed Portobelo by over five hundred miles. A Danish Court later decided that the captains schemed all along to sail to Panama and sell the Company's slaves at a higher price, pocketing the profits.

Lost among shark- and pirate-infested waters, Jamaican fishermen eventually piloted the frigates into the bay of Punta Caretto off Costa Rica. This latest unexpected stopover was no safer than Providence. British and Dutch privateers-turned-pirates, like the dreaded Henry Avery, Edward Mansfield, Edward Collier, Laurens de Graf, and Laurens Prins, had haunted these Caribbean shores rich with cacao haciendas. British masters were known to pay top dollar for African labor. They did not ask where the enslaved came from. In the year when the *Christianus* and *Fredericus* anchored off Costa Rica, cocoa exports to Europe were at an all-time high, all on the back of Black slave labor.

The Danish ships were now uncomfortably close to the lucrative cocoa estates of the Matina Valley. There, pirates and Miskito Indians raided and traded slaves. A charismatic Miskito king called Jeremy, sixty years old and six feet tall, with hair hanging down to his shoulders and a voice like a bear, was thick as thieves with British merchants. Jeremy was contracted to "hunt Negroes."

COSTA RICAN COCOA, FOOD OF THE GODS

Venezuela's cacao plantations at Caracas started declining in the mid-seventeenth century just when the West's love affair with cacao took off. New sources of chocolate included Porto Limón in Costa Rica's Matina Valley, which the local governor called "the best cacao groves ever seen." Around 140,000 cacao trees ringed the valley in the late seventeenth century. Annual crops might reach 107 tons of beans. Other haciendas flourished in the Barbilla and Reventazón Valleys. Chocolate became the region's biggest moneymaker.

Plantation owners hired Spaniards, Blacks, and mulattos at two pesos a day—more than soldiers earned—paid in cacao, clothing, or other goods. African slave numbers rose by 48 percent in the 1700s to service a mini boom in Costa Rica's cacao trade. The strongest men cleared the thick forests; the less robust watered, shaded, and weeded plants. The average farmer owned 1,900 trees.

Compared to the Americas' sugar plantations, conditions were less severe in Costa Rica. Slaves lived in their own wood and palm thatch houses and ate plantains, oranges, avocados, and sapote fruit. Africans from Guinea introduced traditional rice cultivation to the area and owned rice fields. Because cacao beans were legal tender on Costa Rica, slaves had easy access to money. Slaves also transported cacao crops to the coast of Cartago for sale to Dutch, English, and Miskito-Zambo Indigenous group.

Cacao beans exported from sixty-two ports from Mexico to Central America hooked the West. Cardinal Richelieu of France used chocolate as a drug to cure "the vapors of his spleen." It also treated infectious diseases. Cacao beans were traded into Massachusetts Bay by 1668, and chocolate almonds went on sale in French confectioners about the same time.

Italian immigrant Francesco Bianchi opened White's Cocoa House next to St. James's Palace in London in 1693. Women thought chocolate was an aphrodisiac and sipped the drink in the bedroom. By 1701 chocolate was being drunk and eaten in cakes across the West. In the 1720s England imported around 230,854 pounds of cacao beans a year. Rich and pleasurable, the eighteenth-century scientist Carl Linnaeus called cacao the food of the gods.

The Danish frigates were critically low on food supplies, and the Danes were deep in Jeremy-hunting land. The crews were rattled. They demanded the African captives be released to save the provisions and what food was left be divided among them. They also wanted a month's pay to jump ship and pay their way to safety. When the captains refused, the crews threatened mutiny.

Events were fast getting out of hand. Captain Dirk Fijfe had no option but to release the slaves of the two ships "against my better judgment." On March 4, 1710, the Africans vanished into the bush. It was too little too late. The mutiny was on. The crew smashed open the company's chests holding African gold and counted it out among themselves. To hide the crime and cover their tracks, they burnt the *Fredericus Quartus* down to the waterline. The boatswain on the *Christianus Quintus* landed the crew on the beach and cut the ship's anchor cable, leaving the frigate to break up in the surf.

A Jamaican ship took the crew to Portobelo, the captains forcefully traveling with them. Costa Rican colonists rounded up 105 of the Danish frigates' Africans and auctioned them to the local plantation owners. The rest—approximately 700 souls—were never seen again.

Officers' Wine

Searching for the remains of the Danish ships, the team snorkel-dived up and down until they were drunk with dizziness, their faces peering inches above the seabed searching for anything out of the normal. The water felt eerie, silent, and foreboding, unlike the forest so full of light, noise, and life. It was as if the divers could sense that something terrible happened in these waters.

The underwater visibility here is tricky any time of year. On exceptional days, dozens of species of fish flit across light yellow brain, elkhorn, and blue staghorn corals. Sea fans and gorgonians dance in the shallows. Ever since an earthquake in 1991, though, Cahuita's thirty-five types of coral beds have been fighting for survival.

Earthquakes had uplifted a large section of coral reef by about ten feet. At low tide it became exposed to air and sun and rapidly died. When it rains the visibility drops to a few feet as silt floods down in the Estrella River, a threat on the rise caused by the legal and illegal logging of inland forests. The stripped mountain slopes erode swiftly and end up offshore, blocking the sunlight the reefs need to survive.

Even on endlessly sunny days, the reefs are endangered. Too much fertilizer from the local banana plantations creates vast blooms of plankton that again block the sunlight and poison the water. Seven of Cahuita's thirty-four coral species have disappeared. Both reefs and old ships have been wrecked and need saving.

Alannah was for calling it a day and returning to the Robinson Crusoe beach to chill out. Just then Anderson Rodriguez whooped with delight. The divers made their way to where the top of a black glass bottle, its base snapped off, was perched on top of the reef. Kinga and Anderson high-fived underwater. This was more like it.

Kamau Sadiki, a lead instructor with Diving With A Purpose, took a good look and later told the Bribri teenagers that "What we've found here could be significant. It looks like a period bottle. This brown in color, seems like it might have some manufacturing defects on it. But, it's definitely not a modern bottle."

Did the bottle once hold wine drunk by the officers of the *Christianus Quintus* and the *Fredericus Quartus*? Did the date and style fit?

Fanning out from the bottle a carpet of finds started to appear. One discovery led to another. Half of a buff-colored ceramic plate, possibly Spanish, then an intact champagne bottle and a slice of a white dish with a blue border made in Staffordshire in England. The finds were hard to read and could date anywhere between the seventeenth and nineteenth centuries. The next find looked more promising, the lower half of a fancy, must-have stoneware jug decorated with cobalt blue flowers made in the great pottery kilns of Westerwald in the German Rhineland. All European shipping used these fancy table wares. Right time, right place.

Dr. Melody Garrett, a Diving With A Purpose instructor, was impressed. "I've never really seen so many artifacts scattered around in the same place," she told the team.

Anderson Rodriguez was buzzing. "You cannot see very well," he admitted, "but we found many pottery pieces, bottles. I'm very emotional because it's something new and I hope we can keep finding things."

Kramer agreed and felt that "Archaeologically speaking, this is a treasure trove right here. Items all over the place, so now is the time where we need to get back in and start to document and report these things."

From the one snorkel dive it was clear that, despite its remote setting, a great deal of maritime traffic visited the Punta Cahuita over the years. The big question was: Were the finds from two Danish slave ships? Were the discoveries junk, slung overboard by passing ships, or wreckage? Kinga was cautious but optimistic, telling the team that "We don't yet know whether these artifacts are from the slave ships we're trying to identify but finding so many so close together is a giant step forward."

The four small dive boats floated peacefully on a flat sea lit up by a golden sun. Costa Rica was sharing a final light show before night fell. It was time to pack up, collect thoughts, and plan the next day's dive. Would the *Christianus* and the *Fredericus* give up their jealously guarded secrets?

Reading Pottery

Andreas and Melody set themselves up in a sandwich shop, surrounded by tropical trees, to examine photos of the sunken finds scattered across Cahuita National Park on her computer. Melody was still trying to pick apart the meaning of the many artifacts recorded on the last dive. Only Andreas would be able to tell if they matched the two Danish slave ships that may have introduced enslaved Africans into Bribri culture.

"What do you think?" Melody eagerly asked about the white broken piece of ceramic plate with a blue rim border.

Andreas hardly hesitated, reading the past like most people read books. "This plate? I'm quite sure that that is after 1850. So, it's not related to the wrecks," he started out on a low.

Next Melody asked about a gray-and-blue German jug.

"Could be from the right period," Andreas mused, not sold on the date. "It could also be 150, 180 years more modern."

The photo of the jug was now changed for the broken bottle neck spotted by Anderson Rodriguez. Andreas's eyes widened. "Oh, this is an interesting bottle. It's difficult to see in this photo, but it looks like it has the shape of an onion bottle. One of the things that we know from the cargo list is that we have sixty-six bottles of La Combe Brûlée wine. And we also know that we have French brandy."

Andreas ran his finger down the cargo list for the *Christianus Quintus* and *Fredericus Quartus*, tapping the entries showing the crates of Burgundy's finest shipped for sale in the Americas.

"So, this particular piece is quite promising then," Melody checked.

"This is definitely an interesting object," he confirmed.

The finds carpeting Cahuita's shallows were promising but no slam dunk. Artifacts from so many time periods all mixed together made it impossible to be certain any came from the Danish ships. Time to change tack. Andreas decided the team needed to focus on one very specific signature object that could only have come from Denmark.

The Danish marine archaeologist shared his thoughts with Melody, Alannah, Kramer, Maria, and Kinga. "We know that there are all these different types of cargo, handguns, and there's bottles of wine and brandy. But one thing that is very specifically Danish is the yellow brick."

Hoping for something more glamorous, Kinga was at first taken aback. "The yellow brick?" she enquired.

Andreas explained that the archives showed that Danish frigates like the *Christianus* and *Fredericus* typically carried around forty thousand bricks. The thousands of Danish yellow bricks doubled up as ballast and saleable cargo to sell to the European colonies in the West Indies.

Alannah also struggled to grasp what made bricks a big deal. "What would make the bricks 'Danish'?" she checked.

"The size of Danish bricks was very specific," Andreas explained, pulling an example out of his rucksack. This was classic archaeological sleuthing. Often it is not the statement pieces, silver coins or gold bars, that catch the imagination, but the humblest everyday object.

The team handled the brick while Andreas laid out how "This is a brick found in Denmark. This size is specifically Danish. And it's very often that they're yellow. If you were to find bricks of this size and this color, then it would definitely be a smoking gun."

"There would be a lot of bricks?" Alannah asked.

"Probably not going to look like a gigantic pile of forty thousand bricks, but it will be sort of a substantial area of bricks," Andreas said without being able to go into specifics. After three hundred years being battered on the seabed, nobody could tell for sure what the brick pile would look like today.

Bricks were not what Kinga expected the case nailing the discovery of the *Christianus* and *Fredericus*, and the emotional question of Bribri origins, to hinge on. She cleared her mind and refocused. "So, this is what we're looking for. This will be our smoking gun. Ok, follow the yellow brick road," she said to the brick and smiled at her dive buddies.

SOUL FOOD

Jekyll Island, Georgia, is where the second to last slave ship made landfall in the United States. In November 1858 the *Wanderer* brought in 409 people from Angola. Like in the *Clotilda* years, the transatlantic slave trade was illegal. Little wonder its captain chose this well-hidden marsh covered with eel grass and wild rice to dock his cargo and sell the Africans across the Deep South.

Today on Jekyll Island's wild and serene beaches visitors leave their cares at the causeway and film directors check in to shoot the likes of *X-Men* and *Magic Mike*. It is also home to activist, farmer, and chef Matthew Raiford, who learned his trade in the finest international schools of cuisine. Since childhood, he always knew a different way to cook. Not the European way but what he picked up from his grandmother—and *that* was much tastier.

After a military career, and then plying and teaching his trade far and wide, Matthew returned to his family farm on Jekyll Island to celebrate African American culture through food. He learned to cook from his father, who learned from his mother. She used to pick up discarded chicken gizzards from a local slaughterhouse and spice them up with pepper and salt to fry. For Matthew, traditional home cooking—African cooking—is medicine.

He lives on the family farm on land the Raifords have owned since 1874. They are still working the soil today the old ways. Matthew cooks the Gullah Geechee way. Gullah Geechee culture is part of his heritage. It's an African tradition that took root on the Sea Islands along the Atlantic coast of Georgia, Florida, and North and South Carolina. During the

Civil War, white plantation owners fled in fear of former slaves seeking revenge. The African population that was left on its own was forced to hone its survival skills. How do you make a living with no education and are stuck on a barrier island? It was at places like Jekyll Island that much of what the world sees today as Southern cuisine was invented by enslaved and then freed Africans.

Despite being shackled and torn from everything they knew crossing the Atlantic, the culture Africans brought across the waves included their cuisine—spices, salts, and cookery methods. The exiles often carried not just memories but a piece of home with them, braiding seeds into their hair. They planted what looked like ornaments in their new destinations. Every time they ate, the exiles could remember home, preserve a piece of their identity. Gullah cuisine is made up of many ingredients brought west with Africans, including rice, sweet peas, and okra.

The bridge between food preparing and cooking in West Africa and in America survives underwater. An African grindstone turned up on the wreck of the *Fredensborg*, a Danish West India Company ship lost off Tromøy in southern Norway in 1768. Strange ceramic griddle pans and cooking pots went down on the 1622 Spanish fleet off the Florida Keys and Straits of Florida. Their shapes are identical to potting traditions in Ghana and Nigeria. Even on Spanish galleons sailing between Seville, Colombia, and Havana, slaves forced to sweat below deck in kitchen galleys kept their distinct cultural cooking preferences alive for soups and stews.

The Gullah cuisine mastered by Matthew Raiford is one of the oldest world traditions practiced in America today. From South Carolina and Georgia to Jacksonville in Florida, Gullah people from Angola working coastal plantations farmed lima beans and tomatoes, raised pigs, and cooked with oysters, turtles, and shrimp. And into African dishes they mixed peanuts, okra, rice, yams, peas, hot peppers, sorghum, and watermelon. Gullah cuisine has been kept alive and kicking by these cultural exchanges since the mid–eighteenth century. And the Africans also cultivated rice like they were back home on the Rice Coast of Liberia, Sierra Leone, Senegal, Gambia, and Guinea.

Okra and gumbo, the flagship dish of New Orleans, may be a signature dish connected with the American South, but it was made in West

Africa. Louisiana's jambalaya gets its name from *ya-ya*, the West African word for rice. The South's one-pot wonders also owe deep cultural thanks to the Gullah's *dafa*, "cook everything" culinary tradition.

A large part of West African cuisine's survival was the result of women keeping the home fires burning. Emeline Jones was born into servitude around 1840 as the daughter of a slave on the estate of Colonel Benedict William Hall at Eutaw in Maryland. After being trained as a house servant, she was freed before the Civil War by Hall's daughter. Jones made her way, dreaming, to the mean streets of New York.

From working as a private chef for an insurance executive at the Club House in Long Branch, New Jersey, Jones rose to feeding Presidents Garfield, Arthur, and Cleveland at the Carlton Club, where one of her appetizer specialties was crab gumbo and okra soup. On the back of presidential stamps of approval, the White House tried to poach her. One of Emeline's greatest inspirations was introducing the fried potato chip to America from her restaurant in Moon's Lake House in Saratoga, New York.

Today, Matthew Raiford cooks homestyle, vegetarian paella with sweet potato leaves, Cherokee Purple tomatoes, and Sea Island red peas. For diners preferring a bit of bite he adds sapelo clams harvested right off Jekyll Island. These tastes and traditions, typically thought of as the food of the poor or slaves, is big business. In modern Charleston, Gullah cooking lives on in hipster dishes. Every city in the United States is competing to run the best Southern restaurant. And what are they serving? Rice, peas, and fried gizzards. Along with this adoration of soul food there is a growing realization that it is not just "Southern." It's "Made in Africa."

WHERE DO I COME FROM?

Diving With A Purpose and the young Bribri divers were resting on a narrow strip of castaway beach along the east coast of central Costa Rica. The tropical forest's green branches hung over yellow sands, perhaps the very sands where African captives escaped the *Christianus Quintus* and *Fredericus Quartus* Danish frigates in 1710.

Kramer had been chatting to the locals who had dived around Cahuita for years. Diving With A Purpose had learned that there were a few more spots in deeper waters where the kind of wreckage the team was looking for might lie, final proof of the truth behind the legend of the Danish slave ships. As well as yellow bricks, the divers were also on the lookout for larger targets like cannons, cannonballs, gold, and even ivory, objects which would have accompanied slavers arriving from Africa.

Because the team was heading farther out, snorkeling would not cut it. The team would need to dive. Everyone started suiting up, strapping their buoyancy vests to dive tanks and checking that their lead belts were strung with enough weight.

Before taking to the water, above the seabed where denser finds were thought to be hidden, Kamau Sadiki talked dive plans and safety.

"Salvador is going to be the lead youth diver," Kamau told the team. "In terms of safety, I know it's not very deep, but we've had instructors drown in ten feet of water. So be aware of how much air you have remaining in your tank. Don't take any dive for granted, okay? Your life depends on your skills, your equipment, and your attitude. Everybody *comprendé*? All right. Pool's open. Let's go."

The implication did not need spelling out. Blackouts, panic, and running out of air mostly happen in just a few feet of water. Everybody needed to stay alert and keep their minds and eyes peeled.

The divers made final adjustments. Andreas Bloch tightened the straps on his buoyancy vest and checked that his mouthpiece was clear of the tiniest of grit that could block his breathing. Alannah strapped her underwater compass to her wrist. One by one the team dropped backward over the side of the dive boat into the soothing Caribbean.

The visibility was slightly better in these depths. Very soon the team started to come across shards of pottery and a bottle cemented to the reef. Small clues that would hopefully lead to something grander.

And then the shards of hope turned into the motherlode when the team glided across a cluster of cannons—exactly what sunken ships should look like in shallow waters. All of the Danish frigates' wooden superstructure would have been ripped off by currents and pounding waves within weeks and months of the sinking. The exposed ribs would have left the crew's belongings and cargo free to dance across Cahuita Bay. Only the cannons would have been far too heavy to shift, even by hurricanes. But what ship did they come from?

"The more I saw, the more there were. So that was amazing. They're beside each other, they're across each other . . ." an intrigued Melody trailed off.

To Kramer the guns had undoubtedly been underwater for an age. "There are some cannons that just look like coral. They were so heavily encrusted, the ocean's taken them back," he told the team.

Kamau focused on the technicalities. "We know distinctively that they are cannons," he pointed out. "You can see the bore on some of them, some are covered up. Cannons can give us a lot of information. We saw about eight, ten, maybe twelve. But if there's more, it could tell us the size of the vessel. We know the size of the *Fredericus* and the *Christianus*. So that would be very insightful."

And there was more wreckage to come. Even with three hundred years of coral growth covering it, there was no mistaking the shape of the team's next hit, an intact iron anchor.

"The shape of the anchor, it's about three to four meters," Kamau later told the surface support team, perched on the edge of an inflatable boat. "Comes from a very large ship just based on the size. Two flukes are there. Each one is about a foot wide, and maybe another foot and a half long. So, in beautiful shape. That's some incredible stuff. Some more evidence that we can put in the mix and try to figure out what's going on at this site."

For the teenager Bribri diver Sangye Brenes, the discovery was more than a lump of history, hopefully Danish history. "The first time I saw the anchor, for me is amazing," he shared. "I asked my grandfather and my grandmother, they both say yes, I have African ancestors. And they both had, like, connecting histories with slaves. To know that makes me feel more connected to my history."

The human rights activist Maria Suárez Toro felt that diving with a personal purpose was the best way for the local kids to make sense of who they were. "It's not in the history books. It's not in the documents," she emphasized. "And if they find it themselves, they begin asking the right questions. And the right question is, where do I come from? What has that meant in the life of me and my community?"

The pieces of the puzzle were falling into place. But those elusive bricks that would slam-dunk the ship's identity were still missing in action. The team needed to hunt down the start of the yellow brick road.

ROOTS, ROCK, REGGAE

Something in the air—or water—lit the touchpaper of rebellion in Jamaica. The island was not just a hotbed of pirates and smuggling. Its sugar plantation slaves had an exceptionally violent and organized culture of resistance. Britain's largest island in the Caribbean saw a revolt almost every decade for 180 years. Is it any coincidence that reggae's musical fight for freedom took flight in Jamaica?

West Africa's dazzling music and dance echoed across the Middle Passage to the Americas on the back of slave ships, where captives were forced to sing and dance for exercise and distraction. Britain's first Black political activist, the writer Olaudah Equiano, trafficked out of the Kingdom of Benin in 1756, remembered his home tribe the Igbo as "a nation of dancers, musicians, and poets."

Beyond the need to "dance the slaves" to keep them fit for market, some ships' captains encouraged singing and music to keep the Africans' spirits up. Controlling morale dampened revolt, they hoped. Crews kept instruments—tambourines, fiddles, and bagpipes—while on some crossings music was improvised by captives thumping upturned copper soup and stew kettles. The exiles sung sorrowful tunes about their wretched condition and put their ill-fated experiences to music. As "The Sorrows of Yamba; Or, the Negro Woman's Lamentation" sang around 1790:

> At the savage Captains beck;
> Now like Brutes they make us prance:
> Smack the Cat about the Deck,
> And in scorn they bid us dance.

A nineteenth-century slave smuggler also remembered how

> Our blacks were a good-natured lot and jumped to the lash
> so promptly that there was not much occasion for scoring
> their naked flanks. We had tambourines aboard, which
> some of the younger darkies fought for regularly, and every
> evening we enjoyed the novelty of African war songs and
> ring dances, fore and aft, with the satisfaction of knowing
> that these pleasant exercises were keeping our stock in good
> condition and, of course, enhancing our prospects of making
> a profitable voyage.

Elsewhere, the "entertainment" was more like idle sport to distract
bored crews. The surgeon on the Brazilian slaver the *Georgia* described
how a week off Calabar in 1827, "I found that the captain and crew were
desperadoes of the worst kind . . . the ship became half bedlam and half
brothel. Ruiz, our captain, and his two mates set an example of reckless
wickedness. They stripped themselves and danced with black wenches
while our crazy mulatto cook played the fiddle. There was little attempt
at discipline and rum and lewdness reigned supreme."

Slavery in the Americas may have broken African bodies, but it never
destroyed the fierce African spirit. Jamaica's wild, forested countryside,
tall, rugged mountains, and hidden valleys made an ideal setting for guer-
rilla warfare by runaway slaves. The combination of a never-ending fear
of food shortage, foreign invasion, five communities of trouble-making
Maroons that escaped since 1655, and the high slave death rate made
Jamaica a powder keg.

With its three hundred thousand slaves by 1800, most trafficked from
Ghana, followed by Dahomey, the island's slave communities had little
fear about rising up against their British masters when anger bubbled
over into rage. In 1673, for instance, two hundred slaves on Major Selby's
plantation in St. Ann's, almost all Coromantee from Ghana, killed their
master and thirteen whites, then plundered nearby estates. Jamaica's
forest fire of rebellious slaves still burned bright in 1730 when Governor
Robert Hunter reported that "The Slaves in rebellion, from the increase
of their numbers by the late desertions from several settlements . . . are

grown to that height of insolence that your frontiers, that are no longer in any sort of security, must be deserted."

Maroon villages by 1736 had grown into the three rebel towns of St. George's, St. Elizabeth, and St. James, the largest inhabited by a thousand runaways. Africa had won. On March 1, 1739, the Leeward Maroon rebels signed a peace treaty that gave them freedom, the right to own land, hunt hogs, sell goods at market, and seek justice through magistrates if any whites violated the peace terms.

JAMAICA'S SLAVE PEACE TREATY

Articles of Pacification with the Maroons of Trelawney Town, Jamaica, Concluded March the first, 1738:

"First, That all hostilities shall cease on both sides for ever . . . Secondly, That the said Captain Cudjoe, the rest of his captains, adherents, and men shall [live] for ever hereafter in a perfect state of freedom and liberty . . . Thirdly, That they shall enjoy and possess, for themselves and posterity for ever, all the lands situate and lying between Trelawney Town and the Cockpits, to the amount of fifteen hundred acres . . . Fourthly, That they shall haven liberty to plant the said lands with coffee, cocoa, ginger, tobacco, and cotton, and to breed cattle, hogs, goats, or any other flock, and dispose of the produce or increase of the said commodities to the inhabitants of this island; provided always, that when they bring the said commodities to market, they shall apply first to the customs, or any other magistrate of the respective parishes where they expose their goods to sale, for a license to vend the same."

Across the Gulf, on American soil, the African exiles kept their musical traditions alive, too. Just as sea captains encouraged singing and dancing to keep up morale, plantation owners allowed dances to give their workers something to look forward to. As well as the banjo, the fiddle commonly described in early slave dances was not the European violin, but an African gourd fiddle made to an African design. Isaac D. Williams, a former slave, described how:

> We generally made our own banjos and fiddles, and I had a fiddle that was manufactured out of a gourd, with horse hair strings and a bow made out of the same material. When we made a banjo we would first of all catch what we called a ground hog, known in the north as a woodchuck. After tanning his hide, it would be stretched over a piece of timber fashioned like a cheese box, and you couldn't tell the difference in sound between that homely affair and a handsome store bought one.

Music brought a rare breath of fresh air for the enslaved to stay connected to their African heritage and, at the same time, protest against their bleak conditions. Sometimes slave masters took instruments away as too noisy, foreign, or subversive. When Africans found a way to use drums to send coded beats to stage revolts, the likes of the 1740 South Carolina Slave Code banned captives from "using and keeping drums, horns or other loud instruments." No matter. Slaves started using whatever form of rhythm-making could be adapted from household spoons and washboards to "slapping juba"—using their bodies as makeshift drums. The enslaved adapted vocal rhythms in an early form of beatbox.

In dance and song African communities rebelled, mocking their masters' ways without them realizing. The Cakewalk was a subversive in-joke against white control. The humorous dance imitated English slave masters' trendy Regency moves of small skips and hops in the formal Jane Austen style. Africans found stiff dancing ridiculous compared to their own free form of expression. Whoever danced most like the whites won a cake. White masters and visitors to big house dances totally missed the point of the act, and instead were delighted that the slaves were picking up "civilized" ways. The joke—the rebellion—was on them and still is in the modern phrase "to take the cake," or to call something "a cakewalk." It was the simplicity of mocking masters that was easy.

African Americans have been setting trends ever since. Everything from bluegrass and jazz to rock 'n' roll, country, folk, and hip-hop owes a debt of inspiration to traditional African music and the culture African slaves took to America.

One musical form that Christian slave owners approved of was the African American spiritual, whose purity they were sure praised the Lord. Its essence, though, was all about the longing to free the spirit and body, safety from harm and evil, and relief from the ills of slavery. Songs like "Sometimes I Feel Like a Motherless Child" and "I'm Troubled in Mind" released despair. Other spirituals subtly lashed slavery, using biblical metaphors to protest against Black peoples' conditions, most famously the lyrics of "Go Down, Moses": *Tell ol' Pharaoh, Let my people go.* From 1871, the Fisk Jubilee Singers' tour of America and Europe introduced "Negro spirituals" to white audiences for the first time.

Toward the late nineteenth century, African American musicians fused ragtime, sacred music, and the blues to improvise jazz. The trumpeter and singer Louis Armstrong earned international recognition with his "West End Blues" in the 1920s. America's classical music was born. Ragtime may have become the United States' first popular music in 1899 after Scott Joplin's "Maple Leaf Rag" sold over a million sheet-music copies, but it was already being played in the 1870s when Black musicians spoke of "ragging a tune."

From ragtime came the blues by way of slavery in the South, whose full force was felt after the Civil War when African Americans vented their disillusionment with their treatment. Into the twentieth century the blues turned into a country style with a solo singer playing an acoustic guitar from farms to honky-tonk gin joints at the dawn of the industrial age.

W. C. Handy put the style on America's map thanks to his "Memphis Blues" in 1912 and the "St. Louis Blues" two years later. Blues became a worldwide sensation in the 1920s, reaching new heights in the soulful, haunting beauty of Ma Rainey and Bessie Smith's voices. In 1940s Chicago, the likes of Muddy Waters added gritty electric sounds and amplification, electric guitars, harmonicas, drums, bass, and piano. The Rolling Stones, Led Zeppelin, and the Beatles all credited Chicago bluesmen as their musical fathers.

Even hip-hop has a direct thread to Africa through its rapid wordplay, complex rhyming, and storytelling. Through hip-hop, African Americans found a voice in a culture of oppression. Like their ancestors' rebellion, Black rappers put the spotlight on their communities' inner-city hardships, discontent, and politics.

Rap, the most influential form of hip-hop, combines African American blues, jazz, and soul with Caribbean calypso, dub, and dance-hall reggae. Battling even comes from the African American tradition of "toasting," boastful storytelling, often political and aggressive. Today rappers use African-inspired music to tell tragic tales of decaying projects, vicious murders, and police brutality.

Groups like Public Enemy turned their people's alienation into an art, releasing albums the public could not ignore, like *It Takes a Nation of Millions to Hold Us Back*. Most of all, rap lyrics attack economic and political inequality, waging a full-scale assault on institutions that keep African Americans in poverty. Hip-hop lives at the cutting edge of cultural innovation.

Back in the Caribbean, Jamaica gave birth to perhaps the most iconic African American musical style. Reggae's rawness spoke of a time when Africa existed for its own pleasure, a continent rich with resources, traditions, science, art, and people free from the shackles of European greed. From Harlem in the 1920s, Marcus Mosiah Garvey preached "redemption through repatriation" to Blacks and, later, Rastafarians who looked back to the homeland, Africa.

Reggae's message of empowerment and struggle for social change was powerfully captured by Bob Marley's 1973 hit "Get Up, Stand Up." And artists like Papa Levi and his "Mi God, Mi King" remembered everything that came before and set the scene for reggae to become Jamaica's biggest export:

They tek wey we gold, jah man, them tek we silver
them hang me pupa and rape me madda
the ship me from the wonderful land of africa
Fi slave fi dih plantation owner
They take wey we name, jah man, them call we n---a
the only word we know "I isa coming, massa!"

From the early drum players on slavers crossing the Middle Passage to plantation banjo players, Black minstrel shows, and beyond, Africans in the New World have always stood proudly at the cutting edge of popular music. Every single person on planet Earth is now familiar with music influenced by slave songs and dance that came over on the likes of the *Christianus Quintus* and *Fredericus Quartus*.

THE YELLOW BRICK ROAD

O n the shores of Cahuita National Park the dive team got ready for a final push. Dive tanks were lined up against railings, soldiers ready to battle for the truth of these seas' sunken past. Diving With A Purpose and their Bribri friends weaved between small blue and yellow fishing boats pulled onto the beach. They threw their gear into three dive boats, the *Aqualord,* the *Costa,* and the *Gumbe,* and headed into the bay's deeper reaches.

The cannons and the anchor were important clues, but to identify the Danish ships once and for all meant finding yellow bricks. Loads of them. Diving With A Purpose now had an emotional opportunity to search seas and minds with the Bribri youngsters and help them make sense of their roots.

The cultural debris scattered three hundred meters offshore covered a daunting search area. The location of the guns and anchor half a cannon's fire offshore gave the team hope that they were on the right track. Looking at the nearby shore, the thought that captive Africans could have made it to land made perfect sense geographically. Those bricks had to be hiding somewhere out there. Andreas waited topside anxiously while the rest of the team dived.

It did not take long for Kevin Rodriguez Brown's eagle eyes to spot a line of rectangular objects flush with the seabed, just peering above the seagrass and shifting sands. He was sure they were bricks. Kevin surfaced excitedly and shared the promising news with Andreas.

The marine archaeologist slung his dive tank over his head and dropped overboard to explore the discovery for himself. A few hand fans over the silt and what looked like a paved road appeared. Only it was a yellow brick road, the building blocks stacked on their sides by the hundreds. Andreas pulled out his measuring tape and started checking the bricks' dimensions, his fingers crossed.

Dried down on shore, Kinga shared how well the yellow brick road had hid its secrets. "At first glance, it was hard to notice that there was anything different about this spot at all," she shrugged. "But when we looked closer, there was a strange pattern. In that moment, you realize that this cold case that has been lying on the bottom of the ocean for hundreds of years is now right in front of you, about to be solved. To see that, to be in that moment, that's a historical moment."

"This hill of seabed is actually a huge pile of bricks," Kinga realized. "According to the ship's manifest, there should be forty thousand of them down here."

A description of a brick cargo on a slave trader heading to West Africa in a nineteenth-century issue of *Harper's Weekly* reported how bricks were stored on the ship's lowest level. On top were added water casks, both empty and full of rum. Next was stowed a layer of slave food, especially rice and beans, followed by the general trade cargo like cotton, flannel, muskets, and knives. Perhaps the *Christianus Quintus* and *Fredericus Quartus* bricks were loaded in much the same way.

Andreas had managed to get permission from the marine park authorities to bring up one of the bricks for testing. It was the opposite of gold and did not glitter but shone with historical promise under the Caribbean sun. Sometimes the simplest of finds turn out to be archaeological gold.

The Bribri youth high-fived in the water, hollered, and smiled. Their mission had been accomplished. Lab tests later confirmed Andreas Bloch's scientific hunch and what generations of elders had taught the Bribri. The recovered brick measured 21 x 11 centimeters, closely resembling the Danish *flensburger* brick style.

COMPUTING—OUT OF AFRICA

Africa's contribution to art, music, and dance is well-known. Less familiar is Africa's contribution to medicine, agriculture, and science. For example, fractal geometry, the mathematics of which are one of the most important tools for modeling in biology, geology, natural sciences, and information technology. Fractals is the name for patterns that repeat themselves at many different scales. They appear in rawest form in nature: trees are branches of branches, mountains are peaks of peaks, and clouds are puffs of puffs. All use self-organizing processes in their constructions, such as clusters of cells forming clusters of clusters.

Fractals exist in nature in everything from Romanesco broccoli and ferns to snowflakes, the human lungs, and DNA. They combine a maximum surface area with a maximum flow, so trees take in more light, lungs exchange more oxygen, kidneys filter more waste, neurons connect with more neurons.

Fractal geometry was only "invented" in the West in the 1970s, but mathematician Ron Eglash realized that its nature was known in Indigenous Africa over seven hundred years earlier. Looking at aerial photos of traditional villages he noticed how the Kotoko people of Cameroon built huge rectangular building complexes by adding rectangular enclosures to preexisting rectangles in acts of self-similar scaling. The people of Logone-Birni in Cameroon and villages in Zambia made their settlements from rings of rings. Ethiopian crosses found in the architecture of eight-hundred-year-old churches in Lalibela, the traditional Fulani wedding blanket, and the board game *Owari* in Ghana all share identical fractal structures.

Bamana sand divination, found universally across Africa from East to West, is the most complex example of an algorithmic approach to fractals. It is based on a binary code known in the Western world since Hugo of Santalla brought it into Spain in the twelfth century. From there it was picked up by the alchemy community as geomancy (divination through the earth). Later Gottfried Leibniz, the German mathematician, described geomancy in his book *De Arte Combinatoria* in 1666.

Moving on in time, the binary code was turned into Boolean algebra, which ended up making possible the invention of the digital computer and Google's self-organizing properties of the Web. In today's 24/7 world, every digital computer started life in Africa's robust algorithms rooted in Indigenous knowledge.

The shallows of Cahuita turned out to be the hiding place of two lost wrecks. A cluster of thirteen iron cannon and two anchors, one over three meters long, was scattered 32–250 meters from shore down to a depth of five meters. The brick pile, a kilometer away, proved to be the heart of one sunken ship spanning 19 x 9.5 meters with two iron cannons, an anchor, and three millstones for grinding flour in 9–18 meters depth. The bricks were stacked two meters high. Underneath, preserved for centuries, must lie the wooden hull.

Old turtle traders, divers, and tourists had been plucking parts of the wrecks out of Punta Cahuita since 1828 when a local called "Old Smith" was convinced the two wrecks were a French and Spanish pirate ship. Salvaged glass bottles were sold to a Panamanian antiquities collector. Other salvaged finds included copper manilla bracelets, cannonballs, swords, a drinking glass, glass bottles, a barrel, and a pewter tea kettle. Tons more artifacts are no doubt preserved under the sands and river silt.

Kramer summed up what the discovery of two old slavers meant to the Bribri divers. "Now they have an opportunity to rediscover their ties to their past. Rediscover their contact or the connection to the enslaved Africans who were here."

Alannah agreed. "This is about Cahuita. This is about the people of Cahuita. This is about the Bribri. This is about the people who are here, to find out the truth about exactly who they are as a people. And where they came from, and how Africans were very much a part of creating this community."

The history books record just how badly the loss of the *Christianus Quintus* and *Fredericus Quartus* hit Denmark. After the loss, the Danish West Indies Guinea Company lost interest in risking big investments in dangerous voyages. From Costa Rica the ships' captains somehow made their way back home. Anders Pedersen Waerøe survived accusations of deliberately trying to profit from the misadventure by ignoring the terms of the contract to sail to the island of St. Thomas.

His reward? Eighteen years later, from 1728 to 1735, he became governor of the Danish Gold Coast. Waerøe did not change his dubious ways, though. The captain ended up charged with illegal trade and selling African women for sexual abuse in his dungeon at Fort Christiansborg.

Down the years, between 1702 and 1730, the Danish West Indies Guinea Company lost eight of its twenty slave ships, wrecked everywhere from Norway to the Gulf of Guinea and Costa Rica. Eventually, the merchants shut up shop. A meeting of company stockholders in 1734 decided that the trade was "bad business." They voted against continuing slaving. This did not mark the end of Denmark's trafficking of African captives, just a new phase when the industry's gates were thrown open to private entrepreneurs.

By the time the trade was abolished, Danish hulls had shipped 111,040 African souls into the Americas, separating them from their homes and families. Despite cruelty and pain, their spirits endured. Over three hundred years after the sinking of the *Christianus Quintus* and the *Fredericus Quartus*, some of their descendants dove and found their history on the ocean floor off Costa Rica.

RESISTANCE

Dark; and thorny is de pathway,
Where de pilgrim makes his ways;
But beyond dis vale of sorrow,
Lie de fields of endless days.

—Sung by Harriet Tubman,
liberating slaves on the
Underground Railway

FREEDOM SHIPS

Sheboygan—Wisconsin, USA

The ocean floor hides abundant dark traces of the transatlantic slave trade. It also tells a more inspiring story of hundreds of slave rebellions—stories of uprising and uplifting spirit. Trafficked Africans heading for the Middle Passage, and first- and second-generation slaves across the Americas and the Caribbean, did not just accept their fate meekly, hanging their heads and rolling over.

Many Africans fought back. They did not forget. They did not go onto slaver ships and sugar, cotton, coffee, and cacao fields without a struggle. Across Brazil, Haiti, Jamaica, Grenada, and the United States, revolutionaries turned to the religion of their ancestors to find the courage to fight, to endure, to fight for freedom.

The transatlantic slave trade is not just a story of victims. It is a story of heroes.

Trafficking millions of people could never have been completely peaceful. There had to be moments of uprising and resistance. On ships and plantation estates from Ghana's Gold Coast to Whydah and the Deep South, captives and slaves outnumbered ships' crews and masters by the hundreds. Ruling with violence and fear could only get you so far.

Many captives were whipped into complacency by fear, but other Africans who survived the Middle Passage shuffled in chains out of ships' holds changed men and women. A fire burned inside them that would not go out. These resistance fighters refused to accept their destiny and took any measure to escape.

Resistance took pride, guts, and desperation. Rebels with nothing but bare hands had to weigh up the threat to their wives and children before tackling sea captains and plantation overseers armed to the teeth with guns and backed up by police and the law. Resistance had two completely opposite outcomes—liberty or severe punishment.

Resistance came in many forms from the subtle to the subversive. On George Washington's plantation at Mount Vernon, the slaves pretended to be ill, dragged out their work, and damaged tools. Bolder captives risked theft, arson, sabotaging crops, and running away. More than forty-seven slaves (7 percent of all) tried to flee Mount Vernon and other plantations owned by Washington. The largest rebellion of seventeen Africans occurred when their masters' backs were turned and an enemy British warship, the *Savage*, was anchored off the plantation in the Potomac River in April 1781.

At other times, pregnant women took the heartbreaking decision to have an abortion rather than bring a child into a world of slavery. Rebelling against cruelty, hardship, or worse could vary from taking up arms to suicide.

Just how much resistance was out there? What forms did it take and where did the insurrections flare up?

Underground Railroad

In the United States, resistance for many enslaved people meant riding the Underground Railroad, a series of risky stops along a journey to freedom. Diving With A Purpose had circled the globe investigating slave wrecks and their stories from Suriname to the English Channel to Costa Rica. Now they were back on home soil in the United States facing a very different mission. They were not hunting for a slave ship. They were diving in search of the exact opposite, ships of freedom, ships that took runaway slaves from America to Canada. Out of slavery to liberty.

Where did these slaves find the courage to run and how did they stay unseen in the shadows? What kinds of logistics and visionaries kept the Underground Railroad on the tracks?

The small town of Sheboygan nestles between the western shore of Lake Michigan, the second largest of the Great Lakes, and the mouth of the Sheboygan River. For centuries this tranquil spot was home to Potawatomi, Chippewa, Ottawa, Winnebago, and Menominee Native American groups. Their villages and camps studded the shores of every lake and stream. They called their land Schwab-we-way-kum, the "Great Noise Underground," perhaps inspired by far-off thundering waterfalls.

New England Yankees first arrived as trappers, followed in the 1840s by streams of immigrant German, Dutch, and Irish pioneers. The settlers opened dairies making two million pounds of cheese from 116 factories. Water from the lakes and streams powered saw and flour mills making windmills, spokes, doors, blinds, wagons, and barrels. Soon the old population was pushed out. By the terms of a "peace" treaty of September 26, 1833, the Native Americans gave up five million acres of prime land between Lake Michigan and Rock River. This was how the West was won.

Kramer, Alannah, Kinga, and Josh made their way down a wooden boardwalk in Sheboygan's marina carrying dive tanks and maps. They had dived the Atlantic and Caribbean seas, the English Channel, and Maroni River. The Great Lakes was a very different prospect. Diving With A Purpose was back in deep waters and all the risks that come with them.

Richard Stevenson had joined the team again. Like the dive down to 110 meters in search of a Royal African Company trader off England, the team would need his special skills to safely navigate these waters.

The lake's surface was a little choppy and the air chilly. This was hats and windbreaker weather. On the trip out to the middle of Lake Michigan, the author and musician Saladin Allah had joined the team. These waters meant everything to his family. His third great-grandfather, the ex-slave, abolitionist, and minister Josiah Henson, escaped slavery in Kentucky in 1830 with his wife and small children.

Josiah was born into slavery in Maryland where he witnessed daily horrors. His father's ear had been cut off, and both of Josiah's shoulder blades were broken in a beating by an overseer. After being sold to a new plantation in Kentucky, the Henson family decided to flee—enough was enough—traveling by night and sleeping by day. They made it across a lake in Ohio, where a ship's captain called Burnham transported the Henson family to Buffalo, New York. Then they crossed into Canada.

The Hensons founded the fittingly named settlement of Dawn for fugitive slaves near present-day Dresden, between Lake Erie and Lake Huron, where Josiah set up a school for runaway slaves, published his memoirs, and inspired the lead character in Harriet Beecher Stowe's American classic *Uncle Tom's Cabin* in 1852. The novel became the second best-selling book of the nineteenth century, following the Bible. The story is told that when Abraham Lincoln met Stowe at the start of the Civil War, he said, "So this is the little lady who started this great war."

SLAVE LIFE IN MARYLAND

The Life of Josiah Henson, Formerly a Slave, Now an Inhabitant of Canada, as Narrated by Himself (Boston, 1849).

". . . the death of Dr. McP. brought about a revolution in our condition . . . were all put up at auction and sold to the highest bidder, and scattered over various parts of the country . . . My mother was then separated from me, and put up in her turn. She was bought by a man named Isaac R., residing in Montgomery county, and then I was offered to the assembled purchasers. My mother, half distracted with the parting forever from all her children, pushed through the crowd, while the bidding for me was going on, to the spot where R. was standing. She fell at his feet, and clung to his knees, entreating him in tones that a mother only could command, to buy her baby as well as herself . . . Will it, can it be believed that this man, thus appealed to, was capable not merely of turning a deaf ear to her supplication, but of disengaging himself from her with such violent blows and kicks, as to reduce her to the necessity of creeping out of his reach, and mingling the groan of bodily suffering with the sob of a breaking heart? Yet this was one of my earliest observations of men . . ."

Saladin Allah, flat cap covering bright eyes and sporting a long goatee beard, looked at the divers following in the footsteps of his ancestors and started sharing what he knew about how runaways tapped into the road to freedom.

"All of you are going to be diving in an area that is significant in terms of the Underground Railroad," he began. "It was a network of people and places that were significant in helping freedom-seekers that were traveling along routes in order to escape plantations. You're talking about stories of resilience. People being able to make this journey from the South to the North."

The Underground Railroad started running in 1831 when a slave named Tice Davids fled from his Kentucky master. The owner chased him to the Ohio River, where he promptly vanished. The master scratched his head and cried that Davids must have "gone off on an underground road." The Underground Railroad was born as the name for secret routes running from the Southern plantations across rivers and valleys, over mountains, all the way to the free North.

"And it wasn't possible unless you had that network in place," Saladin continued. "The way that people communicated was mouth to ear. People would be able to describe a person in terms of where they lived, what area they were going to, what name they responded to. A network of people who were striving to ensure the freedom of others."

JOSIAH HENSON ESCAPES

The Life of Josiah Henson, Formerly a Slave, Now an Inhabitant of Canada, as Narrated by Himself (Boston, 1849).

"It was not without long thought on the subject that I devised a plan of escape . . . In passing over the part of Ohio near the lake, where such an extensive plain is found, we came to a spot overflowed by a stream, across which the road passed. I forded it first, with the help of a sounding-pole, and then taking the children on my back, first, the two little ones, and then the others, one at a time, and, lastly, my wife, I succeeded in getting them all safely across, where the ford was one hundred to one hundred and fifty yards wide, and the deepest part perhaps four feet deep. At this time the skin was worn from my back to an extent almost equal to the size of my knapsack . . .

When I got on the Canada side, on the morning of the 28th of October, 1830, my first impulse was to throw myself on the ground, and giving way to the riotous exultation of my feelings, to execute sundry antics which excited the astonishment of those who were looking on. A gentleman of the neighborhood, Colonel Warren, who happened to be present, thought I was in a fit, and as he inquired what was the matter with the poor fellow, I jumped up and told him I was free. "O," said he, with a hearty laugh, "is that it? I never knew freedom make a man roll in the sand before."

On shore, Kramer felt the bite of the lake. He had doubled up the warmth factor with two coats. Now in his happy place, on the waves, he was spellbound by one of the most inspiring stories Diving With A Purpose would ever hear.

"So they may know that there's a house or a shelter, three or four miles up the road, right, and then once they get there, they figure the rest of it out," Kramer thought out loud. "I have no idea of where I'm going or how I'm going to get there, but I'm going."

Of course, it was not so easy. Saladin explained that, "At the same time, there were bounty hunters tracking people based upon descriptions. And, if you were caught aiding and abetting a freedom seeker, then you could risk up to six months in jail and a thousand dollar fine at that time."

Kinga sat silent in deep contemplation, trying to figure out just how scary it must have been to dodge informers, tracker dogs, and authorities. Richard nodded respectfully, his hair rustling in the breeze. No hat needed: this was summer as far as the thick-skinned Englishman was concerned.

Alannah, too, tried to imagine how Africans set about summoning up the nerve to make epic, life-changing journeys. "How do you even go about figuring out who to ask or where to go to?" she asked.

Saladin's very personal family history, and the memoir his ancestor left behind, gave a unique window into the art of vanishing into thin air.

"When you're growing up on a plantation and you're not allowed to read, you learn how to read people," he told the team. "It would be an unspoken form of communication where they understood that sense of trust in one another."

"So, my third great-grandfather, Josiah Henson, he was enslaved for forty-one years of his life and he took his four children and made this journey from Kentucky over six hundred miles to western New York. Two of his children were so small, he had to carry them in a knapsack on his back, the entire journey."

As much as Saladin had talked openly about his family history throughout his life, he always got a lump in his throat. He shook his head, letting the emotions pass. This place, this past, was very personal. If fighters like Josiah had not found the strength to rise up and the courage to strike out for freedom, Saladin and his parents would not be here. And America would have been a very different place. The musician finished his tale. "And he was able to cross over into Canada in October of 1830."

Josh felt Saladin's deep sense of history and pain for the past. They were going to dive and find a "freedom boat" to commemorate the resistance. "Here's the waters. Here's the terrain that your ancestors crossed so you can be here. So a lot of us can be here," he understood, choked up, too.

Kramer looked at Saladin and then beyond to the great abyss toward the six thousand ships wrecked in the Great Lakes. How were they going to distinguish one wreck from another? "We'll try and do you and your ancestor justice," he promised.

FLYING AFRICANS

I n most slave ship logs Africans sound like passive captives, walking blindly up gangways onto great ships to be trafficked a world away, never to be heard of again. Time after time, though—in as many as one in ten slaving voyages—the captives resisted. Whether from Ghana, Benin, Nigeria, or Angola, rebel Africans took any glimmer of opportunity to fight or flee.

Resistance even took what some may say was the ultimate form of rebellion: suicide. Captives and captains both knew that the most charged moments were when the homeland was still in sight. Crews took every measure to make sure their "cargos" had no chance to get away. Africans were tightly shackled within sight of the home shore. And slave ships were constructed in careful ways to dampen down any hint of rebellion.

Captives were stowed deep in holds below several decks, as far away as possible from where the crew slept. In these cramped and claustrophobic quarters, just breathing, combined with not catching disease or being whipped, took up all your energy. Organizing rebellions needed exceptional mental and physical toughness to tackle hardened sailors armed with cutlasses, pistols, muskets, and cannons. The Africans were guarded around the clock. Captains had few reservations about turning swivel guns inward to rake fire on rebelling captives if need be. Slave ships were built to be resistance-proof.

Try as they might, few rebellions at sea got anywhere. The fire of resistance was usually swiftly put out, the chief mischief-makers executed, their bodies tied to masts to warn against repeat offenders and then thrown overboard with no burial. Africans knew their chances were slim but still preferred to die fighting, go out on their shields, especially if they had been warriors back on their home soil.

Friends Like These

Rarely has a ship been given such an unfortunate name. The *Amistad*—Spanish for "friendship"—was a slaver working the waters of Cuba. Onboard were fifty-three enslaved Africans, seized and shipped from Dumbomo in Sierra Leone by the Portuguese slaver the *Teçora*. In Havana, José Ruiz and Don Pedro Montez bought the Africans for $450 each and headed out to their plantations on the *Amistad*. The small schooner steered for Guanaja, further west on the island's northern shore, on June 28, 1839. The Africans' names had already been changed to Christian ones with a payoff of $15 apiece for Cuba's authorities to whitewash where they came from. Now they were no different from thousands of other slaves sweating under Cuban skies. No matter the slave trade had been made illegal by Spain since 1820. Cuba's sugar barons snubbed the law.

The slaves were not shackled: the voyage was short, and Ruiz and Montez did not want to raise any suspicion that the Africans were freshly landed. Trouble kicked off when the drinking water ran low on the night of June 30. Two thirst-quenched slaves tried to sip from the water cask and were soundly whipped. The captives' backs were up. Then, when they asked the cook where they were going, he told them they were heading to be killed and eaten. The mean-spirited joke backfired. Led by Cinquè, the chief of the Mendi captives, the rebels grabbed sugarcane cutting knives and killed the captain and his jesting cook. Ruiz and Montez were tied up. The rest of the crew fled on a small boat.

Using a little English and Arabic, the Africans demanded to be taken home, "three moons" toward the east. By day the *Amistad* sailed east. As soon as the sun set, the devious Spanish merchants slowly turned the ship around and zigzagged north for two months. When a shore appeared on August 25, what the Mendi hoped was Sierra Leone turned out to be Long Island, near New York City.

The landing party dressed in handkerchiefs twisted around their loins and blankets thrown over their shoulders made a striking sight. It did not take long for the freed Africans to be retaken by the crew of the naval brig the *Washington*. Ruiz and Montez claimed government protection. A sorry Cinquè's address to his people, heard by the warship's Black cabin boy, was eventually picked up by a newspaper in New London. The fallen chief told his people:

> Friends and Brothers: We would have returned, but the sun was against us. I would not see you serve the white man. So I induced you to help me kill the Captain. I thought I should be killed. I expected it. It would have been better. You had better be killed than live many moons in misery. I shall be hanged, I think, everyday. This does not pain me. I could die happy if by dying I could save so many of my brothers from the bondage of the white men.

A court of inquiry accused Cinquè, going by his enforced Anglicized name of Joseph, and thirty-eight other Africans of murder and piracy. The case was set for trial. The captives were crammed into the county jail with no way to communicate with the outside world. Meanwhile, Lieutenants Thomas Gedney and Richard Mead of the *Washington* filed a salvage award to the tune of $65,000 for rescuing the *Amistad* and its human cargo for their Spanish owners. The hearing was going to be a big headache.

The *Amistad* affair marked a momentous tipping point for the transatlantic slave trade in the United States. Britain had freed eight hundred thousand colonial Blacks in 1833 and its navy was throwing serious manpower to fight the African slave trade at sea. In Cuba and the American South, though, slavery was on the rise.

In the United States, President Martin Van Buren supported sending the *Amistad*'s Africans back to slavery in Cuba. His political power had taken a hit after the economic panic of 1837. Now he feared that the case could damage his bid for reelection in the South. For America's abolitionists in the North, however, the *Amistad*'s plight was the perfect opportunity to attack the evils of slavery.

Three days after landing in New York, the city's antislavery supporters, headed by the Reverend Simeon Jocelyn, a former pastor of a church of Black parishoners, the Reverend Joshua Leavitt, and Lewis Tappan, wrote a public appeal in the *Emancipator* newspaper for funds to cover legal counsel for the Africans and the services of an interpreter. Ruiz and Montez were moving fast too, demanding the prisoners be returned to them or to the Spanish government as their lawful property. The Spanish minister backed their claim to the US State Department.

The trial came to court on January 7, 1840. Among the prisoners' counsel was the powerful figure of John Quincy Adams, the sixth president of the United States. The courtroom was packed with rubbernecking spectators. For eight and a half hours the seventy-three-year-old Adams passionately defended the Africans' right to freedom on legal and moral grounds. In summarizing, the judge awarded the officers of the *Washington* salvage rights to the *Amistad* and its cargo. But not over the Africans.

THE *AMISTAD*'S CAPTIVES JUDGED

Letter from the Mendi Africans from the Cuba-bound *Amistad* slaver, imprisoned in New York, to John Quincy Adams in New Haven, January 4, 1841:

"José Ruiz say we born in Havana, he tell lie. We stay in Havana 10 days and 10 nights, we stay no more. We all born in Mendi—we no understand the Spanish language. Mendi people been in America 17 moons . . . We want you to ask the Court what we have done wrong. What for Americans keep us in prison . . . you have children, you have friends, you love them, you feel very sorry if Mendi people come and carry them all to Africa . . . If America people give us free we glad, if they no give us free we sorry—we sorry for Mendi people little, we sorry for America people great deal, because God punish liars. We want you to tell court that Mendi people no want to go back to Havana, we no want to be killed. Dear friend, we want you to know how we feel. Mendi people think, think, think . . . Mendi people have got souls . . . All we want is to make us free."

The fate of the *Amistad*'s slaves had circled the world to reach the highest seats of power. The British quietly wrote to the US secretary of state, pointing out that the British government knew the Africans were illegally imported into Spanish Cuba by a Portuguese slaver. Because Spain had supposedly renounced the slave trade, Queen Victoria was taking a personal interest in the fate of the abused Africans.

In the end Judge Andrew Judson decided that the prisoners were free-born and kidnapped into slavery. They should be delivered to the president of the United States to be transported home to Africa. The *Amistad*'s Spanish masters had violated the act of Congress of 1808 banning slave trading.

The *Globe* newspaper, the official mouthpiece of the presidential administration, was unimpressed, and attacked "the justice of an American Court, bowed down in disgraceful subserviency before the bigoted mandates of that blind fanaticism, which prompted the Judge upon the bench to declare in his decree, in reference to one of these negroes, that, although he might be stained with crime, yet he should not sigh in vain for Africa; and all because his hands were reeking with the blood of murdered white men. It is a base outrage . . . upon all the sympathies of the civilized life."

Spain appealed and the case went all the way to the Supreme Court, where Justice Joseph Story decided that "it was the ultimate right of all human beings in extreme cases to resist oppression, and to apply force against ruinous injustice." The stolen Africans had every legal right to resist their unlawful kidnapping.

In 1842 the African freedom fighters finally landed home. Thirty-five of the *Amistad*'s fifty-three captives survived.

Slave revolts in the Caribbean were common. The most spectacular, during the eighteenth and nineteenth centuries, took place in Jamaica, Grenada, Barbados and, most significantly, in Haiti. The Haitian Revolution of 1791, was the only revolt that led to the creation of a state. On January 1, 1804, what had been the French colony of Saint-Domingue became the Republic of Haiti. This was the culmination of more than a decade of fighting again French enslavement. The revolt was led by the legendary Toussaint-Louverture and Jean-Jacques Dessalines. The new state was the second independent country in the Americas after the United States. It was also the first sovereign state in the world to abolish slavery.

Death or Liberty?

Collective suicide was not uncommon among enslaved people. Surgeons logs covering the years 1792–1796 show that 7.2 percent of captive Africans killed themselves between being captured, embarking, and sailing the Middle Passage. Rebellion at sea was so common off the coast of West Africa that suicide prevention technology was brought in. Nets were strung up across slaver decks to stop captives jumping to their deaths. Mouth-opening, teeth-shattering braces, the dreaded *speculum oris*, were used to forcibly feed Africans on hunger strike.

The unimaginable trauma of kidnapping, forced migration, rape, brutality, starvation, exile, and family separation gave captives and slaves on land and sea good reason to seek the ultimate release from bondage. Before slaves were converted to Christianity by their masters, which considered suicide a sin leading to hell and damnation, suicide was an act of highest honor among many West African peoples, such as the Yoruba and Ashanti. Death, the ultimate resistance, also brought spiritual relief, a release for Africans to return home.

Western masters were baffled when their laborers took their lives. The British politician Edward Littleton warned planters in 1698 that slaves hanged themselves and that "no creature knows why." Estate overseers tried hard to scare slaves from suicide. When a captive called Roger hanged himself in a tobacco house in 1712, his head was "cutt off and Stuck on a pole to be a terror to others." Through the Civil War years, it was common for the corpses of suicidal slaves to be decapitated, dismembered, and exhibited to warn off like-minded rebels.

The thought of separation was especially painful to bear. After a Philadelphia slave called Romain learned that his family was about to be shipped to the West Indies and separated from him, he became "maddened . . . complicated by misery" and slashed his throat three times with a pruning knife. Female slaves jumped out of windows, plunged into rivers, and cut their throats rather than be separated from loved ones or accept cruel treatment.

Certain African peoples had a reputation for depression among planters who were warned to "fly, with care, from the Moco nation," because "they themselves destroy" and to avoid "Coromontee," who "chuse death before dishonorable bonds." Traders in the West Indies and planters in South Carolina found the Igbo especially suicidal. Still, between 1710 and 1760, 38 percent of all slaves imported to Virginia were Igbo.

The most famous case involving suicide as resistance revolves around a group of Igbo captives that landed in Savannah, Georgia, in the spring of 1803, after a dreadful crossing from Nigeria. They were bought at the slave market in Savannah by agents working for John Couper and Thomas Spalding, loaded on a small boat, and thrown below deck for a trip down the coast to St. Simons Island in Glynn County, Georgia.

The captives were fiercely independent and refused to accept their humiliating fate. The Igbo Africans rebelled. A firsthand witness, Roswell King, a white overseer from the plantation of Pierce Butler, watched aghast as the captives chose death. The slaves grounded their boat on St. Simons Island. As soon as they landed, at a place now called Igbo Landing, they drowned their captors. Then, seventy-five warriors walked singing into Dunbar Creek, led by their high priest, and took their own lives. It was America's first freedom march.

In rich legend, popular from the United States to the Caribbean and Latin America, Africans are described as the only people on earth to whom God gave the power to fly. Using secret chants like *Kum buba yali kum buba tambe*, they could become free as a bird, light as a feather.

According to legend, the Igbo of St. Simons Island did not die. Instead, they took wing, rose high into the sky, turned into birds, and flew back home.

THE NIAGARA FALLS

On Lake Michigan, Alannah, Kramer, Kinga, Josh and Richard were closing in on their first dive in the Great Lakes. Saladin Allah had told the team that all kinds of ships often operated secretly here as "freedom boats." Where were the freedom boats among the Great Lakes six thousand wrecks?

Local knowledge goes a long way. Saladin had introduced Diving With A Purpose to local historian John Polacsek, an expert on sunken ships in these waters. Now John was taking the team out to a very specific spot on Lake Michigan where a steamer called the *Niagara* sank.

The lake's surface was flat. Perfect diving conditions. Only a squawking seagull broke the peace. Not another boat was in sight.

Wearing his SS *William Clay Ford* baseball cap in honor of one of the Great Lake's uncountable bulk freighters, silver wire glasses above his moustache, John told the team to get ready to dive.

"We're out here on the site, this is where the *Niagara* is, about fifty feet down below," he began. "The *Niagara* was part of the Reed fleet, which is out of Erie, Pennsylvania. The Reed family were major abolitionists, and any time you wanted to forward a fugitive slave, you could contact one of the Reed boats. Once they got on the boat, the fugitives would blend in as crewmembers until they had the opportunity to get to Detroit, get on the ferry, go across the mile to Windsor, Canada, and then they would be free."

The journey was not as easy or safe as it sounded. The final road to freedom involved taking the ship to Chicago on the southern tip of Lake Michigan, steaming all the way to the northern end, and then turning 180° east down the full stretch of Lake Huron. It was a distance of over 510 miles. Today Lake Michigan is idyllically peaceful. In the mid–nineteenth century it was the beating heart of industry, business, and communication. Eyes were everywhere.

THE *NIAGARA*

- Sidewheel palace steamer, built 1845 by Bidwell & Banta of Buffalo, New York
- Owner, Charles Manning Reed
- 68.5 meters long, 10.2 meters wide, depth of hold 4.2 meters, 1,084 tons
- Capacity for seventy-five cabin passengers and 180 in steerage
- Up to sixteen round trips from Buffalo to Chicago a year, passengers and general freight
- September 24, 1856, lost to fire. Sixty of three hundred people died; steamer and cargo a total loss
- Wreck 17 meters deep, east of Harrington Beach State Park, Ozaukee County
- Keelson, vessel machinery, engine, walking beam, triple boilers, and paddlewheels well preserved

"Was the *Niagara* a fancy high-end boat?" Kinga wanted to know.

"Yes, it was. There were as many as three hundred people who were bringing their livelihood, their whole families with them," John confirmed.

"And we know that the fugitive slaves worked in the galley," Kinga added.

"That's right. As waiters and other crew members," John explained. But it ended in tragedy. "In 1856 when the *Niagara* was coming back to Chicago, a fire broke out, and it sank."

"Was there a loss of life on the *Niagara*?" Kinga checked.

John told the team that more than sixty people sank on the steamer. He had brought with him surviving examples of the last objects the runaway slaves touched.

"Over the years, a number of divers have been down on the boat," John explained, "and they were able to salvage several artifacts which I have collected. So, what we have is a spoon which was recovered back in the 1960s. At that time it was legal to pick up artifacts off shipwrecks. One of the other items he found was a fork. It has a wooden handle, it's in good shape. It was used to serve the diners."

The team handled the silver spoon, finery once laid out on the *Niagara*'s immaculate dining tables. John had also brought along a white porcelain cup with a blue rim border used to serve coffee and tea. Ivory-colored door handles once opened into first-class passengers' cabins.

Kinga turned a silver ladle around in her hands and wondered out loud. "The fugitive slaves, very likely, they were out there setting out the silverware."

Kramer was ready to roll. The *Niagara* dive would feel very different. No nailed-down hatches like on the *Leusden* in the Maroni River off Suriname.

"It's gonna be interesting diving this ship, looking at it as a freedom boat and not a luxury ship," he shared.

Just because Lake Michigan was calm would not make this dive easy. The team had to be vigilant not to be lulled into a false sense of comfort. Comfort meant danger. Visibility can be as great as one hundred feet. On other days you are lucky if you can see your fingers in front of you due to toxic algae blooms running for miles and caused by modern fertilizer runoff from the fields.

Bad visibility meant a risk getting entangled in fishing nets. Currents can quickly change, too. And on the bottom, the lake is a bed of soft mud. One misplaced kick stirs up a cloud of silt making the view even worse. Little wonder that recreation divers are banned from Lake Michigan. These waters are a no-go for anyone other than advanced divers.

One of the biggest hazards in the Great Lakes is the water's temperature. With every ten to fifteen feet descent into Lake Michigan, the water drops by ten degrees. By the time you reach one hundred feet, the lake hits forty degrees Fahrenheit. Staying safely warm means using special equipment from drysuits to multiple tanks and regulators because colder temperatures make equipment more likely to fail. Normal breathing regulators are not designed for cold temperatures. Falling water temperatures cause free flows when air gushes out of regulators uncontrolled, making it impossible to breathe. Panic sets in.

That is the bad news. The good news is that the Great Lakes' surfaces may be disastrous for wrecking caused by fog, ice, storms, and collisions, but the same chill factor and soft silts make Lake Michigan a wonder for shipwreck preservation—the opposite of what you find in the English Channel. There are very few places on earth where ships survive in perfect 3D glory. Only in the icy reaches of the Baltic, and the Northwest Passage of Canada, the Antarctic Weddell Sea, or the oxygen-free Black Sea do you find wrecks perfectly preserved.

Shipwrecks are the stars of the Great Lakes, six thousand and rising at the last count. Lake Michigan is like a giant refrigerator. And there are no salts or worms to munch through wooden hulls. Ships over two hundred years old stand defiantly amid the gloom, their rigging upright and their figureheads as clear as the day they were carved. You can dive into cargo holds and glide along abandoned walkways. Who knows what is out there? Rumors abound about stolen Confederate bullion jettisoned into a stormy Lake Michigan in the 1890s.

It was into Lake Michigan, the second largest Great Lake and the only one located entirely inside the United States, that Diving With A Purpose was heading in search of resistance fighters. The team took special care suiting up and triple-checked their equipment. To dive these cold waters, they had come prepared with special drysuits used by the military, fire service, and police to keep warm. They were as good as otter skins.

The dive's aim was not to look for objects left behind by the *Niagara*'s fancy passengers but to chase finds handled by the runaway freedom seekers. The plan was to search the galley area behind the boiler where food was prepared and crockery stored for serving fine diners. Because fugitive slaves worked in the kitchen and dining room as a cover to make their way into Canada, it might be possible to match finds to runaways. The wreck told an amazing tale of the logistics of resistance.

Alannah and the team pulled their tight drysuit hoods over their heads and splashed down with double air tanks on their backs—an extra safety net should the main air supply fail.

Palace Steamer

The Reed family were big-time entrepreneurs. Colonel Seth Reed had commanded a regiment during the Revolutionary War and fought at Bunker Hill before making money in the hotel business. His son, Rufus Reed, made a fortune trading furs for liquor with Native Americans. Charles Manning Reed, the colonel's grandson who built the *Niagara*, went on to become the Great Lakes' largest ship owner. After studying law in Philadelphia, he returned home and was worth as much as $15 million when he died in 1871.

By the late 1830s, the world was on the move. On a single day, five thousand people headed west from Buffalo. Reed saw the huge potential for fast luxury steamboat transport and built up the largest fleet on the Great Lakes. The *Niagara*, 245 feet long and 1,100 tons, was the jewel in his empire. The ship took six months to build in 1845, used the finest architects and craftsmen and cost an eye-watering $95,000.

Reed contracted the *Niagara*'s build to the Buffalo shipyard of Bidwell & Banta. Jacob Banta was famous for his colossal side-wheel steamers and as "a genius of high order." For the engine Reed turned to New Yorker James Allaire. The beating heart of the ship cost $32,000—more than the rest of the hull put together.

The *Niagara*'s walking beam steam engine, fourteen feet tall and six feet in diameter, traveled ten feet up and down during every stroke of the engine. It powered thirty-foot-long paddlewheels weighing over six tons each. Every season the steamship burned more than eight million feet of timber, enough to build four hundred houses.

Each year the *Niagara* made fourteen to sixteen round trips between Buffalo and Chicago. Reed's agents sold migrants newly arrived at New York City westbound tickets along a railroad, canal, and steamboat route that he almost entirely owned. The ship might carry five hundred immigrants as well as cargos of furs, dry hides, minerals, beef, pork, flour, wool, and sugar. The *Niagara* held the record for the most valuable cargo ever landed at Buffalo, $300,000 worth of furs and buffalo robes in 1849.

Reed's Great Lakes palace steamers like the *Niagara* were much more impressive than British boats and were said to "make the Englishman blush for his inferiority." The Reed Line advertised its steamers as taking the "most romantic, pleasant, and popular route ever established in the Union . . . the route for the Business Man, the Tourist, and the Pleasure Seeker." At his height of power, Charles Reed was celebrated as a master of the water, "the Napoleon of the Lakes."

The omens for the *Niagara*'s final voyage were troubling from the start. In a previous run from Chicago to Mackinac, several passengers died from cholera. Then a major leak needed $2,000 to fix. In the days before the final voyage a storm, the worst in living memory, sunk schooners and ships. To cap off the bad signs, just before the *Niagara* set sail a poison pen letter threatened to burn the steamer "that very night."

The cross-lake hop from Collingwood, Ontario, to Sheboygan on the 22nd and 23rd of September 1856 passed incident free. The *Niagara* steamed peacefully at twelve to fifteen miles an hour with two hundred passengers. It would have been provisioned like similar steamers with nine calves, twenty lambs, pigs, beef tongues, hams, nearly ten thousand eggs, six hundred chickens, dozens of turkeys, 450 pounds of bass and trout, halibut, live and pickled lobsters, oysters, and four thousand cigars. Cargo included wagons, twenty-one horses, and 105 tons of baggage and cargo containing who knew what. Not checking their contents ultimately sent the *Niagara* to its doom.

The ship was a little world unto itself. On the lower deck a crowd of immigrants sat around their luggage, sharing memories. In the upper cabin's staterooms and salon, lavishly decorated with murals, paintings, and fancy glass, wealthy passengers made merry. Toward evening, a musician started playing the fiddle and cast a spell over the passengers, calling dancers, "boys and misses, dandies and flirts, men and women" to the floor.

At four o'clock on the afternoon of September 24, Captain Fred Miller was resting in his cabin when the alarm of "fire" was raised. Passengers claimed the fire broke out near the starboard paddlewheel, the hottest part of the steamer. Miller turned the *Niagara* toward shore a few miles west of Wisconsin and started manning the fire hoses. Almost at once the engine broke, leaving the steamer four to five miles from the safety of land.

Petrified travelers tried to launch two small lifeboats from the hurricane deck. One capsized. John B. Macy, a former US congressman from Fond du Lac in Wisconsin—a towering, corpulent man of great energy—jumped overboard, fell seven feet, smashed into the second lifeboat, and killed all its passengers. Macy died as well.

What sank the *Niagara* and sixty passengers in fine weather in one of Wisconsin's worst transport disasters is still a mystery. Palace steamers were one large box of kindling with their wooden cabins, long salons, and oil lamps. A possible cause of its fire was an explosive cargo of matches and fireworks. The steamer's failure to carry life preservers turned out to be a foolish error as well.

Chasing Ghosts

The lake was greenish blue and gloomy. The divers followed a rope shot line to guide them straight down to the wood and steel bones. Without any salt in the water fighting buoyancy, it was unnerving to plummet faster than Diving With A Purpose was used to. They carried a diagram of the wreckage with them to orient their position and track down the all-important galley.

The wreck veered into view, fifty feet down. Compared to the flattened ships of the Atlantic, Caribbean, and English Channel, the *Niagara* was a stunner. But for a Great Lakes wreck it had taken a pounding. The fire that ended its glory days burned down much of the structure. Then it broke apart. In an act of cultural vandalism, treasure hunters later stripped the wreck bare, hauling up crates of china and damaging the hull. Finally, zebra mussels invaded the hull, gluing themselves to the wood and snapping off large sections under the shells' weight. Despite it all, the *Niagara* had resisted the ravages of time admirably.

Kramer was impressed. After languishing 160 years underwater, he could still see everything. The thirty-foot-wide paddlewheels, once weighing more than six tons, and now whittled down by nature and man, still dwarfed him. The boiler that powered the engine, twenty-seven feet wide, stood proud as if it was ready to spark into action. There were the charred timbers of a steamer that shaped the Midwest, a ninety-foot-long section of the hull. Its build was exceptionally heavy, finely assembled using thick inner oak frames bolted together with iron fastenings.

Finally, this was a ship that ferried runaways to freedom. Where was the galley where the fugitives worked?

Gliding around the *Niagara* the team could easily imagine the boisterous passengers having a high old time on its luxurious decks in the final days, thanks to a description left behind by Bishop Thomas Asbury Morris, who sailed on the boat in a journey from Cincinnati to the Wisconsin Conference of the Methodist Episcopal Church in Milwaukee in 1848:

> In the cabin were men of leisure and pleasure with their families, seeking new sources of enjoyment—men of business, intent on its accomplishment—invalids traveling for health—peddlers of books and maps—tourists exploring new states—ministers and agents with ecclesiastical business, and smoking, loquacious politicians—some promenading the deck in solitude, some clustered together in social chitchat, others attracted by the sound of music and song.

And then the team spotted something bright glowing among the brown camouflaged debris—half of a white porcelain dish, its edges elegantly decorated with a blue border and floral motifs. This was exactly the kind of fancy dining wares the ex-slaves masquerading as hired help served to guests with no idea of the drama playing out behind the scenes—guests who were free while their servers were scared witless of being exposed at any moment.

To the conductors of the Underground Railroad, Charles Reed's fleet—the *Sultana, Madison, Missouri, Keystone State,* and the *Niagara*—were trusted free boats. Year after year they safely delivered fugitives to Canada. And Reed refused to take a cent for the risk. For more than twenty years his captains "laundered" slaves onto Reed's floating havens as free Black workers.

Alannah rose back up the rope shot line smiling ear to ear and whooped as soon as she hit the surface, buzzing with the thrill of discovery. The marine ecologist from the Bahamas peeled back her drysuit and said to the surface team, "That was awesome. So that plate, that's a direct connection to these lawfully employed but fugitive slaves on board in the galley, right?"

Kramer had tapped into the *Niagara*'s emotional memory. "It was cold. It was dark, and a little eerie," he shared with the team, catching his breath in the stern of the *Seaquest II* dive boat. "But not sad. I know that in previous journeys people on that wreck made it to freedom. Somewhere out there, their descendants are still alive."

Back on shore, the *Seaquest* moored, and the friends shared their experience with John Polacsek.

Kramer was not completely satisfied. Diving With A Purpose wanted to dig deeper to get a handle of what the runaway slaves endured in their flights to freedom.

"So, John, the *Niagara* didn't take the fugitives all the way to Canada," Kramer pointed out. "Close, but not all the way. Can we find a ship that went all the way? Smuggling fugitives trying to get a way to freedom, to Canada."

John knew better than anyone else how tricky it was to match historical records with sunken ships.

"You're talking about boats which are down on the bottom of the lake," he thought out loud. "You have to verify the fact that they actually did carry fugitives. I've been collecting material for at least twenty-five years. What I'm planning on doing now is to come up with something out of the file drawer in the basement . . . something which will give us the name of a captain and the history of his vessel."

John set off to put on his thinking cap and excavate dusty files he had not looked at for an age. Which, if any, ship would fit the bill and bring the dive team closer to the footprints of America's runaway slaves?

CIVIL WAR SLAVE ARMY

On a different body of water, inland, the fate of America's enslaved peoples turned on one morning of mayhem. When, in 1520, the Spanish discovered the Combahee River in South Carolina, they called it the Jordan, after the river that runs in the Holy Land.

On Tuesday, June 2, 1863, two years into the American Civil War, whose central issue was the status of slavery, America's repentance for the slave trade took a turn which only a few years earlier would have been unthinkable. Fog rolled off the rice fields blanketing the river. Slaves were toiling the soil when they stopped, stock-still. With the morning fog lifting they saw an astonishing sight, three hundred Black Union soldiers jumping out of three gunboats, the *John Adams*, *Harriett Weed*, and *Sentinel*.

Even more unbelievable, a Black woman led the charge, shoulder to shoulder with Colonel James Montgomery and the 2nd South Carolina Volunteer Infantry Regiment. Harriet Tubman knew the lay of the land like the back of her hand. Many times, she had snuck into enemy Confederate lines. To the Union army, Tubman was an intelligence asset. To African Americans, she was the Black Moses.

The covert mission planned to remove a torpedo blockade placed across the Combahee River by the Confederate army and then blow up railroads, bridges, and starve the enemy of supplies. At Fields Point the Yankee raiders pillaged and torched eight plantations, mansions, mills, steam engines, and barns. The devastation was swift and sweeping. On the plantation of Joshua Nicholls, eight thousand bushels of rice, his house, out-buildings, and beloved library of rare books went up in smoke. The crops of three years burned. Then the daring raiders vanished into the morning light having destroyed millions of dollars of Confederate stores, cutting down the pontoon bridge at Combahee Ferry, and the enemy's communications as they went. Fifteen miles of fields were torched all along the riverbank.

When the firing started, the terrified slaves had run for the woods. Soon the smoke cleared and they peered out from the trees. Word spread that "Lincoln's gunboats come to set them free." The steamers' whistles blew, and down every road and field the slaves poured to the water's edge. Hundreds crowded the banks, reaching out to be saved. Harriet Tubman would later remember that "Some had white blankets on their heads with their things done up in them . . . Some had bags on their backs with pigs in them; some had chickens tied by the legs." One woman had "a pail on her head, rice a smokin' in it just as she'd taken it from the fire, a young one hangin' on behind, one hand around her forehead to hold on . . . [and a] hold of her dress two or three more [children]." The sight reminded Tubman of the Children of Israel coming out of Egypt.

That morning Harriet Tubman and the 2nd South Carolina Volunteer Infantry Regiment delivered 756 enslaved Africans out of the River Jordan's bondage. By ship their ancestors had forcibly crossed to the Americas. Now by boat they were being liberated to Beaufort. The sound of a slave army singing "There Is a White Robe for Thee" echoed across South Carolina.

River Raiders

The Combahee River Raid was only possible after Abraham Lincoln signed the Emancipation Proclamation on January 1, 1863. For the first time in US history, Black men could enroll in the army and navy and legally bear arms to resist against their lot in life. By the time the Civil War ended, almost 360,000 Union troops died fighting to abolish slavery. Some 300,000 Southern troops died fighting to preserve it. At first, African Americans were not allowed to bear arms. By the end, African Americans had served in 175 Union regiments. Over 179,000 fought in the last two years of the war, making up 10 percent of Union troops. Nearly 40,000 died in combat, paying the ultimate price. In one of US history's great ironies, many of the Union soldiers in the Combahee

River Raid were former slaves. Burning and pillaging the estates that had enchained them for decades was a sweet revenge, a long time coming.

The journey to the Combahee River started in Key West in February 1863 when Colonel Montgomery recruited 130 Black men who marched unarmed to Camp Saxton near Beaufort. Now bearing guns the troops started up the St. Johns River on March 10. Their destination, Jacksonville, was deserted. The troops passed the time learning how to march and shoulder arms. The Black unit pushed seventy miles above Jacksonville, catching and eating pigs, turkeys, and oranges along the way. By June 1, the raw recruits had made it to the Combahee River. When the raid was over, most of the slaves the army freed volunteered to join the war effort.

The Combahee River Raid was the first time Americans heard about the legend of Harriet Tubman. Wearing a coat, federal blue dress, and a large bandanna over short hair, carrying a musket and canteen, and her satchel filled with first aid equipment, the "Black Moses" was a nurse, cook, scout, and spy. She was the first American woman to lead an armed raid into enemy territory and has taken her place alongside some of history's boldest women like Joan of Arc and Florence Nightingale.

Tubman's life changed forever when she started working as a nurse in Port Royal in Beaufort County during the Civil War, where she helped sick and dying soldiers and civilians, ill from contaminated water and food, poor sanitation and hygiene. Smallpox, dysentery, measles, malaria, scarlet fever, typhoid, and pneumonia were killing thousands. To make a living she made and sold daily "about fifty pies, a great quantity of ginger-bread, and two casks of root beer."

Tubman turned out to have a knack for ferreting out information on rebel locations and movements from the local Black population, which she passed on to the Union's generals. Soon the army sent her scouting behind enemy Confederate lines seeking intelligence about rebel troop movements. As she traveled and watched, she peddled chickens and gingerbread as a cover.

Tubman's humanitarian fire brought her into contact with a kindred fellow, the abolitionist and reformer General David Hunter. Hunter had boldly declared all "contrabands"—escaped slaves—in the Port Royal district free. Shortly after, he let it be known that all slaves in the Department of the South, including South Carolina, Georgia, and Florida, were free. It was Hunter who was committed to building the first regiment of Black soldiers.

THE PORT ROYAL EXPERIMENT

When the Union Navy overran Beaufort District after the Battle of Port Royal on November 7, 1861, in the American Civil War, white plantation owners ran. Some ten thousand slaves were left in limbo, freed overnight. As "contraband of war" they were placed under the US Department of the Treasury's control.

In January 1862 General William Tecumseh Sherman arranged for an army of teachers from the North to train the former slaves. Three months later the Boston attorney Edward Pierce was appointed to set up the Port Royal Experiment, a network of schools and hospitals to empower ex-slaves to buy and run plantations. The steamship *Atlantic* sailed from New York City with fifty-three volunteer teachers, ministers, and doctors.

The Port Royal Experiment was a pioneering humanitarian effort to prepare former slaves of the South Carolina Sea Islands to be free American citizens. It covered fourteen islands with two hundred plantations. The experiment aimed to dismantle the plantation slave system in favor of a wage-based one. In its first year of operation, African American field hands harvested ninety thousand pounds of cotton and were paid $1 for every four hundred pounds—the first slaves freed by Union forces to earn a wage in the United States.

The scheme looked like a success. In 1863 President Abraham Lincoln ordered forty thousand acres of abandoned Confederate plantations to be divided among sixteen thousand African families. They had the option to buy the land at $1.25 an acre. About two thousand acres were snapped up. The dark side of government soon returned with Lincoln's death in April 1865. Andrew Johnson decided the following summer to forcefully restore all lands to their previous white owners. Not all white owners returned to the Sea Islands. Thousands of Black landowners and their descendants stayed on.

Harriet "Moses" Tubman, (1822–1913), is one of America's most famous women. She was born Araminta "Minty" Ross on the plantation of Anthony Thompson in the Parsons Creek district of Maryland. She was the granddaughter of a captive trafficked from Africa, and the fifth of nine children. As a teenager she was nearly killed by a blow to the head from an iron weight thrown by an angry overseer. Tubman suffered from headaches, seizures, and "sleeping spells," probably epilepsy, for the rest of her life. The experience gave her an iron will. In the late 1830s and early 1840s she worked for John Stewart, a Madison merchant and shipbuilder. In 1844 she married a free Black man called John Tubman. Minty changed her name to Harriet Tubman.

When her master died in 1849, Harriet and her siblings risked being sold at auction. Tubman ran away in the fall of that year, tapping into an underground organization. Traveling by the North Star by night, she made her way to freedom in Philadelphia. In 1851 Tubman visited Canada for the first time, working out how fugitives might cross the bridge over Niagara Falls. Everything had to be memorized: Harriet never learned to read or write.

Harriet Tubman, one of the most remarkable woman of her age, would go on to earn fame as the fearless "conductor" of the Underground Railroad. No one can say for sure how many slaves she liberated over sixteen years, but Tubman returned to the eastern shore of Maryland perhaps thirteen times. Hiding in drainage ditches, abandoned sheds, and piles of manure, she guided the runaway slaves to Chesapeake Bay, Delaware, Pennsylvania, New York, New England, and finally freedom in Canada. A supposed bounty of $10,000 was offered for her capture, later increased to $40,000. But the Moses of her people was fearless. The lash, bloodhound, or fiery stake would not stop her.

The Combahee River Raid, one of Harriet Tubman's finest hours, saw the largest freeing of slaves during the Civil War. All their lives they had prayed for freedom. Some were now sixty-five to seventy years a slave. And then Tubman arrived with an army of runaway field hands turned warriors. The day of reckoning and resistance shone bright.

Harriet Tubman, uneducated, female, and Black, but a lifelong humanitarian, suffragist, freedom fighter, and leader among men died on March 10, 1913, aged ninety-three. To serve the needs of destitute Black women, African Americans in Boston founded the Harriet Tubman Home in her memory. In World War II the US Maritime Commission launched the *Harriet Tubman* liberty ship. Later she was honored with her face on a first-class US postage stamp.

LET MY PEOPLE GO

B uffalo straddles a vital crossroads by land and sea in New York. To the west the slipper-shaped Lake Eerie runs to Cleveland, Toledo, Detroit, and, for runaway slaves, the most important town of the nineteenth century: Sandusky. To the north the Niagara River separates the United States from Canada.

If Diving With A Purpose wanted to find a freedom ship that ferried runaway slaves on the final leg of the Underground Railroad all the way to Canada, first they needed to do a different kind of deep diving. This time into dusty archives to search out a lake shipwreck that linked its skipper to fleeing slaves.

For the past few weeks, John Polacsek had been buried away in the Buffalo History Museum going through reams of old reports and newspapers like the *Buffalo Morning Express* looking for an elusive clue. It was hard going. The historian was bent over a scanner reading documents copied onto old-style microfiche. None of the lakes' old archives of ship lists and cargos were digitized. Behind John, row after row of gray storage boxes and catalogue filing cabinets held memories long buried.

The good folk of the lakes did not openly advertise their secret role taking slaves to Canada, for obvious reasons. The Fugitive Slave Act of 1850 made assisting enslaved people to freedom illegal. Abolitionists feared it as the "Bloodhound Bill" because of the relentless dogs sent to track down runaways. Anyone helping resist fugitives' capture was fined $1,000, about $31,000 today.

Kramer and Kinga were happy to see John again and find out if he had unlocked any sunken gems. The warm greetings over, Kramer cut to the chase. "Good to see you again. So, what do you have?" he asked, rubbing his hands together.

The divers sat down on either side of John, who was peering over his glasses at a large screen.

"I had a whole bunch of files that I was going through," John began. "The problem ends up being when you look at an Underground Railroad boat or a freedom boat, you got to figure out what happened to the boat. Some of them were abandoned, some of them burned. And what I'm just trying to do is narrow it down so that what we come up with is a boat that's still out there."

Not every ship ends up sunk. And not every sunken ship turns into a wreck preserved decades later.

John paused and added, "Then I came across this schooner, which is a possibility."

"It's called the 'Schooner Home.' It was a vessel coming from Buffalo to Sandusky. However, it ran for a number of months unaccounted for," John exclaimed, pointing to an entry in a local newspaper listing the "Schooner Home, Nugent, Sandusky" in 1848.

"What does that mean?" Kinga wanted to know.

"Well, when we look at the papers from the Port of Buffalo, they have arrivals and clearances to the custom house. Right now, there's kind of a gap in its history. If it doesn't show up in the port for say six months, where was it going?" John asked out loud.

Ships do not just vanish. They leave paper trails, sail in an orderly way. Customs houses list departures, arrivals, and what cargos they carried, goods that the government wanted to tax.

Trying to make sense of the question floating in the air, Kramer filled in the implication. "Do you suspect that because it was missing, that maybe it was smuggling fugitive Africans?"

John had good reason to hope this was the case for the *Home*. "That's a good possibility. I mean, knowing that Sandusky was full of abolitionists."

"So are you saying there's a possibility the *Home* was going to Canada?" Kinga checked.

"You would say that, yes," the historian confirmed.

Kramer and Kinga were busting to know more about the captain of the *Home*.

"Well, it was James Nugent who was the captain. He was an immigrant from Ireland," John set out. "He lived in Sandusky. And it's a good possibility that he was an abolitionist simply because of the people he was running around with in Sandusky."

Focusing on the prize, Kramer understood that the team needed to find out more about the elusive captain.

John agreed and put the divers to work. "Why don't you check out Captain Nugent, and I'll check out the missing months of the *Home*'s routes," he suggested.

"Sounds like a plan," Kramer grinned.

Singing to Freedom

The glory of African American spiritual music is celebrated worldwide. Today it has spread from the plantations to the church and from gospels soared on wings into mainstream culture. Pop stars from Aretha Franklin and Marvin Gaye to Whitney Houston and Jennifer Hudson were schooled in church. Few realize today the pivotal role music played in the African struggle for freedom.

Southern spirituals were more than a theme tune for runaway slaves shuttled along the Underground Railroad to the edge of the Great Lakes. Threaded through songs were hidden codes, secret signals for escaping, hiding, and warning of danger. Slaves were forbidden from being taught to read or write. Harmless singing was encouraged to keep up spirits. Most songs drew on biblical references to people, places, and stories that seemed to be speaking directly to nineteenth-century Black Americans' troubles.

The Underground Railroad ran under the utmost secrecy from the 1810s to the 1860s. Travel for fugitives was full of danger at every turn. Runaways usually only moved by night, walking ten to twenty miles a day to the next in a chain of safe houses, hidden in abandoned mines, tunnels, wagons with false bottoms, closets, and cupboards.

Coded songs were sung along the entire line of escape from preparing to run to safely reaching Canada. Harriet Tubman and of her fellow conductors started off by contacting slaves waiting to flee by softly singing along plantation boundaries. The hymn "Go Down Moses" was Tubman's go-to signature tune:

> *Go down, Moses, way down in Egypt's land;*
> *Tell old Pharaoh, to let my people go.*

Whispered words spread from mouth to mouth and slave to slave that Moses had arrived to shepherd her people north to their promised land. If Tubman sang a verse twice, followed by silence, it meant the coast was clear and the escape was a go. To slave masters the spirituals were just good old Christian tunes that did no harm helping workers pass the time. They might even heal their weary hearts. Little did they know their words were a matter of life and death. Egypt meant the South and pharaoh the slave owners. The Israelites were the slaves and Canaan was Canada. The Jordan River could mean the runaways' place of departure or Ohio.

When slaves heard conductors sing "Follow the Drinking Gourd," it was a map for how to run:

> *When the Sun comes back*
> *And the first quail calls*
> *Follow the Drinking Gourd,*
> *For the old man is a-waiting for to carry you to freedom*
> *If you follow the Drinking Gourd.*

The tune was alive with coded meaning for pinpricked ears, telling slaves the best time to start the long journey in springtime. The drinking gourd stood for the Big Dipper constellation and warned runaways to follow the line of the constellation to Polaris, which pointed to freedom.

When Harriet Tubman sang "Swing low, sweet chariot, Comin' for to carry me home!," the coast was clear for escape. Get ready. The sweet chariot—the Underground Railroad train—was ready to leave the station. Slaves would sing the "Gospel Train" to let others know they were preparing to run. Maybe they were ready to join too?

> *The Gospel train's a'comin'*
> *I hear it just at hand*

I hear the car wheel rumblin'
And rollin' thro' the land . . .
Get on board little children
There's room for many more.

"Wade in the Water" was another crucial signal sung by Harriet Tubman to warn fugitives to head for the water and throw distant bloodhounds off their scent:

Wade in the Water. God's gonna trouble the water.
Who are those children all dressed in Red?
God's gonna trouble the water.
Must be the ones that Moses led.
God's gonna trouble the water.

The hymn also harked back to the biblical story of the Exodus, where God splits the sea for the runaway Israelite slaves. Water is everywhere in American African spirituals because it was central to journeys past and future. Africans' captivity began crossing the Middle Passage between West Africa and the Americas. Later the Ohio River marked the dividing line between slavery and freedom across the Great Lakes. It was a modern River Jordan. The Bible inspired captives. It was their playbook for liberation.

Enslaved African Americans and their descendants left behind over six thousand spirituals, the soundtrack of the American diaspora. Spirituals were rites of passage that lived with the enslaved, fugitives and the free all their days.

When Harriet Tubman lay on her deathbed on March 1, 1913, the last song she sung out loud was a celebration of her life, "Swing Low, Sweet Chariot." The legacy lived on. A century after they were first sung, the same tunes became political weapons for the Civil Rights movement.

Station Hope

Kinga and Kramer had headed to Sandusky, a major center of abolition, to find out if James Nugent, captain of the *Home*, really ferried runaway slaves to free Canada. On the way they grabbed the opportunity to stop in Cleveland to see firsthand one of the shelters used by freedom seekers in the Underground Railroad.

In Cleveland, the Reverend Kelly Aughenbaugh, vicar of St. John's Episcopal Church, took Kinga and Kramer in the secret footsteps of fugitive slaves so close to liberty.

"The building that we're standing in was built in 1838, and from its beginning it kind of had this social justice lean," she explained. "St. John's was a stop on the Underground Railroad. In that time, the Underground Railroad had code names to describe the people and the places that they were traveling, to keep secret, but also so that they would know where they were going next. And Cleveland was known as 'Station Hope.' That was because if you made it to Station Hope, you most likely would make it to freedom."

The church was Cleveland's safest sanctuary. As Kinga and Kramer walked inside, St. John's felt ancient, with mysteries to share. The church stands less than a mile from the shore of Lake Erie, surrounded by a modern concrete jungle. Inside, the light was subdued. White paint peeled off the walls. But the wooden organ and rafter beams defied the passing time. The church, sandwiched between the meandering Old River and Cuyahoga River—the ancient Mohawk "Crooked River"—stood in the perfect place to move fugitives around with the least chance of being caught.

"Where we think people hid is actually the bell tower," the Reverend Kelly went on, "at the time the tallest structure in the city. And so people who were fleeing slavery would hide in the bell tower and they could look out to two places, the Cuyahoga River and to Lake Erie. Bodies of water. People could catch onto boats and then be taken to Lake Erie where they would then hop on ships."

Kinga and Kramer were cautiously led to the bottom of the very tower where runaway slaves hid. The walls were wet from the lake and river moisture, their paint patchy and stripped bare. The Reverend Kelly nimbly led the way up a near-vertical brown wood ladder; as she climbed she warned Kinga and Kramer to watch out for rickety timbers. The ladder could only take one person at a time. The stairs gave way to a narrow door barely high and wide enough for a human to enter without bending over, into a space whose raw walls looked more like a Gold Coast castle than a House of God. The main frame of the sagging old tower was propped up by stiff iron poles.

Kelly pointed into the bell tower where the ladders and landing soared ever higher.

"Can we go up there and take a look?" Kinga eagerly asked, always up for an edgy adventure.

The climb was on. Kramer would wait in the lower tower while his friends climbed the easily snapped ladders. They inched upward warily, keeping to the hopefully more solid sides, while Kelly laid out the scene of new runaways' arrival in Cleveland.

"Often when people traveled the Underground Railroad, it was at dawn or dusk. They didn't travel during the day because people would see you."

Kramer tried to help. "Step on the outside of the stairs, not in the center," he worried.

"It's nice to have a friend who is a former firefighter," Kinga replied through the gloom.

The iron bars propping up the tower's decaying walls crisscrossed one another like a giant industrial spider's web. Kinga and Kelly climbed safely to a narrow landing intersected with vast wooden beams.

The reverend explained that from here "There was a system in place to help these people make it to safety. And so with light signals from the river or the lake, people would know when it was safe to come down from the tower and either run or walk to get on a boat. Or they would sometimes be put in the back of horse-drawn carriages and then covered up."

By the sunlight fighting its way through the dark tower windows, Kinga made out two hidden side chambers. Kelly pointed out a third on the floor above. "Kramer, there are two rooms right here on either side, and they just go deep in and it's really dark. You actually can't see inside but this is probably where people would have hidden," she whispered excitedly.

Kelly led Kinga, her trousers coated in dust, for a careful peek. The diver reached a square hole in the wall, wooden framed, half her height, easy to miss. It was even smaller than the entrance to the Door of No

Return in Ghana's Elmina Castle. A narrow brick-lined space ran inward around fifteen feet toward a sloping roof.

"Be careful. Hold onto the rails and not the stairs," Kramer insisted, his brow furrowed with worry.

"Look at that. Oh my gosh, that's amazing," Kinga whispered down to Kramer. "One of these rooms with a little bit of light is where you can imagine one, two, three people could have stayed," she visualized. "This is your last leg of the journey and you're in this church steeple, and at night you would probably come out and look through these windows here because the signal would have been a lantern, so you would have been able to see it at night. People who were staying here were waiting for that signal."

The big question for Diving With A Purpose was whether one of those signals beckoning fugitive slaves to the water might have come from the *Home* schooner. The jury was out.

HOPE'S HERO

The team had moved base to Sandusky, a small town on Lake Erie. Here, 170 years ago, James Nugent, captain of the *Home*, that today lies at the bottom of Lake Michigan, regularly loaded his boat with merchandise and headed out across the Great Lakes. The burning question was: Did he really also ferry runaway slaves in a final leg to freedom? Was the *Home* a "Freedom Boat"?

Red-brick Victorian warehouses lined generously wide boulevards. Red-hulled Canada Steamship Lines, juggernauts of the water, inched their way from port to port. On the water's edge on a clear winter's morning, Kramer and Kinga had arranged to meet Yvette Darden from the Sandusky Historical Association and tap into her knowledge.

Yvette confirmed that "Sandusky was the great northern depot and was also named 'Station Hope' because of the strong possibility of reaching Canada from here without being captured."

The town was the final location before runaway slaves crossed to the Promised Land, all being well. A light breeze pointed the way northeast across Lake Erie toward Buffalo and liberty.

Sandusky was the most important terminal for one branch of the Underground Railroad. The town is famous for its abolitionist support. In *Uncle Tom's Cabin* it is from Sandusky that Harriet Beecher Stowe has a group of runaway slaves cross the water to Canada.

With his master, Mr. Riley, in hot pursuit on horseback, the first runaway escaped to Sandusky in the fall of 1820. The slave had been hidden by a Captain P. Shepherd, and a local Black man in charge of horses, in a barn next to a tavern. Riley hired a tracker and offered $300 in gold for his slave's capture. After four days of hide-and-seek, the runaway snuck onto the steamboat *Walk-in-the-Water* and sailed for Detroit. Still Riley pursued by sailboat. He was too late: his slave had landed in Canada. He was free.

Yvette pointed out several houses, still standing, where active abolitionists offered shelter, food, clothing, and a place to rest before it was time to come down to the waterfront and start the final push by boat.

"In the whole area, and maybe even the whole state, there were active abolitionists," Yvette explained. "There were a number of attorneys and judges that were in cahoots as abolitionists. There was the Honorable Rush R. Sloane. One time, there were seven runaways caught in a group together. They were hounded by slave catchers. And Rush Sloane asked for documentation of these dark-skinned people."

"Documentation meaning that the slave catchers could prove that these were escaped slaves?" Kinga asked.

"Right. The slave catchers didn't have documentation, so Rush Sloane said, 'There's no reason for you to be held here.' So, a group of citizens rushed the runaways to the waterfront for transport to Canada," Yvette told the team.

"While the slave catchers were still in the courtroom, they rushed them out?" Kramer probed.

Yvette confirmed the story, which is part of a great Sandusky tradition of resisting slavery.

"Wow. So what happened to Sloane because of that?" Kinga wanted to know.

Yvette finished with a twist to the tale. "Well, later on he was charged with aiding and abetting the runaways to get away. Was found guilty, was charged $3,000."

"That was so much money back in the day," Kinga exclaimed.

Yvette listed how "There were court costs that were $1,000 and then the rest of it was equal to the value of the runaways." Judge Sloane was forced to pay for the "property" that he let escape. Fortunately, the good folk of Sandusky pooled in to share the costs.

"The other abolitionists in town contributed toward the amount that he was charged. Rush R. Sloane was a prominent figure in the Underground Railroad movement in Sandusky," Yvette ended.

The burning question for Kramer was who spirited these well-judged slaves away to Canada. "Our research speaks of a Captain Nugent who was involved here in Sandusky. Do you have any records or any knowledge about a Captain Nugent?" he pushed.

To check whether any historical trail remembered who shipped the slaves, Yvette took Kinga and Kramer to an impeccably kept two-story wooden building painted glossy white, the Firelands Historical Society on Case Avenue. The research center with its sprawling library of four thousand books is the go-to place to check local genealogy and history, as well as housing Ohio's oldest museum. It also just so happens that a former vice president of the society was one Rush R. Sloane.

Soon the team was deep in literature and thought sitting around a rectangular dark wood table. Flags of the United States and Ohio stood to attention in the corner of a room next to a cozy brown sofa. The room looked part presidential, part student coffee shop. Kramer was immersed in a green book listing Sandusky's history, year by year.

Yvette and Kinga had taken one end to the table and were absorbed in a paper trail that dated from the time of the Sloane trial. It left an accurate account of the outcome and revealed, finally, just what type of man Captain Nugent was.

"Whose testimony is this?" Kinga asked.

They had come across a letter that had been written by a reliable witness, the mayor of Clyde, a small town near Sandusky. He had witnessed how Rush Sloane freed seven slaves on October 20, 1852. The runaways had arrived by train on the Mad River and Lake Erie Railroad. Just when they thought they had made it, the city marshal, on behalf of their Kentucky owners, dragged them off a steamboat about to sail for Detroit. There had been no authorities by the dock. The commissioner for customs, Earl Bill, had already resigned rather than be forced to respect a Fugitive Slave Act he did not agree with. Under a full moon, Marshal Rice marched the fugitives to the mayor's office. Sloane was found at home and rushed to the scene, where the stairways and halls of the mayor's office thronged with crowds.

Kinga picked up the volume in front of her and read how it all played out well in the end: "That party of fugitive slaves was carried to Canada concealed in the hold of the sailing vessel by a lake captain, then and now a robust Democrat in politics, a man with a conscience and a heart, resident of one of the lake cities."

So, the mayor of Clyde really did see firsthand the slaves' release and the shadowy captain who spirited them away.

The end of the testimony, while impressive for its moral backbone, was unhelpful to the team's quest. "But my lips are sealed for the lifetime of my informant," Kinga read out loud.

"He was sworn to secrecy not to tell the name of the captain that took the seven runaways to Canada," Yvette confirmed.

Kramer was having better luck and had tripped over a crucial piece of the puzzle. The mayor eventually heard the truth from the captain's own lips years later in 1877. Were his eyes deceiving him?

"I'm sorry, can you look at this," he interrupted Yvette, showing her a small red hardback book. "Here they list the names of the slaves . . ." Kramer's finger traced the names of the free fugitives, George Bracken, Emily Bracken, Ellen Bracken, Robert Pritt, Matilda Pritt, Eliza Pritt, and Thomas Pritt. Two families had been released by the good judge.

The final secret remained. "The mayor says his lips are sealed about the identity of the captain who took them to Canada. So how do you know it's Nugent?" Kinga asked Yvette.

"Look what Rush R. Sloane had to say about Captain Nugent," Yvette pointed out, deeper in the red book's pages.

Kinga read out loud the passage Yvette had noticed. "These fugitives were the same night received on a small boat by Captain James Nugent, a noble man now dead, then living at Sandusky and secreted on board the vessel; he commanded these seven and on the second day after were safely landed in Canada."

Kramer smiled and nodded in satisfaction. "We have documented proof now that he was involved as an abolitionist, that he ferried these seven Africans away to Canada," he stressed.

Kinga's mind raced. "So not only did he ferry these seven slaves in 1852 when this happened, it's safe to assume, then, that in 1848 when those missing months happened on the *Home*, he was also ferrying fugitives."

It made perfect sense.

INTO CANAAN

Kramer and Kinga had discovered that Captain Nugent of the *Home* was an abolitionist after all. History remembers the names of seven people he took to Canada. But how did he pull it off?

The divers had jumped camp to the shores of Lake Ontario. In Toronto, the scenery was paradise, a blissful freedom. Perfectly manicured green parks ran down to the lake banks. In the distance modern skyscrapers looked to the future. Here the old and new worlds met, just as they had for Sandusky's runaway slaves decades ago. Their pasts ended. Their futures began.

John Polacsek met the divers on the waterfront with two pieces of hot information to share. First, he wanted to introduce them to the *Empire Sandy* from Thunder Bay, a two-hundred-foot historical schooner built like the *Home*. With its three tall masts it looked and sailed like Captain Nugent's old boat.

The divers took to the water on a small motorboat, flanked by the romantic spectacle of the *Empire Sandy* sailing in full glory alongside. They filled John in on what they had learned about James Nugent and how it was certain he trafficked runaway slaves as an abolitionist.

The historian listened without surprise. His own research had come to the exact same conclusion.

"You've done your research on Captain Nugent, and I also got my part of the story," he added, looking around at Lake Ontario's wide water stretching east to the town of Saint Catharines and south by the Niagara River to Buffalo and into Lake Erie. The other reason why he had brought

Kramer and Kinga to Toronto was to see for themselves the missing piece in the puzzle of the Underground Railroad's last leg.

"This is one of the areas that the *Home* would have sailed through," John revealed. "And the reason for that is something that I found in the Sandusky newspaper." From his bag John pulled out a faded copy of the *Sandusky Clarion* from 1848, written in the years when Captain Nugent sailed the *Home*.

He pointed to the bottom right side of the front page and handed Kinga a magnifying glass. "Down here it says Port of Sandusky," John showed the divers.

Kinga took over and read "Arrived June 8th, Schooner Home, Nugent. So the *Home* went to Sandusky," she realized.

"You need to read a little bit more," John teased.

"Nugent, Oswego," Kinga read. "So, what does this mean, John?" Kinga asked, a little perplexed.

"It was coming back from Oswego, New York," the historian added happily.

"Okay, so it's coming from New York to Sandusky, Ohio." Kinga reconstructed the route in her head. It was quite a slog from the southeast bank of Lake Ontario, south down the Niagara River, passed Buffalo, into Lake Erie and southeast by way of Cleveland to Sandusky. About four hundred miles in all.

"That's right," John confirmed. "But in order to get to Oswego, it had to go through the Welland Canal, which is in Canada. The Welland Canal had been enlarged and it allowed the *Home* to go through it." The historian was enjoying slowly teasing out his sleuthing.

Kramer backtracked to the original mystery of this schooner. "This is the period of time the *Home* was missing," he checked.

"The four-month gap, everyone assumed it was just going back and forth to Buffalo." John had an alternative theory he was ready to share. "I'd like to show you now how Captain Nugent most probably took the runaways to freedom."

The three investigators on their small motorboat, flanked by the *Empire Sandy*, prepared to head out on Lake Ontario, following the exact same route the *Home* would have taken over 160 years ago.

The boats ran down the middle of a straight-side, man-made, waterway. Two narrow spits of land, dense green trees and bushes sprouting off its back, bordered the Welland Canal, a twenty-seven-mile-long and ninety-four-foot-wide artificial umbilical cord linking Lake Ontario and Lake Erie. The divers were in Canadian waters.

"We're at one of the oldest sections, lock twenty-seven," John explained. "In one month they'll put about 140 boats through it. When you come here, you're two hundred feet above Lake Ontario."

To get from Lake Ontario to Lake Erie, Canada to America, relied on a Herculean piece of technology.

John described how "You have to drop down twenty-seven locks. It's time-intensive. And this must've been the moment of truth for the fugitives. The boat is tied there, it comes to a certain level. You could walk off without too much of a problem."

And at Port Colborne that is exactly what the team did. Stepping ashore onto Canadian soil was simple. Kramer and Kinga stared out from the edge of the dock. Over a century ago, thousands of runaway slaves risked their own and their families' lives to step out to freedom. How many waterlogged ditches, risky hiding holes in barns, wagons, churches, and relentless masters hunting them down with burning torches and bloodhounds with bulging eyes, had each and every freedom seeker endured to make it to freedom, to Canaan, the Promised Land in the Americas?

The *Home* had sailed through this very lock taking fugitives to freedom. Kramer felt the freedom coursing through the air. How did the runaways know that they could finally stop looking over their shoulders? "At what point during the course of this journey do I finally get a chance to exhale and say, 'I've made it'?" he asked John.

John pointed north and told the divers that "Just down the ways is the village of Saint Catharines. And it had a number of fugitives who were there and had made a settlement. There were also a number of people who were involved with their welfare. One of the men was Mr. Merritt, who is the one who actually designed the Welland Canal. So, these are all people who were part of the fugitive aid society."

"That's incredible," Kinga exclaimed.

The team had reached the end of the line for Captain Nugent and the *Home* schooner, George Bracken, Emily Bracken, Ellen Bracken, Robert Pritt, Matilda Pritt, Eliza Pritt, and Thomas Pritt and the daring journey of the Underground Railroad.

"So, you ended up in Saint Catharines, you built your life there," John wrapped up.

Around seven hundred Black people settled in Saint Catharines between 1851 and 1858 after the Fugitive Slave Act became law. Their number included famous Southern abolitionists. One of them was Moses herself, Harriet Tubman, the conductor extraordinaire, who settled in the town for a decade from 1851.

Local freedom fighters and newly liberated fugitives would meet at the town's Salem Chapel to pray, give thanks, and plot the next great escape. It was William Hamilton Merritt, founder of the town's Refugee Slave Friends Society and builder of the Welland Canal, who helped them build the chapel.

Outside the church stands a bust of "Moses" defiantly looking South to the land of bondage. Beneath the statue plinth Harriet Tubman's words echo down the decades. After the United States passed the Fugitive Slave Act, she said, "I wouldn't trust Uncle Sam with my people no longer. I brought them all clear off to Canada."

The *Home* tramped around the Great Lakes first as a cargo ship but in the shadows as a freedom boat in the winding chain linking slave plantations and liberty in Canada. Kramer and Kinga headed off for Lake Michigan. It was time to dive Captain Nugent's boat, pay their respects, and close a story of proud resistance.

DOING THE CHARLESTON

Among the many ships of hope, one other stands out. It was called the *Planter*, and a Black skipper captained it. This story took place in Charleston harbor, a great terminus of the transatlantic slave trade. A fine natural harbor fed by two broad rivers, the Ashley and the Cooper, flowing past the city, and inland waterways stretching from the St. John's River in Florida to the Cape Fear River in North Carolina, made Charleston the go-to port for landing slaves to work between the lower Chesapeake and St. Augustine.

Charleston handled the lion's share of arrivals and sales of Africans in the Deep South. Incoming slavers had to stop at the pesthouse slums on Sullivan's Island for ten days of quarantine before being allowed to pass Fort Johnson. Advance notice of auctions was advertised in local newspapers like the *South-Carolina Gazette*, particularly on the docks at Stono Landing, Strawberry Ferry at Childsbury on the Cooper River, at Ashley Ferry at Dorchester on the north end of the Ashley River, and at Jacksonburg on the Edisto River. By the mid-1760s a dozen wharves ran from East Bay Street to the south, and to the north of Broad Street, built of pine piles and a hard core of hundreds of thousands of oyster shells. Some docks like Gadsden's Wharf, the largest in North America, were a staggering 840 feet long.

Slaves brought to South Carolina from American or English settlements in the Caribbean were taxed at five or six times the rate of people fresh off the boat from Africa. The biggest demand was for men aged between fourteen and twenty-five and females aged fourteen to twenty yet to give birth. Africans from Senegambia, the Gold Coast, the

Windward Coast, and Angola were especially valued, with captives from the River Gambia most wanted. South Carolina appreciated these peoples' strength, health, large limbs, and skills in agricultural work.

Slaves made up 70 percent of South Carolina's population. They worked in the rice fields and cultivated indigo. Others toiled as domestics, tailors, blacksmiths, bricklayers, coopers, shoemakers, and bakers. Along the waterfront Black men shouldered barrels and helped sail ships. The most expensive cargo of 220 Africans averaged £52 a person in July 1772, linked to high export prices for rice and indigo. All in all, 260,000 enslaved Africans were landed in South Carolina between 1670 and 1808—40 percent of all North America's slaves. In other words, odds are that most African American people living today had an ancestor that landed in Charleston.

The faces and places of Charleston's rich slave traders are dust. Gone is the workhouse where masters threatened to send unruly slaves "for a little sugar," which meant stripping and whipping girls or forcing men and women to walk the treadmill and run the risk of being crushed in their rollers. Look closely at the bricks cemented into the city's warehouses and you can still see the fingerprints of Africans pressed into the raw clay cut out of the rivers on nearby plantations.

The King of Beaufort County

One of the great heroes of Charleston and the Civil War was Robert Smalls. Smalls was born into slavery in the cotton planter slave quarters of Henry McKee in Prince Street on the Sea Island of Beaufort in South Carolina. As a boy Robert cleaned Henry's boots, carried logs to the fire, and water from the well. The brutality he saw day in, day out lit a burning fire for freedom inside him. He would later remember that:

> I have seen a good deal in travelling around on the plantations. I have seen stocks in which the people are confined from twenty-four to forty-eight hours. In whipping, a man is tied up to a tree and gets a hundred lashes from a raw hide. Sometimes a man is taken to a blacksmith's shop, and an iron

of sixty pounds weight is fastened to his feet, so that when it is taken off he cannot walk for days . . . I have heard of whipping a woman in the family way by making a hole in the ground for her stomach. My aunt was whipped so many a time until she has not the same skin she was born with.

As fate played out, McKee sent Smalls to live in Charleston at the age of twelve to earn bigger bucks for his master. In this flashy city, iron gates were mounted with sharp spikes to protect against slave revolts. Naked men, women, and children were sold like livestock in slave markets near the Old Exchange. Smalls was forced to wear a diamond-shaped numbered metal badge to show his enslaved status.

Hard work did not scare Smalls, who made his way from a waiter to Charleston lamplighter, a stevedore unloading cargo on the waterfront, and a sailor on a local schooner. By the time the Civil War erupted, Smalls was the wheelman of a 147-foot Confederate side-wheel steamer that transported troops, artillery, and supplies. The *Planter*, moored in Charleston's Southern Wharf along the Cooper River, a few miles from Fort Sumter, where the first shots of the war were fired, was among the fastest coastal steamers in the South. The wharf was lined with warehouses storing cotton and rice. It was also the headquarters of the arrogant Confederate general Roswell Ripley, commander of the Second Military District of South Carolina.

River life was subdued compared to the prewar days. An imposing fleet of Union ships had blockaded the entrance to Charleston harbor. The port city was a lifeline for the South, which depended on imports of war materials, food, medicine, and supplies. To make it to freedom, Robert Smalls's daring plan was to steal the *Planter*, escape Confederate lines with his family and deck mates, and gift the steamer to the Union fleet floating ten miles away, ready to blow up any outgoing traffic. The scheme was utter madness.

So, it was in the dawn hours of May 13, 1862, that an enslaved local ran the gauntlet of fortifications. As the experienced pilot of the *Planter*, Smalls knew where all the sandbars lurked and the local secret nautical signals. On the fateful day, to spend the night at home, Captain Relyea had left the ship in the hands of Smalls and a Black crew. It was a direct violation of Confederate military orders. But what mischief could a group of illiterate, cowering Black slaves do in a few hours?

Smalls ran up the steamer's stars and bars Confederate flag and South Carolina's blue-and-white state flag to identify the ship as Confederate. Then he popped on the captain's signature straw hat and glided unsuspected past Fort Johnson, a guard boat patrolling the harbor and a gunboat at anchor.

At 4:15 A.M. the *Planter* neared the final hurdle, mighty Fort Sumter, whose fortifications towered fifty feet above the water. The crew and their families fell to their knees, crying and praying. Smalls calmly blew two long and one short toot on the steamer's whistle, the Confederate signal for permission to pass. Fort Sumter's night sentry waved the ship on and shouted out, "Blow the damned Yankees to hell." The thirteen-mile arc of Union ships was now within sight. Seconds before being fired on, Smalls rushed to hoist a white bedsheet to signal surrender.

Robert Smalls was hailed as a hero. It was not just the four massive cannons recently stripped from Fort Sumter in the *Planter*'s hold that made the Union treat the slave respectfully. He had also brought with him priceless intelligence: a Charleston newspaper, the *Planter*'s secret code book for reading Confederate wigwag signals (coded messages sent by waving flags), and, of course, the steamer itself, a valuable acquisition to the Union squadron.

Rear Admiral Samuel Du Pont was so impressed by Smalls's bravery that he wrote to the secretary of the navy that "This man, Robert Smalls, is superior to any who has yet to come into the lines, intelligent as many of them have been. His information has been most interesting, and portions of it of the utmost importance." The *New-York Tribune* reported that "This man, though black, is a hero—one of the few History will delight to honor. He has done something for his race and for the world of mankind . . ."

The Boston Evening Transcript celebrated Smalls with the front-page poem "Our Country Calls":

> *Hurrah for Robert Smalls, my boys,*
> *Hurrah for Robert Smalls!*
> *He broke secesh's thrall, my boys,*
> *And came without a call.*

His bounty was the flag, my boys,
The flag that waves for all,
He sunk the rebel rag, my boys,
Hurrah for Robert Smalls!

Du Pont took care of his people. Smalls was free from slavery and famous. Eventually, he was made captain of the *Planter*, the first Black captain of an army ship, and paid $150 a month, just $19 less than a Union major. With his salary, and the reward the navy paid him for handing it the *Planter* on a plate, Smalls's rags to riches story came full circle in January 1864 when he bought the large white house on Prince Street in Beaufort where he was born and his mother sweated as a house slave.

At the end of the war, Henry McKee's widow, Jane, returned to town to find her riches and plantations gone. Suffering from dementia, she knocked on Smalls's door. Face-to-face with his former owner, Smalls invited Jane McKee into his house—her old home—on Prince Street and gave her the master bedroom. Never mind that she refused to dine with Smalls. Later, Robert gave money to McKee's widowed daughter and helped her sixteen-year-old son get a job as a midshipman at the US Naval Academy.

The Civil War hero rose rapidly up America's greasy pole. In 1867 Smalls opened a school in Beaufort for African American children. He was a founder of the Enterprise Railroad Company of Charleston and became a major general in the state militia to help end violence between whites and Blacks in South Carolina. Smalls was so popular among the Sea Island's Black community that they hailed him as the "King of Beaufort County." The natural-born politician became one of the first African American members of Congress, serving five terms in the US House of Representatives.

Like Harriet Tubman and Rosa Parks, Robert Smalls refused to play the victim. Today he should be remembered not just as a Union hero but as an all-American hero. As his tombstone reminds America, MY RACE NEEDS NO SPECIAL DEFENSE, FOR THE PAST HISTORY OF THEM IN THIS COUNTRY PROVES THEM TO BE THE EQUAL OF ANY PEOPLE ANYWHERE. ALL THEY NEED IS AN EQUAL CHANCE IN THE BATTLE OF LIFE.

Robert Smalls, congressman and father of public education in the United States, won not just the battle but the war.

A FINAL HOME

As it turns out, several years after Captain Nugent ferried runaways to Canada, the *Home* sank in a collision with the *William Fisk* on Lake Michigan in 1858. Everyone survived. One hundred and twenty-three years later, the schooner's memorable bones were discovered among Lake Michigan's hundreds of wrecks.

Diving With A Purpose were back in US waters to dive for the first time what had been identified with certainty as a "Freedom Boat."

The team could imagine George Bracken, Emily Bracken, Ellen Bracken, Robert Pritt, Matilda Pritt, Eliza Pritt, and Thomas Pritt fleeing across more than 330 miles from Kentucky to the edge of the Promised Land at Sandusky on Lake Erie. They traveled by night, listening for the slightest sound of bloodhounds. By day, they became ghosts, hiding wherever fortune led them, in muddy ditches or unsuspecting farmers' barns before jumping onto a locomotive for the last land leg of the Underground Railroad.

Then they were hauled off a steamer at the eleventh hour and thrown before the mercy of the US law when a miracle happened. The same law that was charged with sticking to the Fugitive Slave Act, in Sandusky, turned a blind eye to big America. The runaway slaves became free citizens. They had made it.

The schooner with so much history, on whose deck the heroic Captain Nugent once strode, now lay far below at a depth of 175 feet. Richard Stevenson would lead the team equipped with the same trimix gases and special gear used on the Royal African Company slaver in the Western

Approaches to the English Channel. In their specialist space-age suits, with wide breathing tubes and double dive tanks, the team looked like they were heading up to outer space. Instead, they were heading down to inner space.

Kramer suited up. Richard was taking nothing for granted. "The deeper you go, you're committed to the water for a longer period of time, so we have to watch topside conditions more carefully on deeper dives."

For this reason, Josh and Kinga would free dive from above to watch out for any signals of diver distress. Richard had devised a simple system to communicate with the topside team. "Red bag comes up, means something's kinda changed, but we're in control of the situation. A yellow bag comes up, that means we absolutely need your assistance," he made clear.

The colored bags were known in diving circles as delayed surface marker buoys (DSMBs). When divers are submerged, they can be inflated, also showing their positions deep down.

A bluish green gloom enveloped the divers, getting darker with every foot they plummeted. Richard and Diving With A Purpose were traveling through space back in time. Kinga and Josh soon lost sight of their friends. Just bubbles left an echo of where they must be.

If the *Niagara* was a sight to behold, the *Home* could hardly be called a wreck. It was still a ship; a whole vessel standing upright on the seabed, resolutely resisting change like the hundreds of runaways it once carried. From above, the outline of the schooner was intact, not broken up like 99 percent of the three million wrecks scattered across the world's seas.

THE *HOME* SCHOONER

- Sailing schooner, two masts
- Built by Redfield, Lower Sandusky, 1843, to trade grain, lumber and general merchandise between Lake Erie and the upper lakes
- 25.7 meters long, 7.1 meters wide, depth of hold 2.2 meters, 128 tons
- Owners, W. D. Winslow, Robert White, and Thomas Jones of Chicago

- Sunk October 23, 1858, in collision on Lake Michigan, bound Manitowoc for Milwaukee, no loss of life
- Wreck mostly intact at 51 meters deep. Collision damage to starboard bow; stern cabin missing; foremast pulled up in commercial fishing nets.

The divers could make out the *Home*'s deck planks and the hatch through which Captain Nugent spirited away the Sandusky seven into the hold, hidden in sight of US soil. They found the same kind of hatches through which more than twelve million enslaved Africans were forced and trafficked across the Middle Passage over centuries. The Welland Canal was not just the final stop on the Underground Railroad, for thousands it was the end of the line for the unfathomable atrocity of the transatlantic slave trade.

There were the railings where the runaways peered out to land and held tight, pinching themselves, as Canada came ever closer into view. The *Home*'s mast that powered its sails to freedom lay unbroken, mute on the deck. The iron anchor was still lashed to the bow, standing upright on the seabed, leaning against the lower hull. Its rope line ran upward to a capstan, ready to be winched up. The wooden rudder, too, was as sound as the last day the *Home*'s steering wheel turned. Nugent's schooner was pristine, apart from the tens of thousands of mussels infesting every wooden surface.

After the divers surfaced, nobody spoke. Everyone was caught up in their private thoughts. Reading about history can be dispassionate. It is something that happened moons ago. Seeing the past through its archaeology, its physical remains, is an emotional privilege. It messes with your mind. No longer does what happened to a group of runaway slaves in 1852 feel faceless when you glide through the very spaces where they stood

Sitting on the research boat staring out over a now flat Lake Michigan, Kramer tried to envision this space, this time and what it meant to his own complicated personal journey. He tried to imagine what somebody would have felt having traveled, three, four, five hundred miles on foot to get to this final point. People carrying their kids any which way to make it to a safe haven like Sandusky in hiding, waiting for an opportunity to get on a boat. And still the fear that somebody can come and snatch and drag you all the way back to slavery.

Then the rare instance of the special people who went back into the lion's den to help others get free, doing it time after time. Some of the conductors who traveled back and forth were inevitably caught and killed.

"The drive for freedom is universal. The sacrifice and resistance of these special conductors, who were not paid a bean for their risk, is what made it possible for me to be here," Kramer mused.

The sands of times past ran out. It was time to return to the present, the land of the living, and move on to hunt down a few final slave wrecks to give voice to the ancestors.

One final act of remembrance awaited. The team had tracked down a poem by an Ohio gentleman named Joshua McCarter Simpson. Simpson taught himself to read and write, and became a conductor on the Underground Railroad, helping runaway slaves get to the Great Lakes and ferrying them to Canada.

On behalf of the divers, Josh read some of his memorable lines written in the early 1850s:

> I'm on my way to Canada,
> that cold and distant land.
> The dire effects of slavery I can no longer stand.
> Farewell, old master, don't come after me,
> I'm on my way to Canada where coloured men are free.

The friends had circled the globe remembering and honoring the voices of the men, women, and children who were taken from West Africa and died in enslaved exile or on slaver ships in the middle of nowhere. In this place nobody died. They lived. Never more so on their journey did the emotion of the moment touch the divers.

Wrecks where Africans died make you angry at the lack of humanity and justice they never got. Freedom boats were success stories, forces of good in a bad world.

Alannah, Kramer, Kinga, Josh, and the team took their time dropping red, yellow, and pink rose petals overboard. They watched them float free on the water, above the final resting place of the *Home*. Nobody spoke. This was a wreck like any other Great Lakes wreck. But it was a wreck that embodies all that is good in the human spirit.

The *Home*, a highway to the Promised Land, was a ship of hope.

ABOLITION

Amazing Grace, how sweet the sound
That saved a wretch like me
I once was lost, but now am found
Was blind but now I see.
—John Newton, former slave
ship captain, 1772

UNSHACKLED

Rapparee Cove, Ilfracombe, Devon—UK

The floor of the Atlantic Ocean is one giant graveyard and for some parts of history a crime scene. The remains of 1.8 million African ancestors, who lost their lives and liberty in these dark recesses of the world, cover the ocean floor.

For centuries, the transatlantic slave trade seemed unstoppable. But it was ground down until it was eventually brought to an end.

The city of London was the beating heart of slave trafficking. England's enormous wealth was in part created by trading enslaved humans. In one decade alone, 1790–1800, British ships made 1,340 voyages across the Atlantic and sold nearly 400,000 enslaved Africans. Another 266,000 were forcibly shackled and shipped from 1801 to 1807. In a twist of historic justice, it would be in London where the first political punches were thrown to knock down such a harrowing chapter in human behavior.

What was the spark that suddenly got so many people fired up in their lifetime to shake up the old ways and refuse to put up with slavery? What made England the first European country to abolish slavery and what made the year 1807 so special?

Rebel Cove

In a small sleepy town on the west coast of England, just at the moment when the tide was finally beginning to turn against the slave trade, a storm shattered a ship called the *London*. It was carrying over sixty Black men and women. Almost all died when the out of control hull smashed onto the cliffs in the Bristol Channel. The tragedy was practically forgotten until recently, when Professor Mark Horton and local explorers began reviving a confused tale.

The Diving With A Purpose team had headed to Ilfracombe in north Devon on a windy winter's day. From the cliff top, where they met up with Mark Horton to get to the bottom of the mystery of the *London*, Alannah, Kramer, Kinga, and Josh peered down the vertical drop into the tiny Rapparee Cove, an old Irish name meaning "rebel." The beautiful bay, almost circular, looked scooped-out by nature. It would take a truly bad stroke of luck for a ship to end up smashing into such a small inlet.

THE *LONDON* TRANSPORT SHIP

- Three-hundred-ton merchant vessel, built at Shoreham, West Sussex, 1764
- Owner James Mather, commander Captain William Robertson
- Sailed to Honduras for cargos of mahogany wood
- A troop transport ship in the Ganges Fleet that attacked the French West Indies, April to June 1796
- Caught in a storm in the Bristol Channel, wrecked off Rapparee Cove, Ilfracombe, North Devon, October 9, 1796
- Supposedly carrying five chests of treasure and ex-slaves turned French soldiers as prisoners of war

"The story starts in 1796," Professor Horton began. "A convoy of ships was coming in from the West Indies carrying loot, but also Africans from the former French Colonies, who'd been fighting for independence in St. Lucia. They had been captured and re-enslaved. And one of the ships, the *London*, got separated."

"A great storm erupted and, as you can see, it's a very dangerous coastline. And in a trice the ship was dashed onto the rocks just here.

The people on the deck survived, but of course the people below decks, shackled in their positions down there as cargo, would have drowned as the ship stoved in. The water would have rushed in. It was a dark night in October. Nobody would have bothered to come and rescue them."

The disaster was picked up by the *Ilfracombe Parish Magazine*, which reported how "It was late in the evening when a gun was heard faintly booming in the distance. A fine vessel was seen in distress . . . loaded with fellow beings as slaves . . . such invaluable treasure—a cargo of human life with gold and specie, the worth of which none shall ever answer . . . the noble vessel sank beneath the gurgling waters, amidst the agonizing cries and shrieks of those on board, thus ruthlessly and desperately deprived of precious life. In the morning the beach was covered with the bodies of the unfortunate Negroes, washed up by the tide . . ."

"So, these people died in shallow water and no one bothered to unshackle them or even give them a fighting chance?" Kinga asked.

"Everyone was looking after their own skin," Mark shrugged.

Alannah wondered what pieces of the *London* might have survived the pounding ocean. "Are any of those remains, any of that, still down there today?" she asked.

"Well, surprisingly, nobody has ever looked," Mark told the team. "And we will be the first to try and explain this tragedy from the very last days of the slave trade."

The great mystery about the *London* was what it was transporting and how it ended up sinking. Local memory tells a romantic tale of a band of West Country rogues who made a living from luring ship captains to the rocks so they could plunder spilt cargos. In exactly this age-old way, the *Ilfracombe Parish Magazine* in 1856 reported how

> It is well known by many old men now living that about sixty years ago a vessel, manned by blacks, ran ashore, and that the then best families in the town (being nothing but wreckers and smugglers) murdered the crew and buried the bodies on the beach, and then plundered the vessel of a very valuable cargo, consisting of ivory, doubloons, jewels, &c . . .

Ilfracombe's scheming townsfolk, so the story goes, pulled off the dastardly deed by tying lanterns to horses' tails and leading them along the cliffs. From afar, the unsuspecting victims mistook the beams for a lighthouse, for salvation. For very good reasons Ilfracombe's wreckers were known as Combe Sharks.

Whether the "lured to their death" twist is partially true for the *London*, nobody can prove for sure. In part, because conflicting versions of what went down on that stormy night of October 9, 1796. The *Ilfracombe Port Book* for 1796, for instance, described how, "Last evening 'The *London*' of London, a transport, William Robinson, master, from St. Kitts with French prisoners aboard, was unfortunately driven on shore at the entrance of this harbor, upward of 40 persons drowned. The vessel was entirely lost." The accident was dismissed as nothing more sinister than caused by the awful British weather.

Another take on the fate, published in the *Transactions of the Devonshire Association*, remembered a very different "cargo" than prisoners and insisted that:

> This Rapparee Cove was the scene of a dismal wreck, nearly a century since, of a Bristol ship, with slaves on board. Their corpses were denied Christian burial, and their skulls are now at times turned up in neighbouring fields. Tradition says that many of them were drowned with iron fetters on their legs.

Mark Horton and Diving With A Purpose's mission at Rapparee Cove was to put a 222-year-old trail of forensic archaeology under the microscope to weigh up which of the versions of the *London* cold case rang true.

Nobody is even sure of the ship's size. Accounts vary from three hundred tons to double that, at six hundred tons, though the smaller size is almost certainly right. The death toll was also counted at forty, fifty, or maybe sixty people, although the *Ilfracombe Customs Book* put the drowned at forty souls. And the biggest conundrum of all? Who were the Black men and women who died, suspiciously shackled in the hold?

Finding out the truth would mean digging on both land and sea, and fast, to beat the rising tide.

A Moral Steam Engine

In the age of the slave trade, it was not easy to spread new ideas like the abolition of slavery. One giant of a man, with bright blue eyes, red hair, and an iron will, bucked the trend to force through irreversible change.

Thomas Clarkson was born in 1760, a native of Wisbech in Cambridgeshire. He had every intention of becoming a deacon in the Church of England. Life's compass steered him in a different direction. While studying at Cambridge University he entered a prestigious Latin essay competition in 1785. Its timely topic asked, "Is it lawful to make slaves of others against their will?" Clarkson scooped up the first prize. And that was supposed to be that. God beckoned.

Soon after, Clarkson graduated, packed his bags, and headed south on his horse for London, wearing the black garb of a clergyman to start a promising career in the Church. As he counted off the miles to his new life, he found his thoughts sidetracked, not by saving Christian souls but by slavery. Along the River Rib in the county of Hertfordshire, Clarkson stopped in his tracks and sat down on the grass, confused and torn.

There on the road to London, Clarkson had his Road to Damascus moment. Two months spent researching the transatlantic slave trade in Cambridge for his winning essay had shaken the student to the core. There and then he swore that "it was time some person should see these calamities to their end." The birth of Britain's antislavery movement can be traced to that single moment by the roadside at Wadesmill in June 1785. Clarkson was radicalized. He was ready to swing into action.

The ex-priest devoted the rest of his life and his very health to the cause. To fuel William Wilberforce's debates in Parliament with facts to change the law on slavery, Clarkson left no stone unturned. He helped found the Society for Effecting the Abolition of the Slave Trade with powerful Quaker friends and funding. Then he set about collecting an unprecedented collection of witness testimony for the House of Commons' committee hearings. The truth had to be so overwhelming that nobody could ignore it.

By the time Clarkson finished his epic fact-gathering exercise, pulling sixteen-hour days, he had ridden thirty-five thousand miles and interviewed over twenty thousand sailors, merchants, and ships' surgeons in taverns and quaysides. Mostly he toured what he called the "fountain head," the major slave ports like Bristol and Liverpool. For a decade from 1783, Liverpool ships had trafficked over three hundred thousand Africans into slavery, while cities like Manchester sold £200,000 (around $28 million today) of goods a year to slave ships.

Clarkson thought that the power of the people was the best line of defense, creating a "ferment in the public mind." He oversaw the Herculean task of pushing Britain's great towns and cities to flood Parliament with petitions written on rolls of stiff parchment. Manchester lit a fuse in December 1787 that took off like a forest fire. A year later 103 petitions in favor of ending the slave trade had been signed by one hundred thousand people. Across the land, petitions were left for signature in town halls, printing shops, hotels, banks, coffeehouses, and pubs. Sheets were signed at Hatchards book shop on Piccadilly, Mortlock China Manufactory on Oxford Street, and in three of London's most popular taverns.

When the first abolition bill was introduced in 1791, Wilberforce lost the debate. Clarkson and the abolitionists responded by presenting 519 new petitions with over 390,000 signatures to Parliament. The message was loud and clear: the public would not be turned. The people had spoken. The petitions overwhelming the House of Commons were not the rarified opinion of nobles, magistrates, clergy, and Oxford or Cambridge professors. Almost all were the signatures of the working man and woman.

JOHN NEWTON: SLAVER, SINNER, PRIEST

John Newton, born in 1725, sailed the seas from the age of eleven. In a colorful life he was flogged on deck by the Royal Navy and gifted by a Guinea slave trader to a Sherbro princess in Sierra Leone, where the infidel and libertine became a servant of slaves in West Africa.

From 1748 to 1754 Newton worked as a first mate and then captain on Liverpool slave ships, where he gave in to his "brutish lusts" and sexually exploited women captives. Later he admitted that "When the women and girls are taken on board a ship, naked, trembling, terrified . . . they are often exposed to the wanton rudeness of white savages . . . The prey is divided, upon the spot . . . Resistance or refusal, would be utterly in vain."

After surviving a storm off Ireland, Captain Newton found God. In 1764 he was ordained as an Anglican priest. The ex-slaver and rapist went on to publish half a dozen books and 279 hymns. But he never spoke a word in public against slavery. He still invested in the slave trade and socialized with old slaver captains at the Jamaica Coffee House in London. His sermons preached that the American Revolution and disastrous hurricanes in the West Indies were God's punishment for Britain's sins. As for slavery—not a word.

Over thirty years after sailing as a slave captain, the abolitionist Thomas Clarkson caught up with Newton in January 1788. The priest was persuaded to publish a powerful pamphlet, *Thoughts Upon the African Slave Trade*. Few today remember Newton's slaving sins. Instead, he is celebrated as the author of the world-famous American hymn "Amazing Grace," ironically made famous by African American singers from Mahalia Jackson to Aretha Franklin.

When all else failed, and Clarkson needed the art of greater persuasion to reach deaf ears, he opened his campaigning chest. What the eye could see spoke louder than words. Clarkson's wooden box was divided into compartments that he called "divisions." Some held samples of African wood, mahogany, ebony, palm, mangrove, and dates. Others a selection of ivory, musk, pepper, cinnamon, rice, tobacco, indigo, cotton, and fruits, all valuable medicines. There was an African loom and spindle with cotton made by Natives, white and multicolored, as well as gold trinkets, iron knives, leather bags, sandals, daggers, and dagger cases.

The fourth and final division held instruments of torture, a thumb screw, a *speculum oris* for forcing open the mouths of captives refusing to eat, chains, shackles, and iron neck collars. Clarkson could talk like a politician when needed but also needed props to perform. Speaking in public, he had to shock and dramatize with great force how Britain could turn a profitable trade with Africa in goods other than human beings.

Eventually, on May 12, 1789, William Wilberforce had enough ammunition to make his first speech to Parliament against slavery. The path to freedom was slow and winding. It would take twenty years, fighting the deep pockets of West India plantation owners, for Britain to take action.

William Wilberforce is credited today as the man who abolished slavery. But it was this other remarkable Briton, Thomas Clarkson, who was the brains. The novelist Jane Austen expressed her love for Clarkson. The poet Samuel Taylor Coleridge, famous for the *Rime of the Ancient Mariner*, called him a "moral Steam-Engine" and a saint.

Feeling Wrenched

The Bristol Channel has the highest tidal range in the world. It can vary by forty to fifty feet. The team at Rapparee Cove had chosen this exact moment, the lowest tide of the year, to investigate the mystery of the *London*. Mark Horton's team was preparing to work on dry land with ground-penetrating geophysical technology. They planned to peer beneath the sand—harnessing an X-ray vision superpower—to see metallic wreckage from the *London* buried on the beach, and then to dig it up. Diving With A Purpose, meanwhile, was heading out to sea to check for more substantial remains underwater.

Kramer was back from diving freedom ships in the Great Lakes, and now needing to make sense of the slave trade as a giant crime scene. The team busied itself running equipment down a narrow, near-vertical staircase to the slippery quay in Ilfracombe harbor.

From the deck of the *Shelley VI* dive boat, while he fussed with his breathing regulator, Kramer admitted that "This mission is disturbing to me because these Africans had actually fought and won their freedom on the island of St. Lucia in the Caribbean." He added, "And within a year of that time, the British came back, and re-enslaved them. Took them back to England. They didn't bring them from St. Lucia to here as prisoners of war, they brought them as re-enslaved Africans. They ended up dying in chains in the hull of that ship in freezing cold water."

The team headed out on choppy water to check out the lay of the sunken land. Taking winds and waves into consideration, they had plotted the likely point where the ship hit the rocks and went down. The advance divers had plotted out some promising targets. The dive would start with the deepest target and move ever closer to the spot where the *London* was probably spiked on the rocky shore. The divers were less than a hundred meters from land.

The sunken terrain was unlike anything Diving With A Purpose had investigated so far. The seabed was a continuation of the rocky shore. Alannah, Kramer, Kinga, and Josh swept through dramatic gullies flanked by steeply cutaway bedrock. No coral, kelp, or flowing seaweed here, just rock, large pebbles, and silt. In keeping with the English weather's reputation, the visibility was rubbish.

Alannah, despite the awful conditions, was buzzing because "For the first time since the *London* foundered more than 220 years ago, an underwater search for the wreck is finally happening." But she had concerns. "It's not a very deep dive, but the visibility is not good. The Northern Atlantic waters are frigid, and the Bristol Channel currents are exceptionally strong." Alannah had suited up with warm gloves for this dive.

To find debris from the wreck, the team scanned the seabed with detectors looking for metallic remains of the ship, pieces of the hull, nails, guns, anchors, chains, and shackles. The divers worked in shifts. Each pair surveyed the shallows for up to an hour. Then the next team jumped in.

Across coarse silt mixed with sand, gravel, and shell fragments, and at the bottom of rocky gullies where shipwrecked artifacts are often trapped, the team swept back and forth. There were tons of hits down there, some modern but also hopefully far older. The detectors kept up a constant beeping, like an overexcited puppy.

As the hours passed, one of the magnetometers lit up with promise. Kramer and the shift team started digging feverishly—digging and fanning and fanning and digging. The divers vanished in a tornado of swirling silt. Soon they lost sight of their dive buddy. Minutes later they could not even see their hands. The Bristol Channel became a fog of zero visibility.

Back on the dive boat, after his shift was over, Josh was cautiously excited. "And you know I found something," he spluttered, handing over a lump of concreted iron the size of a fork to the team archaeologist. "This is what I found. What do you think that is?" He could not wait to hear.

A quick bang of the find against the boat railing knocked off the concretion. From inside appeared in all its glory . . . a modern wrench, no doubt lost by a passing fisherman trying to fix his motor.

"It's a wrench. I found a wrench," Josh exclaimed in good humor.

The hunt continued, a race against the clock. After hours of searching, the team had failed to find even a ship's nail. The tide started to turn, so the team was forced to give up the chase, pack their bags, refocus, and pick up again the next day.

For now, it was time to hand the baton of responsibility to the archaeologists on land. Hopefully they would have better luck.

THE DAY AMERICA SHOOK

On the other side of the ocean, in the United States, slavery was so entwined with the local economy that a groundswell in public opinion was not enough to end it. Here, abolition was earned in blood in the deadliest conflict America has ever known.

In the United States, the struggle for abolition turned on one battle at Antietam in Maryland on September 17, 1862. The Civil War was at a dangerous crossroads. The *New-York Tribune* warned that "For the first time, if I remember, I believe it possible . . . Washington may be taken . . ." Antietam would be the moment of reckoning for the future of the United States and slavery in a crucial border state between North and South.

North and South were worlds apart. The antislavery North's financial and industrial powerhouse was home to twenty-three states and twenty-two million people. It was America's hub of banking, merchandising, shipping, and insurance. The South, stretching from the Potomac River to the Gulf of Mexico in the Atlantic Ocean, was the rural backwater of *Gone with the Wind*. Eleven states with a population of nine million—three and a half million being African slaves—made their wealth from cotton, tobacco, rice, iron, coal, and timber. Getting around was still slow. In 1862, the Southern railway was still incomplete.

President Lincoln was under heavy pressure to end slavery from his military commanders, Congress, and the newspapers. The *New-York Tribune* added to the strain by publishing "The Prayer of Twenty Millions," an open letter to Abraham Lincoln demanding the freeing of all slaves who ran away from the Confederate South and joined the Union North's war effort.

A PRAYER OF TWENTY MILLIONS

Horace Greeley, "The Prayer of Twenty Millions," *New-York Tribune*, August 20, 1862. To Abraham Lincoln, president of the United States:

"We cannot conquer Ten Millions of People united in solid phalanx against us, powerfully aided by the Northern sympathizers and European allies. We must have scouts, guides, spies, cooks, teamsters, diggers and choppers from the Blacks of the South, whether we allow them to fight for us or not, or we shall be baffled and repelled. As one of the millions who would gladly have avoided this struggle at any sacrifice but that Principle and Honor, but who now feel that the triumph of the Union is dispensable not only to the existence of our country to the well being of mankind, I entreat you to render a hearty and unequivocal obedience to the law of the land."

By the late spring of 1862, Lincoln was ready to sign up to emancipation. The wheels of change were rolling ever faster. In July he read a draft proclamation to his cabinet and had dipped his pen, ready to sign. Only his military advisers stopped him in his tracks, pushing the president to hold back until he had the feel-good wind of a military win in his sails.

And so it was that a secret agenda was put in play. For now, Lincoln locked the secret document away in his desk. Antietam would become that turning point in the war between North and South, the battle for freeing America's slaves and the very future of the United States.

At Antietam, rolling hills, thick woods, and sprawling cornfields ran alongside a creek, shallow enough for a man to wade through waist deep or cross by its three bridges. To get in and out of town you took the Hagerstown Pike, the main road north to the towns of Hagerstown and Sharpsburg, thirteen miles away.

President Lincoln spun the battle as the great victory the Union had longed for. No matter the twelve hours of bitter warfare ended in a stalemate. The convenient facts showed that on the night of

September 17, 1862, the commander of the Confederate States army, General Robert E. Lee, crossed the Potomac River and retreated to Virginia. The troops of the North stayed put. The wily Lincoln decided that if his soldiers were still on the field of battle and the enemy was not, he had won. And in one swoop, "God had decided this question in favor of the slaves," the president pronounced.

The cost of freedom was high. The Union saw 2,108 dead and 12,410 casualties; the Confederate wounded reached 10,316 with 1,546 dead. It was the bloodiest single day of the Civil War, deadly even by modern standards. Consider that between 2001 and 2021, 2,448 American servicemen and women were killed in the war in Afghanistan. On one day in 1862 that number was exceeded by more than a thousand.

The sight of the battle shocked everyone who was there. General Williams later told his family that "If all the stone and brick houses of Broadway should tumble at once the roar and rattle could hardly be greater, and amidst this, hundreds of pieces of artillery, right and left, were thundering as a sort of bass to the infernal music." By the afternoon of the fateful day, General George McClellan sent a telegram informing Washington that "We are in the midst of the most terrible battle of the war—perhaps of history."

After the choking smoke lifted, the land had turned red. Bodies were heaped up in the cornfields or draped where they fell over post-and-rail fences. The dead filled every farmhouse, barn, and cabin. Broken wheels, abandoned cannons and rifles, haversacks, and canteens were scattered by the frenzy of war. A stench of burned bodies and horses filled the air. The buzzards circled overhead. The pockets of nearly all the dead had been turned out, robbed of valuables. The needy rebels stole the enemies' shoes, too.

Five days after the Battle of Antietam, Lincoln's cabinet was called to a special meeting at the White House on September 22, 1862. The president had sworn that if General McClellan drove Lee back across the river, he would send the proclamation after him. And so it was that he issued the preliminary Emancipation Proclamation, declaring that if the rebels did not end the fighting and rejoin the Union by January 1, 1863, all slaves in the rebellious states would be set free. America had reached the point of no return. The old ways were done.

The South refused to blink, and so on New Year's Day Lincoln issued the Emancipation Proclamation, putting on notice his intention on January 1, 1863, to set free all slaves in states rebelling against the Union.

ABRAHAM LINCOLN'S EMANCIPATION PROCLAMATION

By the President of the United States of America: A Proclamation:

"That on the first day of January, in the year of our Lord one thousand eight hundred and sixty-three, all persons held as slaves within any State or designated part of a State, the people whereof shall then be in rebellion against the United States, shall be then, thenceforward, and forever free; and the Executive Government of the United States, including the military and naval authority thereof, will recognize and maintain the freedom of such persons, and will do no act or acts to repress such persons, or any of them, in any efforts they may make for their actual freedom . . .

And I hereby enjoin upon the people so declared to be free to abstain from all violence, unless in necessary self-defense; and I recommend to them that, in all cases when allowed, they labor faithfully for reasonable wages.

And I further declare and make known, that such persons of suitable condition, will be received into the armed service of the United States to garrison forts, positions, stations, and other places, and to man vessels of all sorts in said service."

Lincoln's headlines made the world realize what the president had known a year before. In one stroke the proclamation changed the rules of the game, showing that the Confederacy stood for slavery and the Union for freedom. The backward-looking South was unsupportable.

President Lincoln is thought of today as the "Great Emancipator" who unlocked the shackles of millions and delivered them from bondage. It was undoubtedly a great turning point in the history of abolition in America. But the tide had been a long time turning. Dozens of visionaries rose, took great risks, and died for the cause decades earlier. Tennessee had already been publishing The *Emancipator* newspaper, devoted to abolition in America, since 1820. The National Anti-Slavery Tract Society was set up in Baltimore in 1828, and the next year women abolitionists from Philadelphia organized the first boycott against Southern cotton. The printer and radical abolitionist William Lloyd Garrison spent his life disturbing the peace for justice, partly through his Boston newspaper the *Liberator*, which in 1831 championed Black abolitionists' demands for an immediate end to slavery and for political and social equality.

Prudence Crandall started admitting Black girls to her Canterbury Female Boarding School in Canterbury, Connecticut, in 1833. Before she was arrested, it was America's first integrated school. Maryland slave Charles Ball's *Slavery in the United States; The Life and Adventures of a Fugitive Slave* appeared in 1836. Frederick Douglass, born into slavery, would escape to New York and find fame through his 1845 book *The Narrative of the Life of Frederick Douglass, An American Slave, Written By Himself*. In his newspaper, the *North Star*, he fought to "abolish slavery in all its forms and aspects, promote the moral and intellectual improvement of the COLORED PEOPLE, and hasten the day of FREEDOM to the Three Millions of our enslaved fellow countrymen." And in 1852 Harriet Beecher Stowe's *Uncle Tom's Cabin* had a profound effect on attitudes toward African Americans and slavery that helped fuel the abolitionist cause.

From May 1861 onward, Black people had already started escaping to Fort Monroe in Virginia, seeking out the Union army and demanding they be set free to fight their old masters. Lincoln took the door off its hinges that had already been ripped open. Most importantly, the story of emancipation is just wrong if it is told without African Americans claiming their own freedom.

When news of Lincoln's exploits spread, slaves dropped their pitchforks and flocked to Union lines. Days after the announcement, a trickle of fugitive slaves turned into a torrent. Black military units grew to 186,000 as former slaves took up arms. No less than 104,000 of them were recruited in Confederate territory. By the end of the war, 10 percent of Union soldiers were African Americans striking at the heart of the enslaved South.

The thousands who fought to the limits of human endurance at Antietam died to make men free. So history judges the day. Liberating Southern slaves was also a successful war tactic. But the Emancipation Proclamation did not make slavery go away overnight. And it did little to improve racial equality. Lincoln himself expressed ambivilant opinions on letting Blacks vote, hold office, or intermarry.

Like in Britain, political change looked impressive but was a slow grind. In America, the proclamation paved the way for the Thirteenth Amendment to the US Constitution and the total abolition of slavery. On January 31, 1865, the US Congress eventually ruled that:

> Neither slavery nor involuntary servitude, except as a punishment for crime whereof the party shall have been duly convicted, shall exist within the United States, or any place subject to their jurisdiction.

Less than three months later, Abraham Lincoln was shot dead. John Wilkes Booth avenged the South. His motive? To make sure the president never honored his last speech, a speech that talked openly of plans to allow Blacks citizenship in the United States of America.

HELL & DAMNATION

A web of white tape wound around red pegs fixed into the sand crisscrossed Rapparee Cove. Now it really did look like a forensic crime scene. Scientists in rubber boots walked up and down the grid using high-tech kit that would give them X-ray vision.

After hitting bad weather, the *London* came ashore at high tide, crashing onto the narrow beach. Part of its wreckage should be buried deep in its sand.

Professor Mark Horton had brought in the heavy guns, using a flux-gate magnetometer to search out any deeply hidden metal. This kit was first used in World War II to keep an eye on menacing German submarines. The team was patiently walking backward and forward testing the metallic signature of every inch of the beach. They wore rubber boots as insulation to make sure no metal or rivets in normal shoes gave a false reading.

Mark had also brought along a drone, which he expertly piloted below the overcast gray morning sky, taking thousands of photos to build up a three-dimensional map of the cove, cliffs, and coast. The master image digitally stitched together would allow any finds dug up on the beach to be plotted to precise points, like on a map. On top of Rapparee Cove the drone picked out double rings and ditches, maybe from prehistoric barrow burials over a thousand years old. Ilfracombe is ringed by prehistoric standing stones. The cove is as old as time.

Among all the bustling energy thrown at cracking the enigma of the *London*, Alannah could not help but feel that something did not add up. To her there was something very strange about the *London*. Looking out to sea, where her team had recently dived within easy swimming distance of shore, she realized that the ship had almost reached the mouth of the harbor when disaster struck. So why did the *London* crash, rather than take refuge? Alannah put the question to Mark.

"Well, the locals saw the ship was in distress. Lots of people from the harbor rode out to try and help the ship and guide the ship into the harbor," he told the team. "We even had a pilot who tried to come onboard, but the captain refused. Refused help!"

The *Ilfracombe Chronicle* backed up Professor Horton's story. When the town heard a cannon firing in distress:

> An Ilfracombe pilot bravely ventured out in response to the signal, but was not allowed to board her . . . "Pilot away!" exclaimed the captain. "We want no assistance: we're bound to perish!" and, alas!, soon the assertion was realized . . .

Choosing to sink rather than have a sliver of hope of being saved made no sense. Alannah pointed out that "the harbor is right there. Why didn't he just go into the safe harbor? Why was he still out here?"

Mark shrugged and shared the last words the would-be guardian angel pilot heard from the *London*. "Well the captain was reported to have said, 'I've come from hell and I'm going to damnation.' It's a very puzzling thing why he refused help," Mark admitted.

Back on the beach the University of Bristol team had finished plotting every buried metallic target under the sand. The scientists huddled around a laptop, staring at lumps and bumps that made Rapparee Cove look like a vast chunk of Swiss cheese.

"So, we've managed to bring together all the data," Professor Horton explained.

Dr. Henry Webber, the project geophysicist, ran an expert eye over the heat map. One area caught his attention. "There's clearly a lot of metal further down to the end of the beach there, as we went lower," he noted.

Mark also scrutinized the screen. "There's a whole lot of anomalies in there," he was happy to see, both large and small. "And then there's a big anomaly just in there. So our job tomorrow is really clear. We've got an hour and a half of the lowest tide to investigate, get out our shovels, and literally find out what's remaining and whether these really are a part of a shipwreck, and hopefully the *London*."

The pressure was on. Could the team discover what nobody else had managed in the last 222 years?

Water, Water, and Not a Drop to Drink

Olaudah Equiano, a former slave and the leading Black abolitionist in Britain, was taking his morning toast and coffee when he seized on a story tucked away in the folds of the *Morning Chronicle and London Advertiser.* It was March 18, 1783. A Liverpool slaver called the *Zong* had left West Africa on September 6, 1781, carrying 442 captives. The 110-ton ship was dangerously overcrowded. British boats were built to carry 1.7 Africans per ton. The *Zong*'s hold was filled with four people per ton.

The ship had crossed the Middle Passage, traveling 4,000 miles in eleven weeks (two more than normal), and mistaken landfall for enemy territory, French Saint-Domingue. It was Jamaica, its intended destination. The *Zong* sailed on and missed Jamaica by 120 miles. Now it had enough water for just four days. To reach its intended port would take ten to fourteen more days. The math did not add up.

The *Zong*'s eleven crew members and stand-in captain, by profession a surgeon, Luke Collingwood, met on deck and made a decision—destroy part of the "cargo" to save the rest, not to mention the desperate crew. The vote was unanimous.

At 8:00 P.M. that evening, fifty-four women and children were pushed one by one through the cabin windows under the cover of darkness. Two days later on December 1, 1783, forty-two men were thrown overboard from the quarterdeck. Finally, thirty-eight more Africans were murdered. By now the captives had got wind of the foul plan and fought back. Despite their resistance, twenty-six people were tossed overboard with their arms shackled. The surviving 200 of the 442 Africans were auctioned off at Black River in Jamaica on January 9, 1784.

After reading the horror story, the next morning Olaudah Equiano knocked on Granville Sharp's front door. Sharp, a humble clerk in the

Ordnance Office by day, and by night a tough defender of the Black community, called in the lawyers. Messrs Heseltine & Lushington issued legal proceedings against everyone concerned in jettisoning the 130 Africans. The charge? Murder on the high seas.

OLAUDAH EQUIANO, THE OPPRESSED "ETHIOPIAN"

Olaudah Equiano was the son of an Igbo chief in the Kingdom of Benin in Nigeria. He had never heard of white men or the sea when he was kidnapped and enslaved at age twelve. At the seashore, "I was now persuaded that I had gotten into a world of bad spirits, and that they were going to kill me."

Equiano was trafficked to Barbados and sold to Virginia in North America, where a Royal Navy lieutenant christened him Gustavus Vassa. Later he was bought by the Philadelphia Quaker merchant Robert King and taken to Montserrat. Equiano worked as a clerk, barber, and deckhand on King's ships before being put in charge of his stores and trading goods around the West Indies and Atlantic North America. Equiano was given enough liberty to start his own business selling tumblers and gin in Montserrat. Equiano eventually saved enough to buy his freedom on July 11, 1766.

A year later he moved to England with a glowing character reference, where he converted to Christianity and became one of Britain's greatest abolitionists, styling himself as the "Oppressed Ethiopian." In 1792 Equiano married Susannah Cullen in Cambridgeshire. He passed away in London, aged fifty-two, in March 1797.

Equiano died before Britain abolished the very slave trade that turned his life inside out. His autobiography, though, *The Interesting Narrative of the Life of Olaudah Equiano, or Gustavus Vassa the African*, was instrumental in changing public opinion about human trafficking. It remains one of the most important publications of the abolition movement and a unique firsthand account about life in West Africa, the horrors of the Middle Passage, and enslavement.

The public rage against the slave trade coincided with the appearance of Equiano's memoir, which brought the horrors of the trade into Britain, such as the terror of surviving a slave ship:

"The closeness of the place . . . was so crowded that each had scarcely room to turn himself, almost suffocated us . . . the air soon became unfit for respiration, from a variety of loathsome smells, and brought on a sickness among the slaves, of which many died, thus falling victims to the improvident avarice . . . This wretched situation was again aggravated by the galling of the chains, now become insupportable; and the filth of the necessary tubs, into which the children often fell, and were almost suffocated. The shrieks of the women, and the groans of the dying rendered the whole a scene of horror almost inconceivable."

In the conclusion to *The Interesting Narrative*, Equiano left behind a prayer that "I hope the slave trade will be abolished . . . The great body of manufacturers, uniting in the cause, will considerably facilitate and expedite it . . . In a short time one sentiment alone will prevail, from motives of interest as well as justice and humanity. Europe contains one hundred and twenty millions of inhabitants. Query—How many millions doth Africa contain? Supposing the Africans, collectively and individually, to expend 5l, [British pounds] a head in raiment and furniture yearly when civilized, &c. an immensity beyond the reach of imagination!"

The trial had little chance of success. Collingwood had died a week after landing in Jamaica. With the stand-in captain unable to testify, and his ship's logbook, detailing daily events—the prime evidence—conveniently vanished, too. No crew member was called to give evidence in court, either. The version of events told by the sole witness, a passenger called Robert Stubbs, said to be a drunken liar and cheat, was worse than useless.

As much as it "shocks one very much," Lord Chief Justice Mansfield, England's highest-ranking judge, was obliged to stick to the law of the land. The case hinged not on cruelty to humans and murder but on whether the jettison "was the same as if Horses had been thrown over board." The law treated enslaved Africans simply as cargo no better than animals. The argument that the *Zong* was running low on water won the day.

Lord Mansfield found that the Africans were sent to their watery graves by a "perilous necessity." The owners successfully claimed their insurance payout of £30 per lost head of cargo—around $500,000 today—because the letter of the law covered "all other Perils, Losses, and Misfortunes that have or shall come to the Detriment or Damage thereof."

The insurance company, which did not want to pay the slavers, appealed. This time "new evidence" emerged. Mansfield was surprised to learn that rainfall before the *Zong*'s Africans were jettisoned had refilled the ship's water casks. Reports circulated that the slaver reached Jamaica with 420 gallons of water to spare. Judge Mansfield, who had an adopted niece of mixed English and African parents, ruled against the slavers' insurance claim. His decision edged Britain closer to the abolition of slavery.

And yet the trial and murder of the *Zong*'s Africans changed nothing in the great ports and on the high seas—at first. At the time of the scandal, Liverpool had replaced London and Bristol as Britain's leading slave port. Over a century, five thousand slave voyages set off from its docks. Liverpool's Guinea slaver ships were larger and faster than most other vessels, which made them more efficient and profitable.

The head of the syndicate that owned the *Zong* and its enslaved Africans, William Gregson, even enjoyed a rise in his fortunes after the trial. His fleet transported 8,018 Africans from the Gold Coast—and made a killing—between 1781 and 1790. Gregson personally signed off 152 slave voyages and had a stake in the trafficking of 58,201 Africans. 9,148 of them died on voyages to market.

Olaudah Equiano and Granville Sharp's trial for justice of the *Zong*'s murdered 132 may have been lost—no one was ever tried for murder—but wall-to-wall newspaper coverage turned the saga into a tipping point in Britain's thinking about the transatlantic slave trade. The dismissive language heard in Lord Mansfield's court caused great offense, as did the serious accusation of murder swept aside as if the case was dealing with any disposable cargo. Britain woke up to the reality that the trade was brutal, morally bankrupt, and murderous. The *Zong* became the symbol of everything evil about the transatlantic slave trade in what was supposed to be the Age of Enlightenment.

The abolitionists harnessed the *Zong* affair as dynamite ammunition to attack slavery when they launched their campaign in 1787. A snowball of coincidences would be transformed into the smartest political strategy planned in the British Isles.

The abolition of slavery had grown from a roadside ex-priest to a full-scale popular uprising.

Going Viral

Triggered by Olaudah Equiano's breakfast rage, Granville Sharp posted his own fuming letters to the good and the great. Most went ignored. One man who did read his "junk mail," an influential Anglican clergyman called Dr. Peter Peckard, was deeply affected. Peckard was inspired to preach a sermon condemning the slave trade as a "most barbarous and cruel traffick."

A little later the minister became vice-chancellor of Cambridge University. It was then, thanks to Equiano's whistle-blowing and Sharp's poison pen, that Peckard set the theme of slavery's legality for Cambridge's most prestigious Latin essay contest. And from there Thomas Clarkson was inspired to become the chief spin doctor for the abolition movement. This was the chain of coincidences that linked the *Zong* massacre and the eventual abolition of slavery in 1833.

On the back of the transatlantic slave trade's riches, Western Europe's cities like London and Paris became the largest and wealthiest in the world. Rivers of cash brought about technological improvements and these, ironically, helped the abolition movement reach new heights. The printing press, for example, made possible the mass opposition to slavery.

Lord Charles Stanhope devoted his life to science and technology, rather than hobnobbing at court. By 1800 his first all-iron printing press, with its new design of levers turning a central press screw more rapidly and with greater force, boosted the hand press's efficiency. Two men working Stanhope's press could print 250 sheets an hour. And rather than sell his patent to the highest bidder, Stanhope shared his gift with the world. The good lord refused to copyright his design and offered it open source, free to everyone.

Mechanization made print cheap. Newspapers that displayed graphic cartoons were now reaching a mass audience and bringing the slave trade into people's living rooms

Until now the slave trade and slavery were something that happened over the horizon, out of sight and out of mind. The world of print and cartoons thrust far-off horrors under peoples' noses. Nobody could ignore the slave trade any longer.

One of the age's most influential satirical cartoonists was Isaac Cruikshank. Cruikshank had read William Wilberforce's angry speech in Parliament on April 2, 1792, accusing a Captain John Kimber of murdering an African girl on board a slave ship. The *Recovery* was sailing from Calabar to Grenada. Because the girl—a Christian—refused to dance immodestly, Kimber hoisted the slave girl upside down by one ankle and dumped her on the deck time after time until she died. Cruikshank detested what he heard and immortalized the scene. In his cartoon, Captain Kimber stands next to his victim with a grinning leer holding a whip. Cruikshank called his art "The Abolition of the Slave Trade."

Home in London, Kimber was arrested and sent to trial. In line with the times, he was quickly freed thanks to a lack of evidence. Cruikshank, however, made sure that his actions stuck fast in people's minds. Kimber's reputation was shredded. In one image and its subtitle, "The Inhumanity of Dealers in Human Flesh," the abolition of the transatlantic slave trade got unprecedented publicity. Kimber became the unwilling poster boy for the excesses of slave trading and a simple message. Calling the "cargo" on slave ships commercial property was no longer acceptable.

Cruikshank's cartoon made waves across of the pond. In the United States newspapers kept a close eye on Captain's Kimber's arrest, trial, and acquittal. Word spread all the way to the plantations of Virginia and the Carolinas in September 1792, which erupted in solidarity. New York newspapers ran accounts of "insurrections among the Negroes, with the decision on the trial of Capt. John Kimber and otherwise of so many falsehoods and exaggerations circulated . . ." The world was in revolution.

The unlikely epicenter for abolition was James Phillips's print shop at 2 George Yard in London. Phillips was a founding member of the London Abolition Committee in 1787 and the official printer for the Quakers, the deep pockets behind Britain's fight to overturn the land's slavery laws.

In George Yard, the struggle was publicized in permanent ink to forever rid the seas of slavers. James Phillips printed and sold Thomas Clarkson's *An Essay on the Slavery and Commerce of the Human Species* based on his Cambridge essay and Isaac Cruikshank's Kimber cartoon. Out of its doors were carted the length and breadth of Britain James Ramsay's *Essay on the Treatment and Conversion of African Slaves in the British Sugar Colonies* and William Cowper's 1788 poem "The Negro's Complaint," neatly folded and sold under the header A SUBJECT FOR CONVERSATION AT THE TEA TABLE.

Two special forms of media gripped the chattering classes. The world's best-known porcelain maker, Josiah Wedgwood, was another committee member of the Society for Effecting the Abolition of the Slave Trade. He also had mighty friends as the Appointed Potter to the Queen. Wedgwood was a genius of publicity and marketing, the first man to use product placement.

It was Wedgwood who thought up the hit-you-between-the-eyes design of a seal to close envelopes with a wax stamp. The image showed a kneeling African in chains, lifting his hands to the skies, surrounded by the plea, "Am I not a man and a brother?" The logo became the "bumper sticker" for the abolition of slavery, the first designed for a political cause. James Phillips published the image, while Wedgwood made five hundred medallions that Clarkson handed out to influential ladies to proudly wear, on bracelets and as pins for their hair, when promenading around town.

It was another of Phillips's prints that made a serious dent in the pro-slavery lobby. In Plymouth, Olaudah Equiano saw an illustrated diagram made by the local Society for Effecting the Abolition of the Slave Trade committee. The image showed from above the side and end views of a fully loaded Liverpool slave ship called the *Brooks*, which trafficked slaves between the Gold Coast and Jamaica. The diagram sent a lightning bolt through antislavery circles. The image exposed in one glance all the horrors that Thomas Clarkson spent hours trying to talk about.

In Phillips's print works Clarkson reworked the diagram, adding measurements in feet and inches and 482 slaves packed in the hold like sardines. From newspapers and magazines to books and pamphlets, the weapon was fired. The society printed seven thousand copies as posters to be hung on the walls of British homes and pubs. In an age before photography, the *Brooks* diagram sent a shiver down the nation's spine. It was the late eighteenth-century equivalent of the brutal photos of skeletal prisoners found by American and Russian liberators in Nazi concentration camps at the end of World War II or the lone Chinese man facing down a tank near Tiananmen Square.

THE *BROOKS* HORROR STORY

Custom-built slave ships transported African captives across the Atlantic to maximize efficiency. The *Brooks* of Liverpool, owned by Joseph Brooks Jr., was one such slaver that came under the spotlight of antislavery abolitionists. In November 1788 the Plymouth chapter of the Society for Effecting the Abolition of the Slave Trade published an illustrated broadside of the ship.

Its image laid bare the cruelty of the Atlantic slave trade. The public was horrified. Men could be seen chained by their ankles in a claustrophobic six feet by sixteen-inch space per man. The deck above, five feet by five inches high, was too low for adults to stand up. One title on the broadsheet, bordered by a set of manacles and cat o' nine tails, read "Am I not a man and a brother?" It was no coincidence that the *Brooks* was drawn in the shape of a coffin.

The 297-ton *Brooks* was built in 1781 and made ten voyages to West Africa over a quarter of a century, buying 5,163 Africans, of whom 4,559 survived the Middle Passage (almost 12 percent mortality rate). The horrific drawing showed 294 captives. In 1785-1786 the ship actually carried 740 men, women, and children.

The society's work fired activism around the world. The broadside was reproduced in New York and Philadelphia. The London committee went on to publish a gorier version with seven views of the ship. The horror of the *Brooks* was the subject of Parliamentary hearings in 1790. When the politician William Wilberforce, who spearheaded the movement to abolish slavery, saw the image, he wrote that "So much misery condensed in so little room is more than the human imagination had ever before conceived."

Abolition

The man who blew the whistle on the *Zong* affair and brought the *Brooks* diagram south, Olaudah Equiano, was the Black hero of British abolition. The former slave who bought his freedom spoke out for his brothers in bondage and published his autobiography in March 1789 at 2 George Yard. The 530-page *The Interesting Narrative of the Life of Olaudah Equiano, or Gustavus Vassa the African* was a bestseller. It went into eight editions, was translated into French, German, Dutch, and Russian, and was reprinted in the United States.

The timing of its appearance was smart, coinciding with England's Privy Council winding up its hearings about the slave trade in Parliament. For Equiano, his book was a cog in the bigger campaign. He began the text with a petition to Parliament and ended it with an antislavery letter to the queen.

Equiano, like Clarkson, took to the roads on Britain's first political book tour. He did for the antislavery movement what Nelson Mandela did for the antiapartheid movement in South Africa. At the time—107 years after the founding of the Royal African Company in London—lazy Britain still happily dismissed Africans as heathen illiterates from the tropics. Suddenly, a Black man appeared who was Christian, could write English better than most, was a successful merchant, and played the French horn. Equiano's story of rising up out of violence, exploitation, and cruelty on a monumental scale opened people's eyes to what it was like for an African to endure the slave trade.

The road to abolition was a tough slog. The first campaign of 1787–1788 saw over a hundred petitions with sixty thousand signatures presented to Parliament in the space of three months. When William Wilberforce started setting out his case against the trade, backed by the will of the people, the pro-slave lobby used every dirty delaying tactic, bought off people, and paid witnesses.

When the first bill was introduced in 1791, Wilberforce lost the debate. By the end of 1792, the bill to stop the slave trade was passed in the House of Commons but blocked by the House of Lords. Seven years later in 1805, an abolition bill failed for the eleventh time in fifteen years. Finally, the Act for the Abolition of the Slave Trade was passed on March 25, 1807. The slave trade was abolished across the British colonies.

BRITAIN ABOLISHES THE SLAVE TRADE

An Act for the Abolition of the Slave Trade, 25th March 1807:

"Be it therefore enacted by the King's most Excellent Majesty . . . That from and after the First Day of May One thousand eight hundred and seven, the African Slave Trade, and all manner of dealing and trading in the Purchase, Sale, Barter, or Transfer of Slaves, or of Persons intended to be sold, transferred, used, or dealt with as Slaves, practiced or carried on, in, at, to or from any Part of the Coast or Countries of Africa, shall be, and the same is hereby utterly abolished, prohibited, and declared to be unlawful . . .

. . . it shall be unlawful for any of His Majesty's Subjects, or any Person or Persons resident within this United Kingdom, or any of the Islands, Colonies, Dominions, or Territories thereto belonging, or in His Majesty's Possession or Occupation, to fit out, man, or navigate, or to procure to be fitted out, manned, or navigated . . . any Ship or Vessel for the Purpose of assisting in, or being employed in the carrying on of the African Slave Trade . . .

. . . all Insurances whatsoever to be effected upon or in respect to any of the trading, dealing, carrying, removing, transshipping, or other Transactions by this Act prohibited, shall be also prohibited and declared to be unlawful . . ."

In the long shadow of history, 1807 was a momentous year for Britain. A chain of murder and greed going back to Sir John Hawkins trafficking three hundred Africans to Brazil in 1562 was smashed. The campaigners who had fought tooth and nail hoped and thought that slavery was over. They were wrong. The *trade* was theoretically abolished, but not slavery itself.

The good news was that from now on ships caught trading Africans could be seized and sold. Masters and owners were fined £100 per captive and their ships and goods forfeited to the Crown. Bounty hunters made £30 for every man and woman and £10 for every child recovered from illegal slavers.

The bad news was that so many creative ways to skirt around the letter of the law were exploited that it is claimed more money was made out of the slave trade after 1807 than before. The circus of select committees looking into slavery started to feel like a PR exercise. The government was ticking boxes.

Freed Africans were not at liberty to come and go as they wished. Nor were they sent back to their countries of origin. "Liberated" men were enlisted into the military for unlimited service without the right to full pensions. Women and children were apprenticed to local landowners, to the military, and local government for up to fourteen years. The institution of slavery continued conveniently in the profitable plantations of the Caribbean—the sugar islands—on whose economy Britain prospered.

Change was unstoppable, though. The final crushing of slavery through Parliament took in total thirty years to win the day and more lobbying. In 1815, 722 petitions bearing a million signatures opposing slavery—13 percent of England's population—were served on Parliament. The House of Lords threw them out. Finally, Britain passed the 1833 Slave Emancipation Act, freeing all enslaved Africans in the Caribbean, Canada, and Cape Town. Owners were compensated for their losses from a £20 million pot—£1.3 billion today. The trafficked captives got nothing.

The devil had not been completely defeated. A slaving ship was found wrecked off the Essex Coast in 1840 "with hidden equipment for the slave trade," including chains, manacles, and ring bolts. Slavers like John Campbell continued to risk sailing from Liverpool in October 1843, fully equipped for buying slaves and with a cargo of bad old trade goods—gunpowder, cutlasses, coarse cloth, and rum—to swap for captives in West Africa. Other English ships just changed their names and bought Spanish and Portuguese flags and papers to masquerade as foreign slavers. And yet, the tide had turned.

BONES OF CONTENTION

Ilfracombe's fleet of boats was stuck high and dry, grounded on the mud flats. Bored owners sat on deck chairs reading newspapers and waiting for the sea to come in. It was the lowest tide of the year. The water level in Rapparee Cove was fifty feet lower than normal.

While Diving With A Purpose planned the next dive, on land the archaeologists worked frenetically in a race against time and tide. Even on this unusual day, as they cut trenches and test pits to check out the targets the magnetometer had mapped, water rushed in as fast as the sand was dug. The promising targets closest to the shoreline were the highest priority. They had to be examined in a little over an hour.

Amidst the churning mud and search for the *London*, Pat Barrow made his way down the coiled path leading to the cove, his eyes alert as always. Pat lives locally and has been exploring the secrets of the *London* in archives and on this shore for nearly fifty years. After storms he heads out beachcombing to see what gifts nature has sent his way.

"The vision of the wreck on the rocks in this cove has been in my mind for many, many years," Pat told the team. "And I was looking for the story; who were the people on board and what happened to them?"

One unforgettable day Pat made a discovery that changed everyone's thinking about the *London*. News coverage encircled the globe.

"Twenty years ago, I was involved with one of the most shocking finds in this cove: human remains. I saw finger bones, and I found a fragment of a skull and three teeth sticking out of that bank," Pat went on, pointing to the back slope of the cove. He showed the team some of the large iron ship's nails and what looked like shackles picked up on the beach they were digging that very day.

Pat had also dug up handfuls of gold and silver French, English, and Portuguese coins that fit accounts of the *London* losing five boxes of treasure. The day after the wreck, local beachcombers were preparing to bury the bodies when:

> As the waves moved the sand on the beach, heaps of shining coins in gold met the sight of the astonished inhabitants, who were busily removing the dead bodies. The sight was wondrous and not an unwelcome one. Eagerly they rushed to the treasure.

The tiny Rapparee Cove held a rich array of treasure, iron shackles, ship's spikes, and ballast but also human bones that newspapers had reported sticking out of the cliff side since 1856. In the space of a few days in the late 1990s, Pat gathered up more than two hundred human bones from arms, fingers, ribs, shoulders, and skulls from the cliff edge.

A media frenzy erupted. Who were these drowned victims? A *Times* of London headline shouted that the BEACH YIELDS MASS GRAVE OF SHIPWRECKED SLAVES. SHIPWRECK SLAVES GRAVE UNEARTHED, trumpeted *The Telegraph*.

The bones seemed to speak to Pat.

"I felt in my heart, I was convinced it was from the slaves. I started digging into old documents and I discovered shocking descriptions of the morning after the ship had foundered, when dozens of bodies of Africans littered the beach. The morning after the local population came down to try to bury these bodies 'cause they thought they should do because of their religious convictions. They started to move the bodies and then the tide dropped back a bit and then exposed a load of gold that came from a treasure chest that was tipped out of the rowing boat. So, they all rushed to the gold and left the bodies."

The mysterious black people from across the seas, drowned in chains belowdecks on the *London*, were desecrated once more. Who the bodies belonged to and where they came from opened up a hornet's nest of intrigue that bubbled over into anger.

A local politician told the BBC that "The cove symbolizes the struggle for freedom." The people of St. Lucia demanded the return of their people for respectful burial, and the island's high commissioner made a pilgrimage to Rapparee Cove. The War Office sealed off the cove and declared it a war grave, partly to keep out souvenir hunters. Nobody listened. This was an ancient right of way. The African Reparations Movement called for a memorial ceremony to let the dead rest.

There is no doubt what the *London* had been up to. France declared war on Britain on February 2, 1793. The Revolutionary War was just one of the twenty-three times the old foes locked horns throughout history. This time the war lasted until 1802. As well as fighting off the threat of an invasion at home, England had a big headache in the West Indies. France's forces were on the rise after it renounced slavery at home in February 1794 in return for "negro" and local mixed white and Black "mulatto" support. On the other side of the West Indies' trenches, twelve thousand British troops had died from yellow fever. London had no choice but to abandon St. Lucia in June 1795.

That December, General Sir Ralph Abercromby left the English coast of Spithead with a fleet of two hundred ships led by the 74-gun HMS *Ganges* carrying an army of fifteen thousand men. The *London* transport ship was one of them. By then St. Lucia was in open revolt: two thousand ex-slaves had taken the opportunity of the confusion to grab their independence. The battle for St. Lucia, St. Vincent, and Grenada raged from late April to mid-June. When the smoke cleared and England won the day, three thousand prisoners of war—freed Blacks and mulatto volunteers—were rounded up and shipped to Admiralty prisons in England.

The *London* was one of the 103 ships that made the journey home. Their destination was Portsmouth on the south coast, but bad weather pushed the ship up the Bristol Channel. Off Ilfracombe, a great storm of wind, thunder, lightning, and hail, the most tremendous in living memory, struck at 8:30 P.M. on October 9, 1796. The three-hundred-ton *London* was dashed to pieces. The Lords of the Admiralty were advised that:

The London' transport of London, one of 'The Ganges'
Convoy with French Prisoners, in coming for this harbour,

a heavy squall took and forced her upon the rocks; the vessel went to pieces before day light . . .

The thirty to forty Black prisoners who survived the traumatic wreck were locked up in Bristol prison. But who were they? Prisoners of war, slaves, former slaves, or freedom fighters? *Felix Farley's Bristol Journal* called the prisoners "Maroons," the name for escaped slaves who set up free settlements across the West Indies. England's official repository of government documents, the Public Records Office, registered the survivors by their "Nationality" as African or Caribbean and their "Quality" as "Slave." Most notably, Stapleton Prison, where they were held, listed them as "slaves."

The shackled prisoners in the hold of the stricken *London* were former enslaved and free people of mixed race, persuaded to try their luck to support the struggle against Britain with the French revolutionary army that liberated them. The terms of their surrender agreed they would all be treated as prisoners of war, not as slaves. While they were held, waiting to be swapped with France for captured English troops, enemy officers were allowed to wander free in parole towns. The Black prisoners were not. The Admiralty in London decided they were too "violent in their behavior, and savage in their disposition" to be let loose on the local population.

The shipwrecked men are best understood as a mix of runaway ex-slaves and free Blacks who chose to fight for France as freedom fighters. It was a roll of the dice. If they won, their liberty would improve.

In the end, the gamble backfired. Many paid the ultimate price, drowning in the same kind of shackles in which they first arrived in the Caribbean after crossing the dreaded Middle Passage from West Africa.

Mountain of Manillas

While the dive team waited for the tide to come up in Ilfracombe, Kinga, Richard Stevenson, and a small team took the chance to shoot off to the Isles of Scilly, off the southwest tip of England. There lies what's left of an English two-mast ship called the *Douro*, which was lost in 1843, well after the slave trade was supposed to have been abolished.

The plan was to dive remains of the 219-ton *Douro* and search for surviving evidence to back up claims that the apparatus around the illegal trafficking of enslaved Africans went on, even illegally, in the ports of the United Kingdom.

The *Douro* began its final voyage in Oporto, Portugal, on January 17, 1843, its wooden hull sheathed in yellow brass to protect it from shipworms. On Thursday, January 26, a leak opened up in the hull and the limping ship grounded on one of the hundreds of rocks lurking like sharks off the western Scilly. Nobody survived. Bodies, including Captain Thomas Gowland, the logbook, the figurehead, cloth, velvet, and mahogany turned up floating across the water.

THE *DOURO*—AFTER ABOLITION

- 219-ton, two mast wooden trader, built in Sunderland, 1839
- Home port, Liverpool
- Owner Paull & Co., Commander Captain Gowland
- Left Oporto, Portugal, for West Africa, January 17, 1843
- Cargo of cloth, velvet, mahogany bale goods, hemp, munitions, and "brass stops"
- Wrecked, Round Rock, western Isles of Scilly, January 26, 1843
- Remains include three tons of manilla bracelets and glass trade beads

The cargo of bale goods, hemp, munitions, and "brass stops" were all lost. When divers started salvaging the wreck, twenty-five meters down off Round Rock, the brass stops turned out to be thousands of copper manillas—perhaps as many as three tons—stacked four feet high. It was the largest hoard found underwater. The *Douro* shows how ten years after the Slave Emancipation Act of 1833, manillas—perhaps British, made in Birmingham—were still being manufactured in frightening numbers.

The Isles of Scilly are beautiful but deadly. In these waters lie more wrecks per square mile than any other place on Earth: a thousand ships that broke their backs off a hundred miles of coastline. Rocky outcrops rise menacingly out of the deep, hard to spot in the drifting sea mist. The top of Round Rock breaks lightly above the water.

"The *Douro* was supposed to have hit the rock that we can just see right in there. That round rock," Richard told Kinga, pointing a few tens of meters away from their dive boat. "It probably foundered on the reef just behind us. We need to try and find the manillas if we can. See if we can find this currency that was used in the slave trade."

Three divers stepped into inner space and dropped into the Atlantic Ocean, fully kitted head to toe in drysuits and full-face communication masks. As ever off the UK coast, topside the weather was refusing to behave. "Conditions are really making it difficult here," Richard noticed as he prepared to descend. He was not hopeful. "Visibility is probably only one to two meters."

The team swam past sea urchins glued to rocks. The seabed of loose tumbled boulders and gullies looked like the aftermath of an earthquake. Old wreckage was scattered everywhere. The divers swept over an iron cannon and examined two sturdy iron anchors lying on top of one another. Compared to the surface, visibility on the seabed was remarkably good more than five meters down. The absence of sand over the rocky bottom meant no swirling silt clouded the view.

The divers pushed on, looking for manillas. Kinga started sweeping an orange metal detector that looked like a giant carrot over a thin layer of sand caught in the rocky gullies. Seagrass sprouted out of the side of the rock and danced in the water. The detector squealed excitedly at a buried hit. Kinga did not have to fan away much sand to uncover its prey. She picked up the buried object and shook her fist to free it of sand.

Two curved lengths of copper appeared. Kinga pieced them together. They still fit, even after all the decades. It was a manilla from the *Douro*. Even though the slave trade was supposed to be over for Britain, authorities from Spain, Portugal, Brazil, and America either ignored the law or found loopholes to make a killing in the transatlantic slave trade.

Kinga raised a fist in a salute of success at her discovery. It was also a salute to the memory of the fallen.

When she surfaced and clambered back onto the dive boat, Kinga closely examined her star find, too jazzed to take off her dive tank and gear. She pieced the broken lengths together, one rounded, the other widening to a typical flange. Surf broke monotonously over the wild rocks behind her.

"We actually found a manilla with the metal detector," she told the dive support team. "Underneath the sand right by the anchor. In two pieces, it's broken. Here's what the *Douro* was carrying when it went down in 1843. So, this essentially proves that even after slavery was banned, that ship was taking a currency that was used to trade for human lives."

Kinga passed the manilla over to her dive buddy resting opposite her.

"It's hard to comprehend slavery, isn't it, in this world of freedom that we have?" Richard remarked, humbled to think that this was just one manilla among tons that the *Douro* carried for its wicked business. Those manillas were exchanged for flesh and blood human beings. How many Africans could this hoard have bought? "That's quite poignant right? Unbelievable," he added.

Kinga took back her find and turned it slowly in front of her face. From one perspective it was just a lump of metal. Its symbolic value was far greater.

"This was something that was equal in value to a human being, who laughs, and dreams," Kings summed up. "There were thousands of these aboard the *Douro* and they were all taken to the West African coast. And each one of these was traded for a human life."

Seagulls squealed overhead, bird's-eye viewers of thousands of human tragedies in these waters. None stacked up to the three tons of manillas once sent to the Gold Coast on a small wooden ship a decade after slavery was meant to be over.

HEAVY METAL

As always in Ilfracombe, when word gets out that people are hunting for treasure—shiny or not—Rapparee Cove gets overrun with sightseers. Mark Horton's archaeological team was trying to ignore the onlookers. They continued scanning the ground with metal detectors and feverishly digging test pits.

"The tide is coming in very fast now, so we have to pick up the pace if we want to find something," Mark rallied everyone. "We're hoping to find what's called wrought iron, an old form of metal. The *London*'s hull would have been reinforced by that kind of iron."

So far just mud and large pebbles had come out of the holes, nothing ancient and nothing shipwrecked. One of the metallic targets turned out to be shallow, less than fifteen centimeters deep. Mark took a quick look and batted the find away as angle iron used in modern construction. It was twentieth-century and useless.

"Come on, we haven't got long," Mark pushed.

Close to the waterline, another hit uncovered a shiny silver coin. "I'm afraid it's modern. Got a picture of the queen on the back," Mark exclaimed.

Then, twenty feet from the sea, the team's efforts paid off. Mark sat down on the edge of a damp trench and cradled a great lump of flattened iron found over a foot down in the mud. It was wrought iron, bent and torn from some traumatic event.

"It's been thumped, like in a wreck. And it's exactly the right size for the ship, isn't it?" Mark beamed.

The dive team crowded around, eager to know if they had hit their jackpot.

Alannah asked if "This iron is from the time period of the *London*?"

"Wrought iron is spot on for this date," Mark assured her. "We've actually got preserved here a kind of frozen moment in time when the *London* is being smashed up against the rocks behind us, and its actually twisting this strap. Come and hold it. Surprisingly heavy."

Josh and Alannah looked over the humble part of the ship's structure, touching the iron that bent at the very moment of the tragedy. The excavated find bore witness to a ship that traveled all the way from St. Lucia with Africans, freed to fight for France and then re-imprisoned. And whose men and women, shackled below deck, were dashed to their death on a remote English beach.

Alannah imagined this beach covered with a shattered hull, treasure, and bodies. Like the memory of the dead themselves, most of the *London* and its memory were long forgotten. But now they had a find that explained how the London went down . . . but not why.

Facing the Ancestors

Making sense of the transatlantic slave trade's numbers is mentally and visually impossible. The twelve million trafficked and 1.8 million who perished crossing from West Africa to the Americas and Caribbean before abolition became a reality are mind-boggling figures. They just make your head pound.

How can the human mind compute something unparalleled in human history? The 107,600-seat University of Michigan Wolverines college football stadium is the largest sports hall in America. Imagine it filled to capacity. Then imagine the same space filled 111 times more. That was how many Africans were dragged in chains across the Middle Passage. Or try to think about the horror of twenty-eight times its packed seats drowned at sea in chains. At some point the brain just shuts down.

Tracking down and diving the wrecks of slavers like the *London* and the *Douro* humanizes the victims of the slave trade. It brings back to life their stories, their voices, one at a time. The hulls where parents, brothers, and sisters were crammed together, and the objects connected to their trafficking, demystify the big picture. Shipwrecks draw us closer to the time when these people were trapped in West Africa, the conditions they had to put up with at sea, and their final tragic moments. It is one of the truly monumental stories of world history. It is a tale that humanity dares not forget.

Other than the floating coffins where the enslaved millions headed to new destinies, there are few authentic ways to make sense of this dark past. Most of the European forts and castles where captives were rounded up, branded, and sold in coastal West Africa can be visited in Accra, Cape Coast, Elmina, and Frederiksborg in Ghana, the House of the Slaves in Senegal, and Whydah in Benin. The crumbling walls of these sites of conscience, though, are slight shadows of their past infamy.

If the shells of the old forts give a glimmer of what happened, West Africa remembers the painful lines of slaves forcefully herded to the coast. In Libreville in Gabon a more than life-size statue, half man and half woman, smashes its chains between two pillars to seize freedom. A red and white arch at the Door of No Return on the beach of Whydah in Benin, with shackled Africans walking to a ship sculpted on its lintel, memorializes the ten thousand enslaved people who left the town every year. Gorée Island's blood red-painted House of Slaves commemorates the end of the line on the shore of the Atlantic in Senegal.

For most of history it was in Ghana that the bulk of captured Africans were shipped to exile through the "Door of No Return" at Elmina and Cape Castle. They were the last steps the enslaved trod on home soil. After centuries crossing the Middle Passage, English abolitionists demanded that Europe and the New World treat these Africans as human beings. The memory of the captives who perished crossing the ocean has largely floated away on the waves, however.

Kwame Akoto-Bamfo, an artist and cultural activist in Ghana, has started resurrecting the faces of the forgotten millions in a most dramatic way. He sculpts in concrete—to last forever and be resilient like his people—with a goal to make 11,111 heads at his rural studio near Accra, at the heart of the Gold Coast.

Each dramatic head shows a different face and its own personal emotional journey. No two look the same. The memorial heads called *nsodie* pay respect to the ancestral victims of the transatlantic slave trade and bear witness to their torment. Some faces are mirrors of confusion and anger at the moment of being captured. Others are prisoners of war.

Remembering the ancestors' spirit in sculpted heads is an ancient religious tradition in West Africa. When a Supreme Being created a human, life was breathed through the head, which the gods made from divine clay. When leaders and royalty died, they were immortalized in wooden and ivory heads, the most striking art made in places like the Kingdom of Benin in Nigeria. To African society, the human head was the most vital part of a human, the host of its most important organs. The brain was the seat of wisdom and reason. Eyes were the lamp that guided a person through the dark jungle of life. The nose ventilated the soul and the mouth nourished the body. Ears were sound detectors.

Kwame sees his art as a living witness to the knowledge lost to time. His faces from the transatlantic slave trade identity a way to connect with people, not numbers. The faces are inspired by real Africans Kwame has met in Ghana, descendants of the enslaved millions. Perhaps in their eyes and features viewers will spot their uncle, mother, or kid brother and start to think what it was all about.

Eventually Kwame's army of 11,111—the old and the young—will forever keep alive a piece of those lost Africans. People minding their business in their home villages. Or eyes shut, head pushed back in pain and anguish as their fate became clear. And with a vacant stare, unable to make sense of the incomprehensible. Others have their eyes bandaged from torture and wear iron ring collars chained round their necks. Fear, sadness, disgust, and surprise. The ancestors of Ghana show all the emotions of the enslaved millions.

Risking It All

Early the next day, with the tide up, the Diving With A Purpose team was back in the water off Rapparee Cove. For Alannah, a big piece of the puzzle was still missing: what madness made William Robertson, the captain of the *London*, refuse to seek refuge in the nearby harbor? She replayed in her mind the words from the *Ilfracombe Parish*

Magazine. The *London* got in distress late in the evening, but Robertson refused help from Ilfracombe's local sailors: "It was supposed that he had determined to die rather than let it be known that he was trading with human freight: that his vessel was loaded with fellow beings as slaves . . ."

The team had moved further offshore, diving for wreckage in case the stricken *London* recoiled from the rocky shore and drifted back out into the ocean. The seabed was a carpet of monotonous sand. The bright yellow metal detectors kept up a cacophony of beeping at what could be anything buried in the silt.

Then a possible answer why Robertson thought he could stay outside Ilfracombe harbor and survive appeared out of the underwater gloom. A huge iron object loomed into view a couple of hundred feet outside the harbor mouth. It was an old anchor mooring that once offered incoming ships a stable point of anchorage, wedged into the seabed outside the port. Just throw out your rope line until it snagged on the mooring or tie to a float above it.

The design fit the timeline of the *London* and an old account. When John Chiswell, the Ilfracombe ship's pilot, was interviewed at the grand old age of eighty-nine about the fateful night of the wreck, he described how the ship "came into the back of the pier. But the means of securing her to the buoy failing, she drifted in the storm on to the Rapparee rocks and there perished." This must have been the buoy Chiswell spoke about. Captain Robertson had tried in vain to tie to the mooring. But the storm was too severe and tossed the ship aside.

As Alannah touched the old mooring underwater, she instinctively felt she knew exactly why Robertson made for this area just outside of Rapparee Cove, instead of going straight into the nearby harbor.

"He wanted to tie himself to the mooring anchor. He wanted safety without scrutiny. And I think I know exactly what he was afraid of," she shared with the team, dried down and standing back on land in the chilly breeze of Rapparee Cove.

Alannah remembered the case of Captain Kimber hoisting up the girl by the ankle on the deck of the *Recovery* in Isaac Cruikshank's cartoon, and the media storm that broke across Britain four years before the sinking of the *London*. Alannah imagined Kimber forcing his captives to dance and the young girl who refused to take off her clothes. Mad dog Kimber tore off her rags himself, tied her ankle to a rope from the mast and threw her up and down, over and over again, until she stopped breathing.

When the ship's surgeon reported Kimber's horrifying conduct, the tide started to turn against the slave trade. The cause was helped by the dead girl not being "heathen," but a god-fearing Christian. Alannah remembered Isaac Cruikshank's iconic cartoon of that awful scene that shocked Middle England and disrupted people's lives. From that very moment, the gentlemen and gentlewomen of Britain started to see the murdered girl and trafficked Africans as humans, not faceless cargo.

Alannah was convinced that the public fallout of the Kimber case was exactly why the captain of the *London* was hesitant to come into Ilfracombe harbor.

Kinga got her thinking. "Who knows how this captain had been treating his slaves? Maybe there was something he wanted to hide," she suggested.

Robertson had illegally re-enslaved freed people. Maybe he had also committed outrageous acts at sea, which was hardly uncommon on slave ships. No doubt he thought he could get away with anything, even murder. As long as the crossing went smoothly, the Middle Passage was a bottomless pit of casualties.

When ships got caught in terrible danger and captains and crews had to explain their actions to higher authorities, people squirmed to save their own skins. Was this what Captain Robertson feared? Was this why he bizarrely cried that "I've come from hell and I'm going to damnation?"

The past was catching up with the captain's conscience. He had re-enslaved free people. And he knew that the world was not going to sit back and put up with it any longer.

THE LAST GASP

What is not just in law, necessity makes just.
—Proverb of St. Thomas used by Spain
to justify Cuba's illegal slave trade

THE WARRIOR

Florida Keys—USA

The miracle of wood is that it floats. Between the four points of the compass, the blue seas covering 71 percent of planet Earth connect distant lands and peoples. The oceans are boundless. They crisscross borders and are blind to social and cultural differences. For millennia our seas have united the world, allowing the exchange of ideas.

The aims of the transatlantic slave trade had nothing to do with exchanges of ideas or cultures. The trafficking of peoples from West Africa to the Caribbean, Latin America, and the West was knowingly wicked and done solely for the purposes of profit, prestige, privilege, and power. Families were uprooted from their homes and kingdoms. The flesh business ripped the beating heart out of one traditional lifestyle to justify the supposed superiority of another. The industry, which sparked the largest forced migration in history, was meticulously planned to destroy. Thousands of years of culture were left behind. The tragedy of wood is that it can sink. And when slave ships were lost at sea, pieces of Africa's rich culture went down with them.

The beguiling Florida Keys at first sight look like an unlikely paradise to hunt down the cultures dispossessed by the transatlantic slave trade. Under the azure blue heaven and flat sea, you cannot tell where the ocean ends and the sky begins. All is calm, all is content. Only motorboats and thrill-seeking jet skis cut up the flat sheen. Look closely, though, and danger lurks just below the surface. Reefs are scattered across the keys like World War II mines waiting to make fools of the most experienced ships' captains.

Nothing lasts forever. In the early nineteenth century the horrors of the transatlantic slave trade were over. Or supposedly over. It is here, off the southern spear tip of America, where the Atlantic Ocean plunges into the Gulf of Mexico and Latin America, that the panorama of one of the most tainted chapters in history reached its final act. In waters where the last decades of slave trafficking played out, a voice can be given back to the enslaved who died voiceless.

The sights and sounds of the rich cultures left behind in West Africa have faded away. The names of the enslaved millions are forgotten, the kingdoms they were uprooted from are unrecorded. Once shipped across the Middle Passage from West Africa to the Americas, plantation owners gave their slaves new Western names and often forcibly converted them to Christianity.

For centuries, Europe looked at West Africa's religions as a clash of cultures—God and civilization versus savage abominations in a land of human sacrifice, voodoo, and what the West feared as magical *juju*. To Europe, Africa's alleged pagan savagery was the perfect excuse to invade its kingdoms and plunder its natural resources, like palm oil and rubber, into the early twentieth century.

African slaves had been trafficked through the Florida Keys since at least the early seventeenth century. They were locked in the galleys of Spain's mighty treasure ships sailing between the gold, silver, and emerald mines of Colombia, Peru, Bolivia, and Mexico for home: Seville. Traditional African cooking pots and pans turned up on the wrecked galleons the *Nuestra Señora de Atocha*, the *Santa Margarita*, and *Buen Jesús y Nuestra Señora del Rosario* that were wiped out by a hurricane between the Straits of Florida and Key West on September 5, 1622. Below deck, chained Africans were forced to cook for the crews of His Majesty's floating treasure boxes. So much Spanish treasure went down in these waters—home to a thousand wrecks—that the Florida Keys became known as the Bank of Spain.

Gold, silver, emeralds, and sugar were all mined by slave power. At the height of the trade, the English merchant ship the *Henrietta Marie* landed 191 Africans in Port Royal and headed home from Jamaica for England with a cargo of sugar, cotton, dyewood, and ginger. The crew never escaped the Americas, the hull spiked on New Ground Reef, fifty-five kilometers off Key West. The dozens of iron slave shackles found among its wreckage bring home the claustrophobic brutality endured in the name of profit and empire.

By a twist of fate, the Florida Keys are also home to Diving With A Purpose. In these alluringly calm seas, generations of DWP enthusiasts are trained to comb seabeds in search of lost slave ships. As Dr. Melody Garrett, a lead instructor with the group, puts it, "We have to teach our young people where they came from. If we don't do it, no one will . . . ever." The dive team was now ending its journey in seas that saw an illegal sequel to the slave trade.

In their home waters Diving With A Purpose was hunting one of the last slavers to sink off Florida. The Spanish *Guerrero*, which means "warrior," went down somewhere off the Keys in December 1827 transporting Africans to sell in Cuba. The *Guerrero* was up to no good, as the slave trade had already been banned by England and the United States since 1807. The *Guerrero* was a pirate ship illegally busting the blockade.

The *Guerrero* had made it all the way from Nigeria to the Bahamas. It was veering south for Havana when an English antislavery schooner, the twenty-five-meter *Nimble*, spotted its sail. The two ships were locked in a deadly game of cat and mouse. The *Nimble* was armed with eight cannons, but the far more heavily powered *Guerrero*'s fourteen guns could have blown the English patrol ship sky high with a single broadside. Its cagey captain preferred not to risk losing the payday his precious human cargo promised. Anyway, he had complete faith that his slick slaver was a far superior sailor.

The fleeing *Guerrero* gambled on escaping in the Florida Keys' winding coastline. It was a desperate throw of the dice. These waters are a minefield of sharp reefs. Neither the captain of the *Guerrero*, nor of the *Nimble*, had charts that plotted the hazards. Spain surrendered Florida to the United States in 1821. Maps of the shoals were yet to be drafted. Fleeing fast and furiously, the Spanish *Guerrero* sank, while the *Nimble* got stuck hard on a coral reef. The English warship whose mission was to save trafficked Africans inadvertently ended up causing the death of forty-one Africans and great misery to the survivors.

THE *GUERRERO*

- Large Spanish one-deck brig, Don José Gomez captain
- Launched as *James Monroe*, New London, Connecticut, 1813, by shipbuilder Amasa Miller. Home port, New York
- 33.5 meters long, 8.2 meters wide, 3.6 meters deep, 323 tons
- Crew, ninety men; armed with fourteen cannons
- Wrecked off Key Largo, Florida, December 19, 1827
- Carrying cargo 561 Africans for sale to Cuba's sugar plantations. Forty-one captives drowned
- 388 Africans recaptured by Captain Gomez and sold in Cuba
- Ninety Africans eventually returned to Liberia to begin a new life in March 1830

Diving With A Purpose was itching to see what lay below these waters. They started their time travel, though, on dry land, meeting in Key West with Dr. Corey Malcom, the director of archaeology at the Mel Fisher Maritime Heritage Society. Corey has explored a string of sunken ships from the Bahamas to Florida for decades. Nobody knows these seas and their moods better.

Alannah Vellacott, Kinga Philipps, and Joshua Williams found Corey hard at work in his second home, a sprawling storage space stuffed with a treasure trove of shipwrecked artifacts. X-ray photos of odd-shaped concretions stuck to the walls revealed ancient goodies, like weaponry, enshrouded inside them. Sixteenth-century iron cannons lay silenced on wooden floorboards next to refrigerators full of delicate organic finds harvested from the sea. More storage tanks held fresh water, extracting the salts covering tons of historic ceramics fished up off the Keys. Broken Spanish jars once made in Andalusia and filled with olive oil, wine, and even gunpowder lined metal work tops, waiting to be put back together.

The *Guerrero* holds an unwelcome secret about the final years of the illegal slave trade. The ship, Corey told Alannah, Kinga, and Josh, was "sailing to Cuba with almost six hundred African people. They sailed past the Bahamas. Stationed there was a British navy ship, the *Nimble,* whose job was to intercept illegal slave ships. As you know, the *Nimble* tried to stop the *Guerrero.* But the *Guerrero* took off. They got into a chase, they got into a gun battle. Eventually, night fell. Both ships slammed into the Florida reef somewhere off Key Largo. So, beneath these waters now are the puzzle pieces that are going to help us reconstruct the story of these two shipwrecks. And that's really become my passion."

Like Diving With A Purpose, Corey had searched for this major slice of US maritime history for over a decade. To get a handle on the kind of signature finds you might expect to find on a slave ship, Corey invited the divers to join in a little digging above the waves. Finding the *Guerrero* was not going to be easy. The Florida Keys are littered with centuries of wreckage. And to add insult to historical injury, the enslaved have not been left to rest in peace but have been pounded by relentless hurricanes. Wreckage from a ship lost in these waters often turns up tens of kilometers away, scattered to the four winds. Corey knows the chances of finding a pristine ship lying intact are virtually nil. The team would have to take a forensic approach to crack the mystery.

"You know, the story of *Guerrero* is really the story of two ships," Corey explained. "*Guerrero*, the slave ship that we're interested in, and also the *Nimble,* that ran aground and was able to float itself off the reef by jettisoning iron ballast and cannonballs, leaving underwater bread crumbs that might lead to the *Guerrero*."

"When the *Guerrero* sank, taking down forty-one Africans, the *Nimble's* crew said they could hear the screams crossing two miles of ocean," Corey went on. "It had been their duty to save the people on the *Guerrero* but, instead, they accidentally chased them to their doom. We're going to find the *Guerrero* by identifying artifacts that are specific to a slave ship. To know what these might be, I have some things that I have salvaged over the years to show you."

As typical examples of the kinds of finds that would have gone down on the *Guerrero*, Corey set out a number of objects on a table. Among them, a silver spoon no doubt once used by a well-fed captain. The crew would have made do with pewter or wooden cutlery and bowls. But the team's eyes were drawn to sinister looking objects, a hefty iron bar with two U-shaped loops fitted on to it and a strange iron handle with a hook at one end.

"So, what's this guy?" Josh asked, pointing at the hooked metal. Corey explained that back in the bad old days it was known as a tooth extractor.

"I remember in school, we were taught some slaves wouldn't eat in protest," Alannah recalled. "They would remove the teeth so that they could shove food in their mouth. Just visualizing that is absolutely chilling. That my ancestors could've had their teeth pulled to make them eat because they needed to be strong in order to be bought . . ." Her thoughts trailed off, a lump in her throat.

Turning to an iron bar with two U-shaped loops attached, Corey told the team that "here is the real telltale artifact. The essence of the slave trade; a set of shackles. These were the iron restraints designed to hold people two by two."

Shackles are the most explicit objects of shame that identify a wreck as a slave ship. Looking and handling them draws the mind back to an endless procession of people force marched out of West Africa, across rivers and forests into exile.

Alannah wanted to know if they were used to bind wrists, and Corey illustrated how they were sometimes used for wrists but generally ankles. "You slid this 'U' onto somebody's ankle; you took this other 'U,' put it on another person's ankle, and then those people were joined together," he explained.

"It was shackled to two people because it makes it way more effective to keep people from running," Josh realized.

"Right. If you're hobbled to somebody else, you can't swim. You can't run. You can't move. It was horrible," Corey agreed, handing the shackles to Josh. Reading about the history of the enslaved's fate is very remote from handling the tools of terror. Physically touching objects that once intimately enchained millions of West Africans is raw, it is emotional. The young diver struggled to compose his feelings and took deep breaths. Josh stood, his head bowed, examining the shackles once manacled to a sunken ancestor. Just to his right stood the conservation lab's emergency exit door, one quick step to fresh air and freedom. For the enslaved, there was no way out.

Shackles used in the slave trade were known as "Bilboes" in English after their supposed invention in the northern Spanish port of Bilbao. Because iron reacts and dissolves rapidly in seawater, they are hard to find underwater. Manacles, shackles, neck rings, and chains made up the horrific hardware of bondage on European slave ships. The necks of the most rebellious slaves would be locked into large collars to limit their movements. As a rule, men were shackled at the wrist and leg, while women and children were left unlocked. (This relative freedom made women key players in every uprising.) Even when male captives were dragged up to the main deck for air, no risks were taken. Ten men's leg shackles remained chained to a heavy ringbolt, just in case they tried to flee overboard.

THE *HENRIETTA MARIE*

The 114-ton *Henrietta Marie*, commanded by John Taylor with a nine-man crew, was an independent slave trader that paid the Royal African Company of London 10 percent tax of its profits for the right to trade with West Africa. The ship was wrecked off New Ground Reef in the Florida Keys in June 1700. It was returning to England having delivered 191 Africans in Jamaica and picked up sugar, indigo, cotton, and logwood to add to its African elephant tusks.

The wreck's discovery by Mel Fisher's dive team recovered the most important underwater remains of a slaver to date: the largest number of iron slave shackles found at sea, eleven thousand trade beads, and three hundred pewter vessels used to barter for people, gold, and ivory in West Africa. The wreckage is curated by the Mel Fisher Maritime Museum in Key West, Florida.

No crew or enslaved captives survived the sinking. The National Association of Black Scuba Divers honored the shackled victims with a plaque placed on the site. The plaque faces east toward West Africa. It reads HENRIETTA MARIE. IN MEMORY AND RECOGNITION OF THE COURAGE, PAIN AND SUFFERING OF ENSLAVED AFRICAN PEOPLE. 'SPEAK HER NAME AND GENTLY TOUCH THE SOULS OF OUR ANCESTORS.'

Thomas Phillips, master of the London slaver the *Hannibal*, described in 1694 how captives were carefully monitored

> When our slaves are aboard we shackle the men two and two, while we lie in port, and in sight of their own country, for 'tis then they attempt to make their escape, and mutiny; to prevent which we always keep centinels upon the hatchways, and have a chest full of small arms, ready loaden and prim'd, constantly lying at hand upon the quarter-deck guns, pointing on the deck thence, and two more out of the steerage, the door of which is always kept shut, and well barr'd.

A French captain trading in Senegal on the *Brome* claimed in 1693 that "one, or even two pairs of irons is scarce enough for every single captive." As late as August 1804, the *Connecticut Centinel* was still advertising for sale "300 pair of well made Shackles" and "150 Iron Collars" as "suitable for the confinement of slaves." An old former African slave called Caesar living in England remembered those evil times many years later in the 1870s and how, after wearing these chains for so long, "the iron entered into our souls!"

FORCE FEEDING

Thomas Clarkson, the English abolitionist, lifted the lid on torture at sea when he described in 1808 buying in a Liverpool shop tools used on slave ships. They included handcuffs, shackles, a thumbscrew, and a *speculum oris*, or mouth opener, used for force-feeding.

On some slavers, before turning to meaner measures, monitors severely whipped slaves who were forcefully starving themselves. According to one surgeon, "Upon the negroes refusing to take sustenance I have seen coals of fire, glowing hot, put on a shovel and placed so near their lips as to scorch and burn them . . . and this has been accompanied with threats, of forcing them to swallow the coals, if they any longer persisted in refusing to eat . . ."

When all else failed, the vise-like *speculum oris* could be widened by hand, and was used to force-feed captives. These instruments more suited to medieval torture were a matter of pure economics. A weak, unfed slave sold badly.

"So, I know how I'm feeling holding something like this, but this is just a different feeling; it's hard to articulate," Josh tried to explain, his senses running raw. "To just have these in my hand, it hits a different note. I guess you could see in my face maybe . . ."

"No, absolutely," Corey reassured Josh. "There's no denying the cruelty of it when you look at those things, and you know what they did."

After examining the kinds of finds that sank on slave ships and talking over the cruelty they were used for, the team was even more dedicated to hunt down the *Guerrero* and share its story with the world.

With a vast area to search underwater, the divers prepared to suit up. Time to head for the shallows.

HEROES TO PIRATES

Trying to zigzag through the Florida Keys' razor-sharp reefs was a deadly blunder for the *Guerrero*. Bad navigation aside, the ship had no business being there in the first place. The slave trade was over. Britain and the United States had banned it for twenty years. The great profiteer, England, had turned from trafficking to policing, dispatching a Royal Navy squadron to patrol the high seas. Its mission was to seek and destroy slavers and free their captives. In search of blockade busters, patrols mainly stuck to the coast of West Africa, the origin of the illegal "cargos." Later, the navy widened its net to Cuba, the only player left rolling the dice. To Colonial Spain and its fading power, Cuba's sugar trade was vital to stop the royal court sinking under mounting debt.

In the summer of 1827, the *Guerrero* snuck out of Havana, destined for Africa. A report confirmed that "there can be little doubt that her purpose is to plunder of their cargoes of slaves any weaker vessels that she may fall in with on the coast of Africa. This, we have heard, is a very general practice of the Spanish slave vessels fitted out at this port . . ." It was not alone. All in all, 125 ships headed to Africa from Cuba seeking slaves that year. The *Guerrero* carried out its dark plot perfectly and sailed back with perhaps 700 Africans, of whom 561 survived the Middle Passage crossing to Florida.

The *Guerrero* had seen a colorful history, until now successful. Launched in 1813, it started life carrying passengers, wine, brandy, and government dispatches between the United States' East Coast and Brittany and Bordeaux in France. When the chance arose, its crew captured enemy prizes of war shipping a mix of goods from gunpowder to herrings.

In the War of 1812, under the name of the *James Monroe*, the ship earned a reputation as a formidable sailer. And then it changed its name. As the *General Pepe*, well armed with fourteen cannons, its eighty men trafficked 570 African slaves from Gallinas in Liberia into Havana in 1826. Along the way the Spanish ship, flying a false French flag and its commander clad in a fake Colombian officer's uniform, robbed two traders from Maine and Baltimore of ivory, one thousand pounds of tobacco, up to $1,800 silver dollars, $3,000 in cash, and fifteen and a half ounces of gold. To complete the humiliation, the crews had their clothes stripped. The heroic ship had turned to piracy.

His Britannic Majesty's schooner the *Nimble* was cruising the Florida Straits on December 17, 1827, when it noticed a lone straggler. The slaver now trading as the *Guerrero* was sailing through Orange Cay in the Bahamas, down the Florida Straits under the command of Captain José Gomez, in the hope of dodging the British patrolling Cuba's north coast. It almost made it. There were just 250 more miles to Havana's slave markets and a fat payday. As the *Nimble*'s log recorded, "Observed stranger to be a suspicious looking brig. I set topsail, cleared for action & fired 2 guns to bring stranger to whom we observed hauling up to avoid us . . ." The chase was on.

Six miles off Key Largo, the *Guerrero* pretended to surrender. Then it sped off. Day turned to night. Cat and mouse fired relentlessly. All the while the strong breeze propelled the combatants toward the Florida Keys where all hell broke loose. On December 19 the *Guerrero* smashed onto a low-lying coral reef as sharp as a barbed wire fence. After fourteen years of action, the slaver was an old boat. Its masts fell down and the hull ripped open. Forty-one of the West African captives drowned, their cries "appalling beyond description."

The screams echoed across two miles of ocean where the *Nimble* had also fallen foul of the Keys' razor-sharp reefs. While the *Guerrero* turned over and started to slowly sink into Atlantic oblivion, the *Nimble*'s well-drilled naval crew set about lightening the ship's load to float away from imminent destruction. Ballast and cannon shot were thrown overboard. An anchor and rope line were cast to hold the hull tight and stop the wind and waves pushing the *Nimble* higher onto the reef. The rope snapped like thread and the English patrol boat got stuck hard.

Since the early seventeenth century, the Florida Keys have been home to a maverick band of brothers who made their living from misfortune, "fishing" shipwrecks. When the *Guerrero* struck the rocks, the salvage wreckers the *Thorn* and *Surprize* were anchored at Caesar Creek in today's Biscayne National Park. They rushed to the scene of the disaster, joined by the fishing sloop the *Florida*, sniffing profit. The African human cargo alone could sell for $156,000 in Havana. Wreckers expected to take home 50–90 percent of the value of whatever they saved.

Captain Grover of the *Thorn* set about saving the English patrol ship first. Charging to the aid of the Royal Navy made sound business sense. The other opportunists started unloading the Africans. Trafficked from far and wide onto a slave ship, and united in tragedy thousands of miles from home, yet greater uncertainty was about to divide the *Guerrero* exiles.

The *Florida* saved twenty of the slaver's Spanish crew and 142 Africans, and prepared to head for Key West. There the courts would decide what award to pay the salvors. Only the *Guerrero's* tough pirate crew had other plans. The unappreciative Spaniards hijacked the well-meaning *Florida* and sailed the once more condemned slaves to Santa Cruz in Cuba, where they were sold to the island's sugar plantation owners. The *Thorn*, which had boarded 246 Africans and 54 Spaniards, met the same fate. Gomez, the *Guerrero's* captain, and his men turned on their saviors with daggers, cutlasses, and pistols.

A third "cargo" of 122 Africans, shipped on the *Surprize* to Key West, had good reason to hope for a better outcome, even though by the time they landed many were sick with dysentery and going blind. After seventy-five days stuck in town, they were on the move once more, this time 470 miles north to St. Augustine in northeast Florida.

Freedom did not welcome them. The town's former mayor set them to hard labor on the local sugar estates. The rescued Africans were enslaved once more by their supposed saviors. St. Augustine turned out to be little more than a stone fortress all too familiar to the slave forts built by England, France, Holland, and Sweden along the coast of Africa. And so the *Guerrero's* Africans returned to a living hell in what was called the "poorest hole in the Creation . . . the country around nothing but bare sand hills."

It took twenty-three long months in Florida before the ninety-two survivors from the *Guerrero* slaver were ordered to be sent back "home" to West Africa at the expense of the US government. They docked in Liberia on March 5, 1830. With new American names—Brown, Clark, Curtis, Gibbs, Smith, and Tucker—the traumatized voyagers were settled in New Georgia.

Only Liberia was not exactly home. It was not where they were born or even stolen from. The former slaves were almost as lost as when they reached Florida. They had returned to exile.

NIMBLE PUZZLE PIECES

Out on the ocean, looking for sunken slave ships, the surface of the Keys was flat and beguiling. On days like this the tumultuous hurricanes that blitzed centuries of shipping seemed an unimaginable dream. The engines of the *Phoenix* shut down. Diving With A Purpose was nervous. They had spent a decade searching for the *Guerrero*, a slaver that stubbornly guarded its secrets, its voices. Today they hoped would be the day when this African phoenix rose from the ashes.

Silver dive tanks gleamed in the early morning sun while the dive team checked that their mouthpieces were clear, free of blockage. Orange hard cases secured high-tech metal detectors waiting to peer beneath the sands for the faintest shadow of a 190-year-old nightmare. The team covered all ages from sixty-year-old mentors clad in wetsuits inscribed with the logo DIVING WITH A PURPOSE. RESTORING OUR OCEANS. PRESERVING OUR HERITAGE, to youngsters starting out in ocean exploration.

Corey Malcom led the core team and shared his thoughts on the best way to track down the *Guerrero*. From years of diving these shallows he knew that most ships ended up smashed to smithereens by sweeping hurricanes. With any luck intact parts of wrecks may survive under pockets of deep sand, but most structures and cargos had almost certainly ground to dust. In 1827, a large chunk of the abandoned *Guerrero* was salvaged before it slipped beneath the waves a few days later. Around $10,000 of goods were auctioned off in Key West, including "German platillas [cloth], French cambric cloth, thread laces, gold dust, and ivory," the fruits of piracy in Africa. To crack this cold case, the team would need to find and follow a splinter of forensic debris.

Corey rubbed his stubble and shared his best plan. "I think really in order to find the *Guerrero*, we're going to have to find evidence of the *Nimble*," he argued. "*Nimble* essentially left a trail. *Nimble* had run up onto the reef. They needed to lighten their load. They were able to free themselves by throwing over iron ballast blocks and cannonballs. They got anchored up and then their anchor line parted. They drifted onto the reef again and they threw over more cannonballs, ballasts, more shot, and a small cannon."

"So we're looking for things that the *Nimble* threw off," Kramer clarified.

"Exactly. Those are our clues," Corey confirmed. "The biggest clue we have in the historical record in all of this is the position of the *Nimble* the morning after the ships hit the reef. The *Nimble* was towed to safety off the reef and the captain took his bearings. And we know where that spot was; that was right here."

Corey circled on a map a stretch of seabed six miles offshore, where patches of reef rose menacingly close to the surface. Close enough to snap a ship's rudder.

Kinga was concerned that the *X* where the *Nimble* took its bearing could have been miles of drift away from the spot where the ship hit the reef and took on water.

"So, we know that the *Nimble* was anchored here after, but we don't actually know where it hit the reef, right?" she asked.

"Exactly. What we have to do is account for things like the wind and the weather at that time and which direction the ships were sailing when they hit," Corey added, pointing at a map. "When you take in all the historical evidence, it makes it pretty clear that those two ships hit here at Area A, Area B, or Area C. If we can find evidence of the *Nimble* in these areas, I think that's gonna help us pinpoint the location of the *Guerrero*. And of the captive Africans who perished there."

The *Nimble* had been in hot pursuit of the Spanish slaver. They must have hit trouble at much the same time and in the same stretch of water. Since no coordinates were taken for the fast-sinking *Guerrero*, which was in emergency mode pumping water to save its soul, the only option was to follow the trail of cargo and debris the *Nimble* jettisoned in a desperate attempt to free itself from getting spiked high and dry on the reef.

Kramer had dived these waters for decades and saw a possible administrative headache. Today the areas where the wrecks were thought to have gone down are divided. Part of the debris may have been lost in Biscayne National Park and the other in the National Marine Sanctuary to the south. The team would need separate dive boats and permits.

Kramer agreed to head north to explore Area A in Biscayne Park with its rangers, and sped away on a Boston Whaler. Corey, Alannah, Josh, and Kinga headed down to Areas B and C, two miles away, to survey the shallows with the National Marine Sanctuary archaeologists.

The park's crew lost no time making the most of the flat seas. They suited up, ready to splash down, metal detectors in hand. Before going overboard, Joshua Morano from the National Park Service reminded the divers what to look for.

"To the untrained eye, a shipwreck may look like nothing more than a coral reef," he pointed out. "And so there are tiny little puzzle pieces on these wrecks that we as archaeologists look for specifically that help us date wrecks and help us identify maybe nationality; Who made them? How large are they? What they are utilized for?"

Kramer, keen to scour the seabed, was on the same page and recapped with his team that "any artifact we find of British design could be from the *Nimble*. And any artifact of Spanish design, from the slave ship, *Guerrero*. If the *Nimble*'s crew tossed over any large metal objects in this area, our detector should pick it up."

Above him blue skies shone through a gap in the overcast clouds. Underwater too, Kramer hoped to be able to peer behind the curtain of shifting sands and see what was hidden below. On the seabed where the team believed the English slave patrol ship the *Nimble* got trapped, light pockets of sand rippled around reefs, coral, and seagrass. The visibility was perfect.

Kramer and three Biscayne Park underwater archaeologists started sweeping their metal detectors side to side in search of buried artifacts washed into gullies and wedged firm, voices of the transatlantic slave trade trapped for eternity.

Finding remains of the *Guerrero*'s lost African culture in these waters was like looking for the snapped-off tip of a needle in a haystack. The remains were long buried under sand and then overgrown with coral.

Nature had reclaimed its domain, paved over man's monstrosity, covered up the scene of the crime. The seabed was mostly flat and frustratingly sterile. Just broken coral heads were strewn everywhere, a casualty of furious hurricanes. A pair of spirited tarpons joined the chase.

Kramer was having little luck but tapped into his deep reserves of patience and strong will earned from years as a firefighter. Only when he started sweeping across the lower slope of a gentle-sided reef did his metal detector burst into life, peering below the present into times past and beeping manically. Kramer smiled to himself. It sounded like he had caught a whopper.

The sloping seabed looked unspectacular. The Biscayne Park archaeologists stuck a red-and-white iron identification spike over the target between a large boulder and gulley. The team would need to return with serious underwater digging equipment.

WHO DO YOU THINK YOU ARE?

When the *Guerrero's* survivors, dizzy from two and a half years of being uprooted among foreign sights and cultures, were returned "home" to Liberia in March 1830, the United States courts thought they were righting a wrong. The Africans had returned home.

Only they had not. New Georgia in Liberia, where the ninety-one survivors were landed, was not even an African town. Liberia came into existence artificially in 1822 as an American colony where the United States inspired "a stock of civil and social knowledge, as well as an impulse to improvement." The surrounding peoples, the Americans told the world, came from an "utter and unrestrained savage life." To the well-intentioned Robert Finley of the American Colonization Society that founded Liberia, West Africa was previously inhabited by "wild and wandering people." Now the United States had "civilized" three hundred people, and introduced shipwrecked men and women to God and the rule of law. As a tribal proverb from Gabon says, "rather than hear the truth, people love a lie."

Liberia was an American human experiment that assumed what was good and right for a people in their own land. No attempt was made to return the exiles to where they were taken. There were no translators to understand the dispossessed, no interviews were attempted, no reports filed. Survivors trafficked by the slavers the *Dallas* in 1820, the *Antelope* in 1827, and the *Guerrero* were forcibly settled on Bushrod Island in New Georgia, re-rooted to agricultural plantations founded in the mirror image of Western civilization and Christianity.

The lands of Liberia were originally home to sixteen tribes. The Vai people controlled fifty miles of coast between the Gallinas River and

Grand Cape Mount, while Cape Mount to Cape Montserrado was home to the Dey people. History has forgotten where exactly the *Guerrero's* enslaved were taken, but most of the Africans seem to have been Igbo from southern Nigeria. In Liberia they were marooned more than 2,800 kilometers from their homeland.

Three decades later, in 1861, the American naval officer Robert Wilson Shufeldt admitted in a report to a US judge that "To those acquainted with Africa the utter difference in the language, customs & religion of the various tribes—increased frequently by hereditary hostility, it need not be told how far is the prospect of the poor negro ever seeing his home again when landed upon the Soil of Liberia, as foreign & as strange to him as the coast of Arabia . . ." Back on West African soil, the cultures left behind were still a world away.

Going Back Home

In the eighteenth and nineteenth centuries, Europe's superpowers sliced up West Africa into new countries, ignoring the rich cultural traditions that ruled the continent for centuries. To Europe, Africa was a plum pie whose natural resources were ripe for the picking to be dished out as she saw fit. Today the kingdoms, villages, wildlife, much of the forested landscapes, and entire tribal art collections have vanished as the Gold Coast and Guinea—Angola, Benin, Gabon, Gambia, Ghana, Cameroon, Congo, Côte d'Ivoire, Nigeria, Senegal, and Sierra Leone—fell to European flags. The damming of West African culture and the continent's progress was World War 0.

The character of the cultures left behind is a chasm that the world increasingly demands to understand. For most of history, people of color were left with no way to figure out how they ended up in America, Brazil, the Caribbean islands, Cuba, Denmark, England, France, Holland, Portugal, Spain, and Sweden. Uprooted, they ended up rootless. A minority might manage to track family descendants back a few generations by drawing on oral memory.

All that is changing fast. Leaps in science are shifting the narrative, letting people across the globe tap into ingenious DNA analyses to finally discover their identity. The talk show host, author, and philanthropist Oprah Winfrey has found out she is 89 percent sub-Saharan African, descended from the Kpelle of Liberia and Guinea. The actress Whoopi Goldberg's ancestors come from the Papel and Bayote tribes of Ome in Guinea-Bissau. Record producer Quincy Jones and film director Spike Lee have traced their roots to the Tikars of Cameroon. The family of the actor Forest Whitaker was once a member of the Igbo tribe in Nigeria.

DNA analysis has become a powerful grassroots test of time and origins. More than twenty-six million people worldwide have swabbed their mouths to find out who they really are and fulfill their birthright experience. The boom in affordable at-home DNA testing has also fueled a new wave in travel for people of color connecting with their African ancestry and "going back" home. Ancestry trips, pilgrimages, genealogy tours, and DNA travel are a $3 billion industry.

ART OF BENIN

The art and culture of West Africa has long been called primitive and unsophisticated, a belief born in the city of Benin in modern Nigeria. When British troops razed the royal court of Benin between February 9 and 27, 1897, the attack was justified to stop its king's evil customs, slave-raiding, sacrificing humans on crucifixion trees, and cannibalism. The West called Benin a city of skulls and blood.

In days, the Kingdom of Benin, ruled by an unbroken line of Obas (Kings) since 1440, was destroyed by three hundred British troops arriving on ten Royal Navy ships wielding machine guns, rockets, 1,200 rifles, and three million bullets. The Oba was exiled to Calabar and six chiefs executed in the marketplace. The sacred landscape of royal and religious power was leveled to the ground. A golf course was built over it. The soldiers dug fifteen-foot-deep holes to plunder ten thousand cultural masterpieces now scattered among 161 museums and galleries in New York, London, Toronto, Berlin, Moscow, Los Angeles, Abu Dhabi, and beyond.

West Africa's royal art was virtually unknown in Europe before 1897. The Benin bronzes are today appreciated as masterpieces in brass representing one of the oldest artistic traditions on the African continent. Over one thousand rectangular cast relief plaques once decorated the hardwood pillars of the Royal Palace, illustrating the history of ancient Benin through figures of kings, courtiers, priests, warriors, and Portuguese soldiers trading manilla bracelets. The art of Benin shows the faces and customs of the ancestors. In the Edo language of Benin, the verb to remember means "to cast a motif in bronze." Crafting brass was the act of immortalizing historic memory. The burning of Benin severed the kingdom's history forever.

Other art included brass heads and ivories arranged on thirty-five royal shrines, one for each of the Obas since the rule of Ewuare I in 1440. The stolen art included hundreds of brass, copper, iron, wood, coconut, and coral-bead body ornaments in the form of elephants, humans, rams, and crocodiles. The troops seized staffs of office made from ivory, iron, wood, and brass, fly whisks used in rituals, objects for healing and divination, walls, drums and gongs, and ceremonial swords and axes that hung on palace walls.

After the slave trade ended, Britain's economic imperialism turned to trading palm oil, palm kernels, and rubber between 1854 and 1904. Palm oil, 20,394 tons of it, left the Niger Delta every year for soap, candles, lamps, and cooking. Ivory, mahogany, ebony, coffee, cocoa, indigo, hides, and nuts were also bought for the European market. When West Africa's kings refused to sign treaties making them British protectorates, they were forcefully removed from power.

Since 1936, Benin has demanded its art be repatriated. The Nigerian government has bought looted objects when they appeared on the open market. In a new scramble for decolonisation, Berlin is negotiating return of the bronzes, helping build a Royal Museum in Benin City and supporting excavation of the ancient ruins. The National Museum of Ireland, Horniman Museum in London, and Church of England are sending loot back. The British Museum with its nine hundred artifacts and many other institutions have so far refused to send the Benin bronzes home.

What life was like in seventeenth- to early nineteenth-century West Africa can be felt but is hard to visualize in the modern day, however. Here and there pockets of authenticity live on. The activist and Hollywood actor, Samuel L. Jackson, one of the lead producers of the *Enslaved* series's hunt for the sunken ships of the transatlantic slave trade, recently took a DNA test and discovered he is descended from the Benga tribe of Gabon. Jackson went to Gabon and reconnected with the tribe of his ancestors. He was accepted as a lost son returned and initiated into the tribe. He was given a Benga name, Neteti, which appropriately means star. His journey was unique and he chose to use it as a platform for educating millions about the transatlantic slave trade.

The Benga are a perfect example of a minority people who beat the odds to stake a place in the modern Gabon. Their story shows just how hard it is to dig deeply into the African origins of displaced peoples. History books hardly mention the Benga. Their own oral history, passed down the generations every year in reenacted foundation ceremonies, paints a fuzzy picture of intrepid deep-sea fishermen, merchants, and sailors spread thinly along the coast of northwest Gabon, centered on Cape Esterias and Cape Santa Clara near what became French Libreville. They were fluent in all the languages of the coast. But the Benga were not a local sea people. They were refugees forced out of their home by Ikieki warriors who attacked the dense forests of modern Cameroon around the Muni River, over a hundred kilometers north of Gabon.

The name Benga is thought to come from the word *Ibenga*, to follow. They were the people who followed their chief Massangué and the setting sun down to the sea. Along the way they gave names to the landmarks they passed. Ndendé was the Slippery Place, Mégombiè the River of Luck, Myondi the Home of the Fairies, and Mwalika the Place of Abandoned Regret. The Bengas' arrival on the Atlantic coast coincided with the appearance of English traders around the 1760s.

The Gabon slave trade started in the south and slowly spread north. Into the mid–eighteenth century the Benga were mostly left alone to profit from their ties with the inland peoples from southern Cameroon to Angola. Dutch ships soon arrived, hunting for ivory, ebony, and other natural wealth. The coastal people are thought to have rarely raided for captives. Unlike in Ghana and the Gold Coast, the clans managed to monopolize access to the interior, scaring off Westerners with tales of cannibals and savages. Ironically, ships' captains repeated these tales back home, which later justified the invasion and colonization of West Africa in the name of God and the Cross.

As pressure mounted to end the slave trade, and after it was banned, traders increasingly turned to remote Gabon after 1800. With England reinventing itself as chief savior of Africa's enslaved, Spain and Portugal shifted their operations away from the Gold Coast to sleepy Gabon and nearby shores. Gabon became a middle ground for trafficking Africans across the Middle Passage.

Little can be gleaned from history, ethnography, or archaeology about Benga daily life or religion. The clan shrouded itself in secrecy through oaths to the spirit Ukuku. The sacred was everywhere. Nothing was left to chance in this deeply spiritual society, not birth or death, to ensure reincarnation. The people of the shadows, from spirits of ancestors to phantoms of the unfulfilled dead, were sensed in the realm of the living. The Benga made and used works of art—statues, masks, reliquary figures, jewelry, and weapons—to communicate with the Beyond and appease supernatural forces in the here and now. Vast swathes of this ancestral heritage were swept up by European collectors and museums in the nineteenth century. Little is left to study in the place where it was created.

Mary Henrietta Kingsley, a British traveler, managed to glimpse the Benga in 1895 in her *Travels in West Africa*. In the "Gaboon" she learned how, by the end of the nineteenth century, this powerful and proud nation had become "indolent." The Benga were believed through trade in ivory and slaves to have been encouraged to buy goods on credit. Over time they fell into debt to European traders. Rum corrupted their culture. Even the free turned into slaves addicted to the West. Only two thousand Benga were left by the late nineteenth century.

The Benga are just one of thirty-five ethnic groups that thrived in Gabon and were trafficked into slavery. West Africa as a whole was home to around three thousand tribes speaking two thousand languages. The names of few of these are known to the wider world today. The cultures left behind can only be glimpsed in the shadows.

THE DEVIL'S GUN

Separated by just a short boat ride, the National Marine Sanctuary is a forest compared to where Kramer was diving in Biscayne Park. Green coral fans waved gently in the light current. The underwater fauna among these 3,801 square miles of protected water was as dense as the forests of Gabon. The divers could hardly see the reefs on whose backs the vegetation sprouted. Corey, Alannah, Kinga, and Josh were diving on eggshells, finning cautiously through the unspoiled silent world. The team scoured the seabed with video and cameras, sweeping in and out of gullies. Tiny almond-shaped bluehead wrasse and yellow grunt fish, foraging among meadows of seagrass, darted between the human fishmen and fishwomen.

The team had homed in on an area where Corey Malcom believed they had the best chance of discovering a trail of evidence tossed overboard by the British crew of the *Nimble*. The devastation was well hidden under a thick mantle of marine grass. After a decade searching, would Diving With A Purpose finally crack the mystery of where and how the Spanish slaver the *Guerrero* was doomed by finding artifacts from the *Nimble*? The team's eyes were peeled looking for cannons, cannonballs, anchors, and pretty much anything that may have been jettisoned or broken away from a nineteenth-century Royal Navy ship.

To add to the difficulty of seeing the seabed and camouflaged cultural finds, in this protected park picking up historic finds is forbidden. The team instead turned to a high-tech tool to help visualize any discoveries. When the divers spotted forensic clues, they planned to shoot them with 3D photographic cameras. Back in the lab, Corey would convert dozens of photos into a single three-dimensional image so the finds could be scrutinized safely without being disturbed.

In a light pocket of sand, sitting proud of the seabed, Corey suddenly pointed out an unassuming rectangular concretion. It was a key piece of fossilized archaeology that had been there long enough for coral to sprout off its sides.

"Oh wow, this is a big block of iron ballast," he alerted the team through the underwater communications speaker built into his facemask. "It's about three feet long. It was used in the bottom of the ship to make it bottom heavy, so when the sails filled with wind the ship didn't tip over. It fits exactly with what we know the *Nimble* threw overboard. But all ships have ballast onboard, so we can't say for sure that this is from the *Nimble*. We're going to have to keep looking for a needle in a two-hundred-year-old haystack."

Later, back in the lab, Alannah, Kinga, and Josh huddled around a computer screen as Corey demonstrated what marine archaeology looks like in the twenty-first century. Without having touched the find, he had processed their underwater photos into a seamless 3D image that could be rotated to any angle and flown around virtually. With the luxury of limitless time, and no fear of running out of air underwater, the team encircled the iron ballast block.

Navy ships preferred iron ballast, rather than the mix of sand and pebbles used by most merchant vessels, because it was rigid and stiffened the bottom of hulls. In rolling seas iron ballast helped warships sail better and faster because it was less likely to move around the hold. Blocks of iron were a more mathematically controlled way to get the most out of a ship's limitations and stop them being what the Navy called crank, drunken sailors.

Whereas Spanish ships were usually ballasted with large river pebbles, English men-of-war chose iron ballast cast in England. Ballast like this was stamped with a broadarrow, the Royal Navy's calling card. Any objects marked with an arrow-shaped motif, from a sail to a cannon, was recognizable property of the British admiralty. One downside of not being able to pick up finds in the Florida Keys National Marine Sanctuary was that there was no way of cleaning off centuries of concretion to see if it was marked this way. The ballast may not have been a trophy find, but it was an encouraging clue. The team was on the right trail of the *Nimble* and *Guerrero*.

Giant's Knuckles

Two miles north in Biscayne National Park, maritime archaeologists unfurled blue and red hoses over the side of their dive boat and cranked up its generator. The team's metal detectors had struck a big hit in what the archaeologists were calling Area A. Unlike in the south, the team was allowed to investigate what lay below using traditional tools of marine archaeology. There was only one way to figure out what the find was: sucking sand.

In the shadow of an imposing reef outcrop looking like a giant's gnarled knuckles, Kramer and the sanctuary's archaeologists hand fanned sand and dead coral through the head of the dredge. Using the power of the dive boat's generator, water was forced through the hose at such a high velocity that it created powerful suction. Dredges are the equivalent of industrial underwater vacuum cleaners. Slowly, the upper layers of sand and crumbled coral peeled away. The sterile sediment was left to settle through an exhaust, tens of meters away, so the sand stayed in its natural environment.

Half a meter down, the edges of a large concretion started to appear. It was about a meter long and gently slumped, its mouth pointing downward and one end hitched up toward the surface. No marine life grew off its back. Whatever this object was had been buried for an age, not exposed and covered by coral and sea fans.

"When we first saw it, I didn't know what it was," Kramer admitted. "But as we kept on working, it just kept on getting bigger and bigger. And I knew at that point it was going to be something good."

Eventually the team fully uncovered the discovery. Its shape was obvious to everyone.

"It's a gun, which is a very exciting find," Joshua Marano confirmed.

Cannon like this had a very specific shape and were known as carronades. Even better, small carronades were a kind of ordnance especially favored by the Royal Navy.

Joshua Morano drilled deeper into the gun's history, explaining to Kramer through their underwater communications that "right here you see a very fine taper. This is called the nozzle, and it's particularly date-able. They didn't have these on most carronades before 1815. So this particular gun probably dates from about 1815 to 1830. It's a single piece of a puzzle. But this is a very big piece to that puzzle."

Kramer was quick to appreciate the gun's meaning, confirming that "This carronade is about two hundred years old. And it fits the time of the *Nimble*. So, I think we're on the right track to finding the slave ship the *Guerrero*."

Only serious naval ships boasted iron carronades. These types of guns were the sawed-off shotgun of the seas. They were far shorter than regular cannon and were designed at the Carron Iron Works in Falkirk in Scotland—hence their name—to fire a heavy shot at short range like an antipersonnel weapon. In a new twist, the technology was mounted on wooden slides, rather than fixed carriages. Carronades could take a run up and hurl wooden shot cases filled with 250 lead balls to smash through the sides of a wooden ship. The blast sent a surge of wood splinters into the air, bloodily wiping out the crew on an enemy's main deck in one shot.

France and Spain had nothing to compare with this gun's killer ferocity. The carronade played a key part in demolishing French forces in the Napoleonic Wars in 1803–1815, sealing Britain's empire and fate as ruler of the waves. America caught onto the carronades' deadly intentions and armed super battleships like the USS *Constitution* with them in the War of 1812. British sailors called these weapons of deadly intent "smashers" or the "devil's gun."

Kramer and the Biscayne National Park team had made a big win in the hunt for the lost Spanish slaver and its silenced Africans. It was time to head home for the day. The team finned upward toward the bright Florida sky. They were getting close. They could almost hear the faint voices of the enchained starting to rise again.

ANCHORS AWEIGH

In the southern search area of the Florida Keys, Diving With A Purpose, and Corey, continued scouring the seabed for a trail of debris left behind by the badly wounded *Nimble*. Find the *Nimble*, they kept repeating, and you discover the Spanish slaver the *Guerrero*.

Corey had checked the logbooks and shared exciting news. The dusty, brown-cracked spines of Royal Navy logbooks confirmed that the English antislave patrol boat the *Nimble* did throw a small carronade gun over the side into these waters to lighten its load and try to re-float its hull off the reef. The seismic plates of history and archaeology were merging to reveal the voices behind one of America's darkest slaving memories.

Kinga stood back from the evidence piling up and assessed where the team stood. "So we're adding the discovery of the ballast to the carronade that Kramer and Joshua discovered less than two miles away. Really we just need to keep compiling that evidence."

The divers needed to crack on. The Keys' mirrored veneer was starting to get agitated. Because the seabed was shallow—just over three meters deep—even mild wind could throw up dangerous breakers and scuttle the mission. Time was running out. Furious air bubbles cascaded up from the divers' regulators, seeking freedom.

Back in the water, Kinga soon zoned in on a large iron anchor, around nine feet long. Vivid live coral sprouted off its arms and crown. It lay proud and silently unchanged since the day it was lost above a flat sandy sea bottom carpeted with turtle grass. Two flat black-and-yellow-striped angelfish nosily darted around the divers.

Corey finned close to the end of the ship's anchor. "You can see this anchor is set into the ground," he noticed. "One fluke is completely buried, one sticks up. Somebody was actively using this when they lost it. Now it's kind of hard to say for sure if this is indeed the *Nimble*'s anchor, but I'll say this, it's the right size for what the *Nimble* would have carried. It's the right design for the time period, and it's in exactly the right location."

"Isn't that awesome? And *Nimble* lost two anchors," Corey continued after a few gulps of air. "This anchor, I think, is an important part of evidence for the story of the *Guerrero* and *Nimble*. Really matches closely with the evidence that we have. This anchor, along with the ballast and the carronade, shows that the evidence is really piling up. It all points to the hazardous line the *Nimble* took on the high seas chase for the slave ship *Guerrero*."

England's meticulously kept logbooks again confirmed that the *Nimble* lost its anchors near Carysfort Reef. Lieutenant Edward Holland, the warship's commander, wrote how what was called a stream anchor sank in four fathoms, while a second-best bower was lost in two fathoms. The great anchor lying in the National Marine Sanctuary waters was the right size and shape for a 168-ton English ship like the *Nimble*. It fitted with accounts of the patrol ship casting an anchor in a desperate bid to drag itself off the entombed reef using a rope line.

The *Nimble* did not just lose crucial weaponry and its all-essential breaks when it got stuck hard and fast. Iron shot and cannonballs went overboard in a last-ditch bid to save the ship and crew. The forensics were piling up and the scattered debris left no doubt that a ship was once caught in troubled seas at this spot. The dive team was hot on the trail. Soon copper nails were spotted on the reef where a hull's wooden walls once burst open. The team had to double down their powers of concentration as the seagrass got thicker and thicker. Mother nature was covering up a historic crime scene.

In the underwater forest, Corey pointed out a couple of iron cannonballs concreted together. Alannah and Kinga quickly noticed similar missiles all around them, at least twelve, just dropped on top of the reef. These five-kilogram (eleven-pound) cannonballs could inflict serious damage on enemy decks. The sea resembled a battle zone. But this battle had been between ship and nature, not man.

"It's amazing. There's just stuff everywhere," Corey exclaimed. "This fits our scenario of the *Nimble* throwing over lots of iron cannonballs. When you combine all these iron cannonballs with the rest of the evidence, it just fits the historical record perfectly."

The team surfaced to change their dive tanks. Kinga was lost in thought scrutinizing the underwater photos she had taken of the finds. What she saw made her smile. There was now no doubt. The team had successfully confirmed the spot where the *Nimble* crashed onto a Floridian reef on December 19, 1827.

Alannah felt energized. The sea had taken a lot out of the experienced diver, but she was desperate to push on. "Gosh, if this is the actual site of the *Nimble*, then the *Guerrero* is around here somewhere. I think we can find it."

The end game for the slave ship *Guerrero*, with 561 Africans on board 195 years ago, was close by.

SWEET HAVANA

By the time the *Nimble* intercepted the *Guerrero* on its lawless last voyage, all the legal markets where Europe could turn a profit from man's greatest inhumanity had been shut down. Spanish Cuba, out of step with these revolutionary years, was the only player left hanging onto the colonial dream.

Over the years, Madrid had sold the monopoly to the slave trade to the highest bidder. Willing companies banged on Spain's door: royal licenses were handed out between 1696 and 1713 to the Portuguese Guinea Company, the Royal French Guinea Company, and the English South Sea Company. Baker & Dawson of Liverpool put their hands on the rudder in 1783, shipping 5,306 slaves into the Antilles. By the time war and antislavery movements demanded an end of the royal permit favor in 1789, a million slaves had been legally imported into Spanish America. Another million arrived as contraband.

By then, soul-searching had overturned backward thinking. The people rose up in the French Revolution in 1789. The United States had grabbed its liberty with the end of the Revolutionary War in 1783. England's courts had ruled that all the land's slaves must be freed. The Society for Effecting the Abolition of Slave Trade embarrassed Europe into hanging up its shackles. Human rights were finally triumphant.

In 1792, Denmark was the first European country to abolish the importation of slaves to its colonies. It was followed by England in 1807, banning the slave trade as a whole, Sweden in 1813, and Holland a year later. In 1808, the United States also outlawed the trade but not the institution. Only Cuba clung to its slave trading past, swimming against the tide. Why? Because Madrid, increasingly stripped of the trappings of empire, relied on Cuba's sugar revenue as the lifeblood of its treasury.

Back in 1762, when English forces captured Spanish Havana during the Seven Years' War, they found almost one hundred sugar mills on the island. Cuba enjoyed the right setting and climate to seize the mantle of world leader in sugar. The only drawback was the lack of labor. England supplied the solution. After the invasion, English merchants trafficked the same amount of Africans in just eleven months as previously reached Cuba in fifteen years. The Sugar Island was born.

To Europe, and increasingly the United States' new breed of get-rich-quick entrepreneurs, Cuba was a golden goose. A freshly independent United States cut ties with the English Antilles and Barbados and offered the hand of friendship to Spanish Cuba for its coffee habit and distillery needs. By now Massachusetts was pumping out the finest rum in the West Indies, which sold by the fleet load to England, where its army and navy doled it out as merry military rations.

There was no going back. The Spanish Crown followed the English model by keeping unlocked the chains to free trade in sugar, hides, beeswax, coffee, and tortoise shell. A monthly packet line sailed between Spain and Havana. The six merchant traders that docked in Havana in 1765 rose to 1,057 by 1828, excluding slave ships. Cuba's fortunes were tied to one major drug—sugar. A slave rebellion that kicked off on Haiti's plantations in November 1791 only added to Cuba's attraction as a haven for unlimited free trade in African slaves, even as other nations outlawed it.

To keep the island's sugar estate machinery whirring, and to meet the ever greater need for Africans for cutting, grinding, filtration, evaporation, and crystallization, the slave population had to be massively boosted. As King Ferdinand VII of Spain put it in December 1817, "The impossibility of finding Indians . . . to do the work of breaking and cultivating the land demanded that this work. . . be delivered to more robust arms." Cuba's leaders dreamed of an island populated by a half-million-strong African slave army. To feed the dream, everyone got in on the act: the Santa Clara monastery took a cut of profits from over twenty mills. The number of sugar estates on Cuba almost doubled to one thousand by 1827. The enchanting mahogany, cedar, and ebony forests that took centuries to grow were cut down in the space of a few years to fuel the ovens. Sugar fever shook the world.

CUBA'S SUGAR RUSH

In just a decade between 1790 and 1800, the amount of sugar exported each year from Cuba rose from 77,896 to 142,097 boxes weighing over 28,000 tons. Whereas some 2,534 captive African were docked in Havana in twenty-seven ships in 1790, 25,841 were trafficked in 1817. The years spanning 1790–1820 saw 225,574 Africans uprooted for Cuba. At first, the United States and Britain controlled about two thirds of the market, but by 1794 the US share reached 50 percent of total imports. The United States bought up a million pesos a year of boxed sugar.

Cuba's old Spanish families, many living on the island since the sixteenth century, raked in the cash. By 1844, twenty-nine marquises and thirty counts were squeezed onto the island. The bulk of these sugar noblemen bought their positions, paying Madrid up to $50,000 a pop for the title.

In the years before justice caught up with the Spanish slave ship the *Guerrero*, England pressured Spain to abandon its slave trading ways. King Ferdinand agreed in September 1817 to ban the trading of slaves north of the equator in Africa. Ships masters caught breaking the rules risked being thrown in jail for ten years. In May 1820 the ban was expanded south of the equator. The British government put aside a £400,000 nest egg to cover Spanish merchants' trade losses. The nightmare of Europe's scramble for captive Africa should have been over.

Instead, the trade went underground. Risks and costs rose, and sugar profits nose-dived. Cuba went into overdrive. Sugar was more in demand than ever. An unprecedented clandestine network arose, and Cuba's leaders found creative words to justify their actions. They quoted St. Thomas's proverb at any opportunity. "What is not just in law, necessity makes just," they claimed. The island blamed the past for the present.

"The Negroes have come and are here to our misfortune," Havana told the world, "not by our fault, but that of those who first initiated and encouraged this commerce in the name of law and religion." The message was loud and clear: Spanish Cuba was still open for business with all comers.

It was now that Britain sent out its first antislavery patrols. In 1819, the navy stationed a permanent squadron off West Africa. The scheme sounded impressive. At its peak in the mid-1840s, Britain's West African squadron was made up of thirty-six ships and four thousand men. Around 15 percent of all Britain's warships and one tenth of its naval workforce were mobilized to sink the slave trade.

London smugly patted itself on the back for what it felt were charitable motives. In 1869, William Lecky claimed in his *History of European Morals from Augustus to Charlemagne* that "The unwearied, unostentatious, and inglorious crusade of England against slavery may probably be regarded as among the three or four perfectly virtuous acts recorded in the history of nations." History had a short memory, however.

The Royal Navy had always treated Africa as a training ground where sailors were battle-hardened to keep Britannia ruling the waves. Up to October 1807, English ships trafficking Africans to the Americas had been protected by naval frigates. Now, England's xenophobic sailors, often racist, were not impressed by the possibility of dying to save people with whom they had nothing in common.

Perhaps this is why the ships the navy sacrificed to antislavery patrols were slow old tubs without enough speed or firepower to catch America's fast clippers. Even when slavers were caught in the act, they copied pirates' ways by showing forged documentation about their home port to escape capture. The navy's hit rate did see successes though. Between 1808 and 1867, more than 1,600 slave ships transporting 160,000 slaves were arrested heading for the Americas.

On the other hand, 543,882 slaves were shipped illegally to Cuba from Africa from 1821 to 1867. Over 85 percent of captures were made off West Africa. The Sugar Island's 2,000-mile winding coast, studded with thousands of small offshore islands and keys, made patrolling its waters virtually impossible. And which of the 1,500 ships coming and going every year were slavers or innocent traders? Not everyone could be boarded. A fraction of the total traffic ended up policed.

By the time the pirate ship *Guerrero* sailed, the transatlantic slave trade with Cuba was close to its peak. Despite its Spanish commander and catering to the Spanish Cuban market, the *Guerrero* almost certainly had a US crew. Most slave ships were built in New England (Maine, Vermont, New Hampshire, Massachusetts, Connecticut, and Rhode Island). If pulled over by a Royal Navy patrol, these traders doing Spain's dirty work hoisted the stars and stripes and sailed off over the horizon. As the American naval officer Robert Wilson Shufeldt wrote to Judge Truman Smith on January 6, 1861:

> However humiliating may be the confession, the fact nevertheless is beyond question that nine tenths of the vessels engaged in the Slave trade are American. There are two reasons for this; the first is the vicinity of a good market for the purchase of cheap vessels—the facility with which they can be cleared for the coast, & the equal facility with which they can escape conviction if caught, owing probably to an ill-concealed sympathy for the institution of Slavery which seems to extend from the head of our present government to every subordinate officer! But the main reason why American vessels are employed is the immunity which our National flag gives to the combined rascality of Christendom . . .

Cunning slave traders improved their chances of busting the blockade by shifting their base of operations away from the strongly patrolled Gold Coast. West Central Africa, where patrols rarely visited, saw a sharp increase in its business with Cuba. It was now that the Kingdom of Loango and the Congo estuary emerged as the most important hunting ground for Havana's slaves. The trade simply sidestepped into places which were out of sight and reach of the British navy.

End of the Line

When the *Guerrero* was chased to its watery grave off the Florida Keys, Cuba was still illegally pumping African labor into the island. To keep the sweet deals rolling, Spain flew in the face of the world's antislavery spirit and laws. The *Nimble*'s deadly pursuit of the slaver in American waters, however, marked the beginning of the end of the line.

Spain twisted and turned to keep its interests alive. Madrid passed a new royal decree in March 1830 that empowered Cuba's captain-general to issue heavy fines "upon so inhuman traffic." And yet, Spain did not even bother publishing the law in Cuba. Slavers continued to come and go at will. Madrid's Criminal Law Regarding the Slave Trade treaties with Britain in 1835 and 1845 also made little headway. A Spanish Abolitionist Society was only formed in 1864—and by a Puerto Rican.

By the mid–nineteenth century, half a million Africans were enslaved in Cuba. The more sugar Cuba produced, the more foreign luxuries its high society wanted. The United States became the island's strongest trading partner, shouldering 34 percent of imports and 44 percent of exports. Havana's commerce rocketed to $92 million by 1862, fed by over two thousand American ships. By the last quarter of the 19th century, 94 percent of Cuba's sugar went into feeding the American dream.

CONDITIONS ON CUBA'S SUGAR PLANTATIONS

Before the introduction of the labor-cutting steam engines onto Cuba's sugar plantations, 10 percent of African slaves died on the plantations a year. The technological change saw the death rate drop on some estates to 2.5 percent. On others it stayed as high as 10–15 percent in 1829. A steam engine allowed farmers to grind as much cane in twelve hours as in twenty-four using manual labor.

During the four-month grinding season from January to May, living conditions were especially harsh. Slaves were badly sleep-deprived cutting cane or processing sugar loaves, working seven-day weeks and getting just four hours rest a day. On some plantations, slaves were flogged to death. Twenty percent of Blacks were always in the infirmary.

In 1834 Henry Tudor saw on newly docked slaves "marks on their skins, of bruises or blows, probably received from rubbing against the panels of the vessel, in which they had been unmercifully crammed, like herrings in a barrel." Many plantation Africans looked "jaded to death, listless, stupified, haggard, and emaciated: how different from the looks of the pampered, petted, well-fed, idle, domestic slaves of the Dons of the Havana! . . . They lived here in huts, near the Ingenio [mill engine], but very miserable places, unfit for the habitation of wild beasts . . ." (Richard Madden, *The Island of Cuba*, 1849). On less ruthless estates, slaves ate three meals a day of Indian corn, salt fish, tassajo, and plantains.

To prevent rebellion and encourage hard work, Cuba's slaves had the "privilege" of buying their liberty. They could pay their masters small sums on account to become co-owners of their selves or be freed for the sum of $50 to $100. Slaves might earn up to $3 a day. Estates ran small shops "with everything they may wish to buy that is proper for them; cloth cheap and showy; garments gay and warm; crockery; beads; crosses; guano, or the American palm, that they may form neat hats for themselves; little cooking pots, etc" (Abiel Abbot, *Letters Written in the Interior of Cuba*, 1829). Even granted supposed liberty, "they are unchained but the collar remains on their necks. They are subject to most of the restrictions imposed on the slave, such as respect carrying weapons, being out after dark without a lanthorn, etc. and they are equally deprived of information, their freedom by no means extending to their minds" (Robert Jameson, *Letters from the Havana, during the Year 1820*, 1821).

Spanish merchants like Facundo Bacardi worked their way up from apprentice to millionaire through the kitchens of Santiago de Cuba. Bacardi's sugar-thick amber rum may have been detested as substandard liquor on the island, but the United States was addicted. From Havana to Madrid, New York, Philadelphia, Baltimore, London, and Shanghai, Bacardi's booze circled the world. King Alfonso XIII of Spain even claimed Bacardi's rum saved his life from the flu. Bacardi marketed his drink as the Rum of Kings. It took its place at the high table of luxury next to Havana cigars.

Cuba's illegal trade in Africans that the *Nimble* fought hard to stop in it tracks officially ended in 1886. By then the island's sugar crop was valued at over $60 million. Each newly trafficked slave was said to generate a ton more sugar. The horrors of the transatlantic slave trade conveniently passed into the fog of history. The world quickly forgot that for a century Havana was a "banqueting place of death," as Robert Francis Jameson described the city in 1820. The hunt for the wreck of the *Guerrero* gives a voice back to hundreds of thousands of enchained Africans sent to Cuba, and ensures their story is told and remembered.

SHIP'S BONES

The *Phoenix* sped across the smooth mirrored blue, under low-lying bridges interlinking Florida's keys like the spines of prehistoric beasts. The mangroves dripped silently, mysteriously, as they had for centuries. The bones of a steel wreck lay collapsed and listing in the shallow breakers, given up the fight for survival. Desperate Cubans, fleeing Communism, many descendants of the enslaved, fled to asylum in America on the crammed backs of crude chugs like these deep into the twentieth century. They rode anything that floated. Their wrecked hulks litter the keys.

Diving With A Purpose, led by Corey Malcom, had made a good start. The trail of shipwrecked debris showed they were on the right track. Would the efforts pay off? They had spent days diligently chasing a fragmentary puzzle. The carronade believed to come from the *Nimble* was discovered in Area A. Then the jettisoned ballast and the cannonballs were spotted further south in Area C on the same patch of reef as the iron anchor.

Corey summarized how far the team had traveled. "We're connecting the dots," he said. "These are really looking like the strike points where *Nimble* hit the reef while pursuing the Spanish slave ship. And considering that, we could right now be on top of *Guerrero*."

Spurred on by the chance that the end goal was in sight, once more the divers enthusiastically suited up.

Alannah, Josh and Kramer, who had rejoined the team, stepped over the side of the *Phoenix* together. All for one and one for all. Today's mission was to try and pinpoint conclusive evidence that would tie this location to the resting place of the slave ship the *Guerrero* and the 561 Africans it had on board.

CROSSING TO CUBA

Robert Wilson Shufeldt, an American naval officer, to Judge Truman Smith on the secret history of the African slave trade to Cuba, January 6, 1861. During sea crossings: "Each negro . . . is compelled to wash out his mouth with vinegar—and occasionally to eat a pickle—this is done to prevent scurvy . . . After this the 'Doctor' examines them—pitches overboard the dead & the dying—and gives medicine to such as are not beyond the hope of recovery; the principal diseases, with which they have to contend are dysentery and opthalmia, both generally fatal & both owing to the confined space & foul atmosphere; During the day the 'contramaestro' . . . the very sight of whom makes my blood boil with rage—goes about among them with his whip & cows down the boldest—& silences the noisiest with his merciless lash—& sometime he takes a few of the weakliest to a less crowded space & makes them dance & jump—to the tune of his cowhide—as an exercise & to restore circulation!

At night they are compelled to lie down 'spoon fashion' . . . a canvas covering is hauled over them—& it is *impossible* for them to change their position until daylight the following morning . . . [these are] the thousand and one incidents which must make the soul of every American sicken at the bare idea that such abominations are practiced every day under the guarantee of his Nationality."

On the seabed they joined Corey and Kinga. Was it their imagination or did this patch of seabed look different from the last few days' surveys? The reef was more thickly strewn with man-made objects and slivers of shipwrecked hulls. The dive buddies swept by a lonely ballast stone. It looked uninspiring, far from treasure, but its presence was telling to Corey's knowing eye. A rock isn't always a rock, he told Kinga through their communication speakers.

"Around here in the Keys, it's all limestone," Corey explained about the natural geology. "So, if anything is not limestone . . . it was brought in. And if it's underwater, it probably was brought in on a ship, and that's what we're seeing here. Rocks that just don't fit the natural landscape."

If the British navy's *Nimble* carried iron ballast blocks, the *Guerrero's* hull would have relied on more mundane weights. The one ballast stone quickly turned into a carpet of foreign stones. The trail was heating up. Alannah, her hands serenely grasped together in front of her as she planed through the water, pointed out lengths of concreted iron that looked out of place. They had all the symmetry of a ship's structure.

"This looks like an iron knee or some sort of a brace," Corey told the team. "It looks like it's from the right time period. Iron braces like this could've been used to reinforce the hull structure of ships like *Guerrero*."

Corey pointed out how a right-angled lump of iron was supported by a triangular brace. Right next to it a pin once held part of a ship together. Marine archaeologists call these finds fasteners. Maybe the pin once bolted the *Guerrero's* keel together. The brace could have supported a deck, maybe even the low ceiling of the hold where the Africans were packed like sardines. Iron fasteners replaced wooden beams by the late eighteenth century and stayed popular into the middle of the nineteenth century.

Diving onward, the sunken world turned into a debris field of strewn wreckage. And then. . . finally. . .a smoking gun veered into view, another length of concreted iron, forty centimeters long, with wide flanges at both ends.

Corey had seen horrors of warfare like this before. "This is a really interesting piece," he shared with the crew, speaking slowly as he sucked in air between talking. "This is a type of cannonball, and was meant to go whirling around, tear out rigging, and kill people. This oddly shaped piece of iron with these two flat heads. It's called a bar shot."

And then the clincher. "Looks to be Spanish," he added upon contemplation. "And fits the time, fits the nationality for *Guerrero*. This is exactly what we'd expect to find on a Spanish slave ship like the *Guerrero*."

Cannon bar shot are not common in US waters. To Spanish sailors a *palanqueta* was "a small iron bar with two thick heads, which, instead of round-shot, was used in the loading of shipboard artillery to damage the rigging and the spars of enemy ships," as artillery manuals explained. *Palanquetas* became popular flying monsters in the eighteenth century and continued frightening enemy ships into the nineteenth. Spain famously hoped bar shot would give it the edge in the Battle of Trafalgar in 1805, alongside their French allies led by Napoleon Bonaparte. In the end, bar shot witnessed defeat and the fall of the Spanish empire. Here, in these waters, it signaled victory for Diving With A Purpose.

They had found what they came looking for in the Florida Keys: enough accumulated evidence to be sure they had tracked down the tragic *Guerrero*. The crew clambered back onto the dive boat, exhausted but elated. A shaft of light broke through the clouds, lighting up their ascent.

Josh was jubilant. "The evidence is there. It seems like a wreck definitely was in this area. It's beautiful and sad all together to be down there amongst that stuff, amongst the wreckage," he concluded.

Corey dried himself off and in the shadow of a giant red steel lighthouse, the oldest in the Florida Keys, built in 1852, he summed up the wreck hunt. The sights the team shared in these silent seas, not words, spoke volumes. But in his mind, Corey was clear. Smiling, he said, "I feel absolutely confident that we have found the wreck of the *Guerrero*."

The *Guerrero* was no longer an intact space. It was an echo of a ship. The trader was wrecked and then flattened by hundreds of hurricanes, its shackles and timbers scattered far and wide. All that was left next to the memory of the enslaved were a few bones of the slaver: artillery from the top deck, ballast from the hold, and fasteners like ribs that once pinned the ship together.

To the dive team, the archaeology was a grave site. Anyone who dives a wreck with such a profoundly tragic past, pounded by time and tide, understands that the remains are enduring symbols of lives, deaths, and memories. The team felt deeply humbled.

Kramer summed up the crew's sense of achievement. In his imagination he peered far back into the early nineteenth century when a Spanish ship that should never have been allowed to sail with African captives was chased onto the rocks in the Florida Keys.

"It's a sombering kind of experience," Kramer whispered into the sea breeze. "It's giving voice to people who don't have a voice anymore and that's what this entire experience has been all about."

The *Guerrero*, one of America's worst atrocities and disasters in transatlantic slave trade history, was lost no more. A final link was put back in a chain of broken Afro-American memory. Through discovery, touching the past, Diving With A Purpose started repairing the horrors the ancestors endured by exposing a shameful fate.

As for the *Nimble*, the well-intentioned English patrol boat escaped the clutches of the Florida Keys and continued fighting the illegal slave trade for a few years to come. In the end it sank again trying to save Africans. On November 4, 1834, the *Nimble* caught the schooner *Carlota* near Nuevitas off Cuba. The crew rescued 272 Africans. Abruptly the weather worsened and this time the cursed *Nimble* was wrecked on another reef. The fury of the enslaved, free for a matter of hours, was drowned out by the sound of the breakers smashing onto Cayo Verde on the northern tip of Cuba. Seventy Africans died.

As of today, Spain, the last champion of the transatlantic slave trade, has never apologized for its past inhumanity, what it did to people on the *Guerrero* and in the sugar mills of Cuba. And so the wounds fester and the atrocious memories continue. The scars are unhealed. The descendants of the enslaved live on. They rise. And the ships sunk at the bottom of the world's seas scream for justice.

EPILOGUE

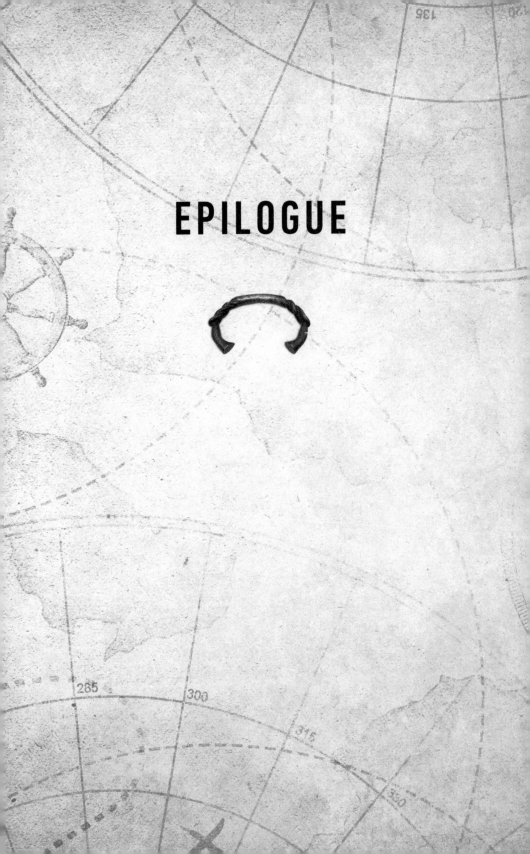

GOOD TROUBLE

Over four years, Diving With A Purpose—Kramer Wimberley, Alannah Vellacott, Josh Williams, and Kinga Philipps—dived Earth's blue seas and investigated sunken slave ships all over the world, from the Florida Keys to the English Channel, Suriname's Maroni River, Cahuita Bay in Costa Roca, Lake Michigan, the Isles of Scilly, and Bristol Channel. Nine shipwrecks on four continents. No one has ever dived so many slave wrecks.

Now, with the underwater hunt coming to an end, Kramer and Alannah had been invited to Washington for a very special meeting with the legendary civil rights leader Congressman John Lewis, months before his passing. Lewis was born into segregation and took the lead in protests as a young man when America was wracked by civil rights storms in the 1960s. He stood in the front line of many epoch-changing and dangerous events. As a leader of the Nashville Student Movement in Tennessee, John Lewis was arrested endlessly while organizing sit-ins against the city's segregated restaurants and bus services.

Lewis was an original Freedom Rider who challenged federal law and segregation on public transport while traveling through Southern states. He was the first rider to be assaulted and kicked while trying to use whites-only facilities in a bus station in Rock Hill in South Carolina. Later he was beaten up by the Ku Klux Klan and the police and spent forty days in jail in Mississippi.

As the chairman of the Student Nonviolent Coordinating Committee (SNCC), Lewis was one of the "Big Six" who organized the 1963 March on Washington where Martin Luther King gave his "I Have a Dream" speech. Two years later he jointly led freedom marchers across the Edmund Pettus Bridge in Selma, Alabama, when they were attacked by state troopers, police, and bystanders. The violence, broadcast coast to coast in America, showed Lewis bloodied by a baton that broke his skull. President Lyndon Johnson was forced to take action. It was a crucial crossroads when public support for equal rights was won. Throughout it all, Lewis fought with his words and feet as a lifelong advocate of nonviolent protest.

Alannah and Kramer were shown, starstruck, into Congressman John Lewis's office in Washington. His walls were thickly covered with historic black-and-white photos of him fighting for freedom and equal rights. A bronze bust of Bobby Kennedy stood in front of the photos.

Alannah wanted to know how many times John Lewis had been arrested.

"During the '60s I got arrested forty times," Lewis confirmed. "For sitting in at lunch counters in restaurants, going on a freedom ride, we were arrested, we were jailed, we were beaten, we were left bloody, left unconscious. Just by sitting in places that only white people were supposed to sit."

"Do you remember the first time that you were arrested?" Kramer asked.

"I remember the first time I was arrested. I can never ever forget it. I felt free," the congressman replied.

Kramer was completely thrown. How could being slung into jail make you feel free?

"I felt liberated, because my mother and my father and grandparents had said, 'Stay out of trouble,' 'Don't get in trouble,' and I got in trouble. What I call 'good trouble.' Necessary trouble."

Diving With A Purpose had got into their own good trouble searching for the sunken transatlantic slave trade. The trouble of deep and dangerous waters, brimming with stingrays. The cold water that could make your regulator stop oxygen flowing in an instant. The trouble of making people who would rather forget the past understand the atrocities that West Africa's enslaved victims endured, the horrors of the Middle Passage, and the anguish of being separated from loved ones. Diving to expose those slave ships worldwide, each one with its own unique story—sad and uplifting—was necessary trouble.

Alannah thought about her own journey that had brought her to this surreal time and place.

"I didn't quite understand my own history," she told Congressman Lewis, "and I have so many questions that each time I go diving some of them get answered. We dove and saw relics, remnants, of the chaos of the brutality, of the abuse. Sometimes it's just too much, but we have to tell this story. This story needs to be told."

Kramer, too, was wondering how he fit into changing thinking about what his ancestors endured. "And that's where I guess I'm stuck, right," he explained. "All of the places that we've been, you can see the beauty of it, and the wonder of it. You see these islands, or shorelines. When we were in Suriname, we're standing on the shoreline of the most beautiful scenery that you ever wanted to see, but to know that 664 Africans were murdered within a couple of hundred yards of the shoreline . . . I'm conflicted all the time," he admitted.

John Lewis had experienced more than most African Americans alive at that time. He had crossed the mighty Rubicon of segregation. Like Robert Smalls of Beaufort, he climbed his way from nowhere to create irreversible change.

"I understand very well what you're saying. And we cannot sweep it under the rug," the congressman advised. "We've got to bring it all out. Make it plain. We have an obligation, a mission, a mandate to do just that, so the whole world can feel this."

Congressman Lewis ended the special meeting by encouraging Alannah and Kramer to "Keep the faith. Don't give up."

"No, sir," Alannah promised.

"Never that," Kramer whispered.

So many faceless millions paid the ultimate sacrifice so Alannah, Kramer, and Black America could be free. The friends slowly made their way down the steps leading away from the Capitol, back to their daily lives. They thought about the hundreds of lost slave ships still littering the world's seas waiting to be discovered. Waiting to give up their drowned voices.

The journey to explore the sunken past is just beginning.

Out of the huts of history's shame
I rise
Up from a past that's rooted in pain
I rise
I'm a black ocean, leaping and wide,
Welling and swelling,
I rise.
Leaving behind nights of terror and fear
I rise
Into a daybreak that's wondrously clear
I rise
Bringing the gifts that my ancestors gave,
I am the dream and the hope, of the slave.
I rise

—Maya Angelou, "Still I Rise"

ACKNOWLEDGMENTS

This book would not have been possible without the series *Enslaved: The Lost History of the Transatlantic Slave Trade*, and the series would not have been possible without the support and participation of Samuel L. Jackson, LaTanya Richardson Jackson, Eli Selden, Rob Lee, and Ric Esther Bienstock.

This book, *Enslaved: The Sunken History of the Transatlantic Slave Trade*, would not have evolved from concept to reality without our dedicated agent, Joelle Delbourgo (Joelle Delbourgo Associates Literary Agency) and our supportive editors, Jessica Case and Claiborne Hancock (Pegasus Books), all of whom believed in this project and passionately backed the book.

A project of this complexity involves hundreds of contributors over many years. The following is a list of some of the most important dive coordinators, divers, filmmakers, researchers, supporters, and family members that helped maked this book a reality.

Dr. Enenge A'Bodjedi, Saladin Allah, Nicole Austin, Dr. Leo Balai, Patrick Henry Barrow, Prof. Audrey Bennett, Prof. Joe'l Lewis Billingsley, Andreas Bloch, Prof. Christopher Bonner, Anderson Rodriguez-Brown, Kevin Rodriguez-Brown, Prof. Marcus Carvalho, Prof. Ana Isabel López-Salazar Codes, Yvette Darden, Prof. Wilhelmina Donkoh, Prof. Ron Eglash, Alenna Emer, Dr. Jerzy Gawronski, Rhiannon Giddens, Felix Golubev, Dorrick Gray, Fallon Green, Jeff Grigg, Sacha Hall, Richard Hanet, Kieran Hatton, Ellai Himel, Terry Hiron, Afua Hirsch, Lawrence Hoo, Prof. Mark Horton, Randi Kirshenbaum, Dr. Paul Kwami, Rep. John Robert Lewis, Dr. Corey Malcolm,

Joshua Marano, Justin Martin, John McGinley, Avi Merkado, Robin Mirsky, Steve Moore, Prof. Elena Moran, David Morrison, Yaron Niski, Dr. Richard Oslisly, Kinga Philipps, John Polacsek, Josh Ponte, Althea Raiford, Matthew Raiford, Ulious Raiford, Jovan Sage, Sarah Sapper, Stacey Shemtov, Richard Stevenson, Kenneth Stewart, Dr. María Suárez Toro, Salvador Van Dyke, Alannah Vellacott, Prof. James Walvin, Dr. Lee White, Joshua Williams, Laura Wilson, Kramer Wimberley, Prof. Natalie Zacek, The Jacobovici Family, The Buffalo History Museum, St. John's Episcopal Church, Jekyll Island Authority, Ilfracombe Museum, History of Diving Museum, Florida, Gabon National Parks, Florida Keys National Marine Sanctuary, Firelands Historical Society.

Sean Kingsley offers a hope that books like this, in a small way, will help make the world in which his son, Felix Sky, grows up and lives, a more tolerant space.

In memory of Frida and Ida Jacobovici, who were enslaved and redeemed.

FURTHER READING

FOLLOW THE MONEY

Alden, Dauril, and Joseph C. Miller. "Out of Africa: The Slave Trade and the Transmission of Smallpox to Brazil, 1560–1831." *Journal of Interdisciplinary History* 18, no. 2 (1987): 195–224.

Araujo, Ana Lucia. "Afterword: Ghosts of Slavery." *International Review of Social History* 65 (2020): 225–36.

Baktir, Hasan. "From Turkish Renegade to a Penny University: The Introduction and Negotiation of the Coffee-Houses in England." *Sosyal Bilimler Enstitüsü Dergisi* 24 (2008): 141–57.

Balai, Leo. *Slave Ship Leusden: A Story of Mutiny, Shipwreck and Murder.* Amsterdam: UTS, 2015.

Bosman, Willem. *A New and Accurate Description of the Coast of Guinea, Divided into the Gold, the Slave, and the Ivory Coasts.* London, 1705.

Curtin, Philip D. *Capitalism, Feudalism, and Sugar Planting in Brazil.* Cambridge: Cambridge University Press, 1998. Eisenberg, Peter L. "Abolishing Slavery: The Process on Pernambuco's Sugar Plantations." *Hispanic American Historical Review* 52, no. 4 (1972): 580–97.

Ellis, Markman. "Pasqua Rosee's Coffee-House, 1652–1666." *London Journal* 29, no. 1 (2004): 1–24.

Fatah-Black, Karwan, and Matthias van Rossum. "Beyond Profitability: The Dutch Transatlantic Slave Trade and Its Economic Impact." *Slavery & Abolition* 36, no. 1 (2014): 63–83.

Ferreira, Maria Teresa, Catarina Coelho, and Sofia N. Wasterlain. "Discarded in the Trash: Burials of African Enslaved Individuals in Valle da Gafaria, Lagos, Portugal (15th–17th Centuries)." *International Journal of Osteoarchaeology* 29, no. 4 (2019).

Hoogbergen, Wim. "The History of the Suriname Maroons." In *Resistance and Rebellion in Suriname: Old and New,* edited by G. Brana-Shute, 65–102. Williamsburg: VA: College of William and Mary, 1990.

Lurvink, Karin. "The Insurance of Mass Murder: The Development of Slave Life Insurance Policies of Dutch Private Slave Ships, 1720–1780." *Enterprise & Society* 21, no. 1 (2020): 210–38.

Postma, Johannes. "The Dimension of the Dutch Slave Trade from Western Africa." *Journal of African History* 13, no. 2 (1972): 237–48.

Postma, Johannes, and Victor Enthoven, eds. *Riches from Atlantic Commerce: Dutch Transatlantic Trade and Shipping, 1585–1817.* Leiden: Brill, 2003.

Price, Richard. "Scrapping Maroon History: Brazil's Promise, Suriname's Shame." *New West Indian Guide* 72, no. 3/4 (1998): 233–55.

Russell, Peter. *Prince Henry "The Navigator": A Life.* New Haven, CT: Yale University Press, 2001.

Russell-Wood, A. J. R. "Iberian Expansion and the Issue of Black Slavery: Changing Portuguese Attitudes, 1440–1770." *American Historical Review* 83, no. 1 (1978): 16–42.

Schwartz, Stuart B. *Sugar Plantations in the Formation of Brazilian Society: Bahia, 1550–1835.* Cambridge: Cambridge University Press, 1985.

Stedman, John G. *Narrative, of a Five Years' Expedition, Against the Revolted Negroes of Surinam, in Guiana . . . from the Year 1772, to 1777 . . . Volumes I & II.* London, 1796.

Van Lier, R. A. J. *Frontier Society. A Social Analysis of the History of Surinam.* Leiden: Brill, 1971.

Verrest, Hebe. "City Profile. Paramaribo." *ScienceDirect* (2009).

RATIONALIZATION

Davies, K. G. *The Royal African Company.* London: Routledge, 1957.

Dobson, Neil Cunningham, and Sean Kingsley. *A Late 17th-Century Armed Merchant Vessel in the Western Approaches (Site 35F).* Tampa, FL: Odyssey Papers 2011.

Evans, Chris, and Göran Rydén, "'Voyage Iron': An Atlantic Slave Trade Currency, Its European Origins, and West African Impact." *Past and Present* 239 (2018): 41–70.

Habib, Imtiaz. *Black Lives in the English Archives, 1500–1677: Imprints of the Invisible.* London: Routledge, 2016.

Herbert, Eugenia. *Red Gold of Africa: Copper in Precolonial History and Culture.* Madison: University of Wisconsin Press. 2003.

Inikori, Joseph. "Transatlantic Slavery and Economic Development in the Atlantic World: West Africa, 1450–1850." In *The Cambridge World History of Slavery. Volume 3, AD 1420–AD 1804,* edited by David Eltis and Stanley Engerman. Cambridge: Cambridge University Press, 2011.

Jordan, Winthrop. *White Over Black: American Attitudes toward the Negro.* Chapel Hill: University of North Carolina Press, 1968.

Law, Robin. *Ouidah: The Social History of a West African Slaving "Port," 1727–1892.* Athens: Ohio University Press, 2004.

Manning, Patrick. *Slavery, Colonialism and Economic Growth in Dahomey, 1640–1960.* Cambridge: Cambridge University Press, 1982.

Morgan, Kenneth, ed. *The British Transatlantic Slave Trade, Volume 2: The Royal African Company*. London: Routledge, 2003.

Mtubani, V. C. D. "African Slaves and English Law." *Pula: Botswana Journal of African Studies* 3, no. 2 (1981): 71–75.

Osei-Tutu, John Kwadwo. *Forts, Castles and Society in West Africa: Gold Coast and Dahomey, 1450–1960*. Leiden: Brill, 2018.

Pettigrew, William A. *Freedom's Debt: The Royal African Company and the Politics of the Atlantic Slave Trade, 1672–1752*. Chapel Hill: University of North Carolina Press, 2013.

Richardson, David. "Slavery and Bristol's 'Golden Age.'" *Slavery and Abolition* 26, no. 1 (2005): 35–54.

Walvin, James. *Black and White: The Negro and English Society*. London: Penguin Press, 1973.

NEW WORLD CULTURES

Bailey, Jay. "Historical Origin and Stylistic Developments of the Five-String Banjo." *Journal of American Folklore* 85 (1972): 58–65.

Beoku-Betts, Josephine A. "We Got Our Way of Cooking Things: Women, Food, and Preservation of Cultural Identity among the Gullah." *Gender and Society* 9, no. 5 (1995): 535–55.

Bialuschewski, Arne. "Black People under the Black Flag: Piracy and the Slave Trade on the West Coast of Africa, 1718–1723." *Slavery & Abolition* 29, no. 4 (2008): 461–75.

Borrelli, Jeremy, and Lynn B. Harris. "Bricks as Ballast: An Archaeological Investigation of a Shipwreck Site in Cahuita National Park, Costa Rica." *Advisory Council on Underwater Archaeology Underwater Archaeology Proceedings* (2016): 8–16.

Burnard, Trevor, and Kenneth Morgan. "The Dynamics of the Slave Market and Slave Purchasing Patterns in Jamaica, 1655–1788." *William and Mary Quarterly* 58, no. 1 (2001): 205–28.

Diouf, Sylviane A. *Dreams of Africa in Alabama: The Slave Ship Clotilda and the Story of the Last Africans Brought to America*. Oxford: Oxford University Press, 2007.

Dubois, Laurent. *The Banjo: America's African Instrument*. Cambridge, MA: Harvard University Press, 2016.

Eglash, Ron. *African Fractals: Modern Computing and Indigenous Design*. New Brunswick, NJ: Rutgers University Press, 1999.

Floyd Jr., Samuel A., Melanie L. Zeck, and Guthrie P. Ramsey, eds. *The Transformation of Black Music: The Rhythms, the Songs and the Ships of the African Diaspora*. Oxford: Oxford University Press, 2017.

Geggus, David. "The Enigma of Jamaica in the 1790s: New Light on the Causes of Slave Rebellions." *William and Mary Quarterly* 44, no. 2 (1987): 274–99.

Gøbel, Erik. *The Danish Slave Trade and its Abolition*. Leiden: Brill, 2016.

Grivetti, Louis Evan, and Howard-Yana Shapiro, eds. *Chocolate: History, Culture, and Heritage.* Hoboken, NJ: Wiley, 2009.

Hall, Neville A. T. *Slave Society in the Danish West Indies: St. Thomas, St. John, and St. Croix.* Mona, Jamaica: University Press of the West Indies, 1992.

Harris, Lynn. "The Serendipitous Saga of Danish Slave Trade Frigates *Christianus Quintus V* and *Fredericus Quartus IV,* Wrecked in 1710." *Coriolis* 10, no. 1 (2020): 1–31.

Harris, Lynn, and Nathan Richards. "Preliminary Investigations of Two Shipwreck Sites in Cahuita National Park, Costa Rica." *International Journal of Nautical Archaeology* 47, no. 2 (2018): 405–18.

Holm, John A. "The Creole English of Nicaragua's Miskito Coast: Its Sociolinguistic History and a Comparative Study of its Lexicon and Syntax." PhD diss. University College London, 1978.

Hurston, Zora Neale. *Barracoon: The Story of the Last "Black Cargo."* New York: Amistad, 2018.

Kinkor, Kenneth J. "Black Men under the Black Flag." In *Bandits at Sea: A Pirates Reader,* edited by C. R. Pennell, 195-210. New York: New York University Press, 2001.

Lohse, Russell. "Cacao and Slavery in Matina, Costa Rica, 1650–1750." In *Blacks and Blackness in Central America: Between Race and Place,* edited by Lowell Gudmundson and Justin Wolfe, 57–91. Durham, NC: Duke University Press, 2010.

Loveman, Kate. "The Introduction of Chocolate into England: Retailers, Researchers, and Consumers, 1640–1730." *Journal of Social History* 47, no. 1 (2013): 27–46.

Raiford, Matthew. *Bress 'n' Nyam: Gullah Geechee Recipes from a Sixth-Generation Farmer.* New York: Countryman Press, 2021.

Sullivan, Megan. "African-American Music as Rebellion: From Slavesong to Hip-Hop." *Discoveries* 3 (2001): 21–39.

Voloshin, Metro. "The Banjo, from its Roots to the Ragtime Era." *Music Reference Services Quarterly* 6, no. 3 (1998): 1–12.

Westergaard, Waldemar. *The Danish West Indies Under Company Rule 1671–1754.* New York, 1917.

RESISTANCE

Baldwin, Simeon. "The Captives of the *Amistad.*" *Papers of the New Haven Colony Historical Society* 4 (1888): 331–70.

Barton, William F. *Old Plantation Hymns.* Boston, 1899.

Bradford, Sarah H. *Harriet. The Moses of her People.* New York, 1886.

Donkoh, Wilhelmina, with Fredericka Dadson. *The Just King: The Story of Osei Tutu Kwame Asibe Bonsu.* Oxford: Woeli Publishing Services and Worldreader, 2013.

Fireland Pioneer. Firelands Historical Society, July 1888.

Foner, Eric. *Gateway to Freedom. The Hidden History of the Underground Railroad.* New York: W. W. Norton, 2015.

Grigg, Jeff W. *The Combahee River Raid: Harriet Tubman & Lowcountry Liberation.* Charleston, SC: The History Press, 2014.

Henson, Josiah. *The Life of Josiah Henson, Formerly a Slave, Now an Inhabitant of Canada, as Narrated by Himself.* Boston, 1849.

Jensen, John Odin. *Stories from the Wreckage: A Great Lakes Maritime History Inspired by Shipwrecks.* Madison: Wisconsin Historical Society Press, 2019.

McDaniel, Lorna. "The Flying Africans: Extent and Strength of the Myth in the Americas." *New West Indian Guide* 64 (1990): 28–40.

Marsh, J. B. *The Story of the Jubilee Singers, with their Songs.* Boston, 1881.

Peeke, H. L. *The Centennial History of Erie County, Ohio.* Sandusky, OH: Firelands Historical Society, 1925.

Schraff, Anne. *The Life of Harriet Tubman: Moses of the Underground Railroad.* Berkeley Heights, NJ: Enslow, 2014.

Snyder, Terri L. "Suicide, Slavery, and Memory in North America." *Journal of American History* 97, no. 1 (2010): 39–62.

Young, Jason R. "All God's Children Had Wings: The Flying African in History, Literature, and Lore." *Journal of Africana Religions* 5, no. 1 (2017): 50–70.

ABOLITION

Barrow, Pat. *Slaves of Rapparee: The Wreck of the London.* Bideford, UK: Lazarus Press, 1998.

Bonner, Christopher. *Remaking the Republic: Black Politics and the Creation of American Citizenship.* Philadelphia: University of Pennsylvania Press, 2020.

Clarkson, Thomas. *An Essay on the Slavery and Commerce of the Human Species, Particularly the African.* London, 1786.

Clarkson, Thomas. *The History of the Rise, Progress, and Accomplishment of the Abolition of the African Slave-Trade by the British Parliament.* London, 1808.

Drescher, Seymour. "The Shocking Birth of British Abolitionism." *Slavery & Abolition* 33, no. 4 (2012): 571–593.

Drescher, Seymour. "Whose Abolition? Popular Pressure and the Ending of the British Slave Trade." *Past & Present* 143 (1994): 136–166.

Hochschild, Adam. *Bury the Chains. Prophets and Rebels in the Fight to Free an Empire's Slaves.* New York: Mariner Books, 2005.

Lineberry, Cate. *Be Free or Die. The Amazing Story of Robert Smalls' Escape from Slavery to Union Hero.* New York: St. Martin's Press, 2017.

Martin, Justin. *A Fierce Glory: Antietam—The Desperate Battle That Saved Lincoln and Doomed Slavery.* Boston: Da Capo Press, 2018.

Odumosu, Temi. *Africans in English Caricature 1769–1819: Black Jokes, White Humour.* London: Brepols Publishers, 2017.

Oldham, James. "Insurance Litigation Involving the *Zong* and Other British Slave Ships, 1780–1807." *Journal of Legal History* 28, no. 3 (2007): 299–318.

Pawlak, Kevin. "'The Heavyest Blow Yet Given the Confederacy': The Emancipation Proclamation Changes the Civil War." In *Turning Points of the American Civil War*, edited by Chris Mackowski and Kristopher D. White, 80–101. Carbondale: Southern Illinois University Press, 2018.

Penny, John. "The Shipwrecked West Indians in Stapleton Prison, Bristol, 1796–1798." *Regional Historian* 11 (2004): 11–20.

Rawley, James A. *Turning Points of the Civil War*. Lincoln: University of Nebraska Press, 1966.

Sadler, Nigel. *The Legacy of Slavery in Britain*. Stroud, UK: Amberley Publishing, 2018.

Sears, Stephen W. *Landscape Turned Red. The Battle of Antietam*. New York: Mariner Books, 2003.

Swaminathan, Srividhya. "Reporting Atrocities: A Comparison of the *Zong* and the Trial of Captain John Kimber." *Slavery & Abolition* 31, no. 4 (2010): 483–99.

Walvin, James. *The Zong: A Massacre, the Law & the End of Slavery*. New Haven, CT: Yale University Press, 2019.

Webster, Jane. "The *Zong* in the Context of the Eighteenth-Century Slave Trade." *Journal of Legal History* 28, no. 3 (2007): 285–98.

White, Tim. "Robert Smalls: From Slave to War Hero, Entrepreneur, and Congressman." *Objective Standard* 15, no. 2 (2020).

THE LAST GASP

Aimes, Hubert H. S. *A History of Slavery in Cuba, 1511–1868*. New York: G. P. Putnam's Sons, 1907.

Burroughs, Robert. "Suppression of the Atlantic Slave Trade: Abolition from Ship to Shore." In *The Suppression of the Atlantic Slave Trade: British Policies, Practices and Representations of Naval Coercion*, edited by Robert Burroughs and Richard Huzzey. Manchester: Manchester University Press, 2015.

Corwin, Arthur F. *Spain and the Abolition of Slavery in Cuba, 1817–1886*. Austin: University of Texas Press, 1967.

Drake, Frederick C. "Secret History of the Slave Trade to Cuba Written by an American Naval Officer, Robert Wilson Schufeldt, 1861." *Journal of Negro History* 55, no. 3 (1970): 218–35.

Fraginals, Manuel Moreno. *The Sugar Mill. The Socioeconomic Complex of Sugar in Cuba*. New York: Monthly Review Press, 1976.

Hicks, Dan *The Brutish Museums: The Benin Bronzes, Colonial Violence and Cultural Restitution*. London: Pluto Press, 2020.

Klein, Herbert S. "North American Competition and the Characteristics of the African Slave Trade to Cuba, 1790 to 1794." *William and Mary Quarterly* 28, no. 1 (1971): 86–102.

Knight, Franklin W. "Origins of Wealth and the Sugar Revolution in Cuba, 1750–1850." *Hispanic American Historical Review* 57, no. 2 (1977): 231–53.

Malcom, Corey. *A Brief History of the Sailing Brig Last Known as the Pirate-Slaver Guerrero*. Key West, FL: Mel Fisher Maritime Heritage Society, 2006.

Malcom, Corey. *Continued Investigations of Sites and Artifacts Believed to Relate to the Pirate-Slaver Guerrero and HMS Nimble, 2005–2014*. Key West, FL: Mel Fisher Maritime Heritage Society, 2017.

Micheletti, Steven J., Kasia Bryc, Samantha G. Ancona Esselmann, William A. Freyman, Meghan E. Moreno, G. David Poznik, and Anjali J. Shastri. "Genetic Consequences of the Transatlantic Slave Trade in the Americas." *American Journal of Human Genetics* 107 (2020): 265–77.

Moore, David D., and Corey Malcom. "Seventeenth-Century Vehicle of the Middle Passage: Archaeological and Historical Investigations on the 'Henrietta Marie' Shipwreck Site." *International Journal of Historical Archaeology* 12, no. 1 (2008): 20–38.

Rodrigo-Alharilla, Martin. "Spanish Sailors and the Illegal Slave Trade to Cuba, 1845–1867." *Journal of Iberian and Latin American Studies* 27 (2021): 97–114.

Sommerdyk, Stacey. "Trade and the Merchant Community of the Loango Coast in the Eighteenth Century." PhD diss., University of Hull, 2012.

Swanson, Gail. *The Slave Ship Guerrero*. San Carlos, CA: Infinity Publishing, 2005.

Swanson, Gail. "The Wrecking of the Laden Spanish Slave Ship *Guerrero* off the Florida Keys, in 1827." *African Diaspora Archaeology Newsletter* 13, no. 3 (2010): 1–9.

INDEX